AGE DISCRIMINATION
BY EMPLOYERS

AGE DISCRIMINATION BY EMPLOYERS

by Kerry Segrave

McFarland & Company, Inc., Publishers
Jefferson, North Carolina, and London

Library of Congress Cataloguing-in-Publication Data

Segrave, Kerry, 1944–
    Age discrimination by employers / by Kerry Segrave.
      p.   cm.
    Includes bibliographical references and index.
    ISBN 0-7864-1010-8 (softcover : 50# alkaline paper) ∞
    1. Age discrimination in employment—United States—
History.   2. Age and employment—United States—History.
3. Aged—Employment—United States—History.   I. Title.
HD6280 .S44   2001
331.3'98—dc21

                                 2001030770

British Library cataloguing data are available

Manufactured in the United States of America

Cover image ©2001 EyeWire.

McFarland & Company, Inc., Publishers
  Box 611, Jefferson, North Carolina 28640
  www.mcfarlandpub.com

Contents

Preface

This book looks at age discrimination in employment in the United States during the twentieth century. It focuses on how the issue was treated by the media, the extent of age bias, how older workers were viewed, the reasons and rationales presented by business enterprises for their refusal to hire older workers, and the responses of governments to the problem.

Age bias has existed over this entire period, sometimes in the public eye and sometimes not. A look at foreign data—sometimes cited in this book for comparison purposes—indicates that age bias exists in all industrial societies, regardless of the type of government. Also consistent across the period, and from country to country, is that age discrimination in employment creates more difficulties, and begins earlier, for women than for men. The "deadline" for men has more or less always been in the 40- to 50-year age range. It was no coincidence that when laws were passed banning the practice, they all were written to protect people between the ages of 40 or 45 and 65—the age range in which men experience the most discrimination.

Racial bias targets people for what they are. Age bias targets people for what they become.

CHAPTER 1

The Deadline
Surfaces, 1890s-1926

"Take the sum of human achievement ... subtract the
work of men above 40 ... we would practically be where
we are today."
— *William Osler, 1905*

"A man who has failed to make good at 45 is not wanted
to-day; he will never make good."
— *Anonymous personnel executive, 1910*

"It is more delightful to be surrounded by the young,
with hopefulness, gladness, and outlook in their eyes."
— *Daniel Motley, 1915*

"That disinclination to hire older workers is actually a
decent thing, proportional to the employer's kindness of
heart."
—New York Times *editorial, 1916*

Back in 1907 when a middle-aged woman wrote a letter to the editor of the *New York Times* setting forth the difficulties in getting a job,
the editor remarked that the lot of such women was hard, but not any
harder than that of the middle-aged man who suddenly found himself

out of work. He added, "Employers, naturally, look to the young. A man or woman of advanced years is too apt to be given to old-fashioned ways of doing things, and open to suspicion of having the unforgivable fault, in modern business, of slowness." Though admitting that such faults could also be found in the young, the editor argued that at least they could be trained. In conclusion, he stated, "The competition of the old with the young is a pitiful spectacle." This was one of the earliest editorials on the subject of age discrimination in employment by the newspaper of record. It would not be the last. Snarly and unsympathetic in tone, most of the *Times* editorials of this period downplayed the problem as barely existing or blamed the victims of such discrimination.[1]

Two years earlier a *Times* editorial remarked that someone in Chicago was attempting to form a league devoted mainly to the interests of those over 45. It was meant to fight age ostracism such as it believed it found in the recent remark of Admiral George Dewey, who said, "The Nation assuredly will meet with disaster in a naval war unless younger men are given command of the ships of the navy." Dewey was then about 67 years old. Allowing that the league could be commended in a general way, the editor noted that since hardly a fifth of the population was in the age range between 40 and 60, "it might seem as though interest in this topic is confined to a few." Noting that the average age of all native-born whites at death was 36, the editor declared that "those who are working at 45 appear to be working on another man's time."[2]

As early as 1903 the state of Colorado passed legislation indicating an awareness of the difficulties regarding older workers and employment. That law didn't apply to hiring but did affect their discharge. It specified that no employer could discharge anyone between the ages of 18 and 60 because of age. Like so many of the early pieces of legislation designed to deal with age discrimination in employment, this law was not enforced.[3]

As far back as 1866 witnesses testified before a special Massachusetts commission that woodcarvers and cabinet workers were economically old after the age of 40. Later, in 1890, when Judge Altgeld reviewed the arguments for the eight-hour work day, he wrote that at 35 or 40 men "break down in the wake of exhausting toil and exposure and at 40 too many of them are in their graves." In 1900 the New York Commission of Labor Statistics put the deadline for women at 45 and for men at 50. Appearing before the Industrial Commission, the Labor Statistics Bureau pleaded for the man "whose hair is gray but who is physically a strong man and looks to be in the prime of life."[4]

While the above examples would seem to indicate that the problem was firmly entrenched by 1900, there is little agreement on the question of when age discrimination began and when it flourished. David Hackett Fischer described an intense age prejudice in employment in the late 19th and early 20th century. A cult of youth, he said, developed in America during the 19th century and grew rapidly in the next one. W. Andrew Achenbaum settled on the two decades after 1910 as the crucial period in the development of diminishing job opportunities for older workers. He argued that articles in popular and scholarly journals and help-wanted ads in the newspapers appearing after 1914 clearly revealed that the elderly's presumed value and apparent status in the labor market was steadily deteriorating. For Achenbaum it was the decade of the 1920s when age discrimination took its worst toll. Gerald Gruman wrote that in the 1890s and early 1900s it became a standard practice for industry to shut out workers over the age of 40. On the other hand, Tamara Hareven believed that age-related standards of usefulness and productivity were only beginning to be imposed at the turn of the century. The Amoskeag Corporation, her primary object of research, began to lay off slow, older workers only after 1920. William Graebner thought that age discrimination was well established by 1900 and that more older workers were affected by it with each passing decade, including the 1920s. Carole Haber placed the beginnings of age discrimination in employment back somewhere into the mid–19th century and believed that age limits on hiring and firing were widespread by about 1900.[5]

Explanations for age discrimination were equally diverse. Fischer pointed to the factory system, the assembly line and labor unions that wanted retirement systems, and to the fundamental transition from an agricultural to an industrial system: Older workers tended to be employed in the farm economy; they tended not to be employed in the industrial economy. Haber found the urban/industrial explanation less than fully convincing. She settled on several factors, including scientific management, pensions, and especially an ongoing oversupply of labor in the early 20th century that encouraged employers to get rid of the less efficient. Hareven looked largely within the firm, to scientific management, pensions, and the bureaucratic and standardized personnel arrangements and procedures common to larger firms. Largely agreeing with these reasons Graebner also set those microeconomic factors in the context of competitive pressures initiated by the spread of the eight-hour day.[6]

Graebner examined the help-wanted columns of Buffalo, New York's daily newspapers at five-year intervals from 1895 to 1935. Discrimination was defined as any reference which clearly implied a preference for youthful workers, such as "girl," "boy," "young woman," and so on. He found discrimination existed at each interval, actually declining somewhat in the middle part of the period. By five-year intervals the percentage of discriminating help-wanted female ads were as follows: 1895, 66 percent (30 percent if ads for domestics—overwhelmingly requested to be young—were excluded); 1900, 78 percent (62 percent); 1905, 58 percent (33 percent); 1910, 50 percent (31 percent); 1915, 58 percent (n/a); 1920, 37 percent (n/a); 1925, 44 percent (33 percent); 1930, 36 percent (22 percent); 1935, 60 percent (n/a). The percentage of discriminatory help-wanted male ads for those nine periods were, respectively, 31 percent, 32 percent, 22 percent, 20 percent, 20 percent, 19 percent, 14 percent, 19 percent, 19 percent. It was a problem that hit women more than it did men.[7]

Those results, thought Graebner, offered little comfort to those who claimed that age discrimination emerged late, after 1920 or so. As early as 1895 Buffalo job-seekers encountered some form of age discrimination. A 40-year-old reading the want ads in 1895 was at least as likely to encounter age discrimination as a counterpart in 1935. Those early discriminatory ads requesting, say, a "young man" revealed what employers wanted, not whether or not they could actually get it. Nor did they reveal what they did not want. By the 1920s and after, discriminatory ads more and more listed specific age cut-offs, such as under 35, or 25–40. Graebner concluded, "In any event there is evidence here to support the view that age discrimination worsened in the 1920s."[8]

One of the major changes that took place in the years revolving around 1900 was a drastic fall in agricultural work. Between 1870 and 1930 the proportion of male workers in agricultural jobs fell from one-half to one-quarter of the labor force. Farm work was mostly family work with each member, from the youngest to the oldest, contributing according to his ability. The move to wage-labor, to city-labor, to factory-labor, meant a loss of independence and a rigidly structured work day. As firms increased in size, the impersonal personnel department took over the hiring and firing functions, compared to smaller companies where the owner might also do the hiring.[9]

When James J. Davis was United States Secretary of Labor, he made a speech in 1928 before an employees' group. He recalled an earlier time when he was a youth, perhaps in the 1880s or 1890s. Davis (born in 1873, Labor Secretary from 1921 to 1930) remarked: "Many a time, I remember, when I was a boy at work in the iron mill, I saw a faithful worker who had rounded out fifty years of life. The custom was to present him with a gold watch, in token of his age, but he was also presented with a discharge. It was assumed that at his years a man had outlived his usefulness. A man that old was thought to be old indeed. A man that old thought so himself."[10]

Canada's federal Unemployment Insurance Commission briefly traced the history of the older worker problem in a 1960s pamphlet and came to some pessimistic conclusions. The agency concluded that generations earlier when Canada was a pioneer country, "The aged were of limited value to the community. Only youth could survive. In those days, of course, people were considered old at 40 (life expectancy in 1900 was only 46) and at 50 they were often regarded as dead wood, useless both to themselves and to their families." In fact, said the report, often it was "a relief to the surviving relatives when they were finally laid to rest in the churchyard."[11]

Judith Hushbeck looked at age discrimination and the American worker in the period 1860 to 1920 and concluded that institutional barriers to the employment of older workers began to appear in America from around the time of the Civil War, as the economy moved into the industrial era. The nature of that transformation gave rise to a new phenomenon, age discrimination. In contrast was the situation in colonial America and the early part of nationhood when older people were looked to for economic and political leadership. Advancing years were an increasingly negative factor in the time between the Civil War and World War I as age joined class, sex, and race as markers of a person's prospects for labor force participation.[12]

That period saw the rise to dominance of the corporate form of capitalist business along with the separation of ownership from control, at least among the largest entities. Prior to 1860 America was mainly agrarian in its economic base, rural in its living patterns, reliant mainly on self-employment and small-scale production, and oriented toward the family as the provider for those in their nonproducing years. In 1860 fewer than 20 percent of Americans lived in a city larger than 2,500; by 1920 more than 50 percent lived in such settlements. That mainly urban, industrial workforce of 1920, separated from the ownership of the means of production, was predominantly engaged in wage-work for others. Technology and labor specialization greatly reduced the skill level in most production jobs. As firms grew increasingly larger and impersonal, scientific management started to be important in establishing work procedures, rules, and hiring standards, often in arbitrary fashion. Production in industrial America became known for its rigor, its rapid pace and long hours of work. As a result, one of the most valued traits of a prospective employee was youthfulness for physical reasons of stamina and general health and because younger workers were considered to be more amenable to new methods and could be paid lower wages. Background and experience mattered less and less since jobs had been de-skilled to a great extent. Thus, Hushbeck concluded, "Age discrimination in employment began to be introduced into the economic system through the management practices of the largest firms in the nation's most centralized and fastest-growing industries." By the early 1900s, she wrote, men found it difficult to secure employment at ages as low as 35 or 40; for women it was even younger. Increasingly, middle-aged and older workers were found in occupations that had been relatively unaffected by technological change, specialization, and de-skilling. Those jobs, however, were of decreasing importance to the economy, and were found in the shrinking industries of the era.[13]

If age discrimination was widely entrenched and pervasive by 1900, as it appears to have been, it warranted only limited coverage in the popular media and in the newspapers. It would be 1927 before the problem began to be covered in any consistent way by the popular press. A brief flurry of attention focused on the problem around 1905, in the wake of remarks made by Doctor William Osler. What he said was, "Take the sum of human achievement in action, in science, in art, in literature; subtract the work of men above 40, and while we should miss great treasures, even priceless treasures, we would practically be where we are today. It is difficult to name a great and far-reaching conquest of the mind which has not been given to the world by a man on whose back the sun was still shining. The effective, moving, vitalizing work of the world is done between the ages of 25 and 40."[14]

In counseling his own professional physician colleagues, he recommended that to keep their minds receptive and impressionable, older physicians should walk with the "boys"—those men between 25 and 40 who were doing all the work of the world. Osler, a pioneer in preventive medicine and an influential force in the practice of internal medicine, was 55 when he made his infamous remarks.[15]

One of those who rose to dispute Osler was Doctor Felix Adler, who gave a speech in 1906 before the Ethical Culture Society. First he noted the impact of Osler's comments: "The attention paid to Dr. Osler's remarks on old age was as remarkable as the remarks themselves. They eclipsed for a time in the newspapers foreign and home news of the greatest interest." He added that Osler expressed a real tendency in the industrial world; that the old and middle-aged "are crowded out, and those who can keep up the pace and even with feverish energy accelerate it are preferred. This is one of the gravest problems of modern civilization." Adler cited Dante who wrote *Divine Comedy* when he was past 50, Milton who wrote *Paradise Lost* when past 50, and others such as Titian, Kant and Leibnitz, all of whom did their best work when they were well advanced in years.[16]

A couple of years later, in 1908, those remarks were still in the news. At that time *The Medical Record* trade journal, after an extensive investigation, declared editorially that its research proved beyond a doubt the "absurdity" of Olser's assumption that all of the important meaningful work of the world was done by 25- to 40-year-olds. In response to his idea that subtracting all of the work done by those who were older would have left the world essentially unchanged, the periodical pointed out that what would have been lost would be: printing from type, the discovery of dynamic electricity, vaccination, railroads, the Bessemer process of making steel, and so on. Also summarized was the work of W.A. Newman Dorland who had computed the average age of 400 of the "great benefactors of the race" at which each achieved his masterwork. Dorland concluded that for workers the average age was 47 and for the thinkers it was 52. The problem with this type of refutation was that it was limited to a relative handful of people who had achieved genius status, or close to it. It held little relevance for the average employee, who was aging, in an average job.[17]

Five years after his remarks the Osler controversy remained alive, and his name briefly made its way into the American lexicon. In a 1910 letter to the *New York Times* the writer, identified only as W.N., said that he was sending in his letter since he believed the newspaper was opposed to the "spirit of Oslerism" and that a man should be able to be hired regardless of age. W.N. was a 63-year-old former railroad clerk who admitted to lying about his age in his search for a job, but to no avail. He pleaded with the *Times* to tell him if there was still ground left upon which his belief that a man should be able to be hired regardless of age could rest, and where that ground might be.[18]

A response was published as an editorial the very next day. In regard to whether "Oslerism is back," the editor acknowledged "some basis" existed for the assertion that older workers had trouble, but that was not "a novel phenomenon or one indicative of a special coldness and cruelty in a 'commercialized' era.... Certainly the age is not harsher or crueler than other ages were"—rather it was "gentler, more considerate, and wiser." Business had always been business. Explaining the situation further, the editor declared, "The fact is that the old man out of a job is not burdened by his years alone. For one thing, it is not the best of recommendations that his experience and his skill did not cause his previous employer to retain him. Nobody maintains that competent men are discharged because of gray hair." Also pointed out was that the older worker usually would not or could not accept a beginner's place and salary, and no others were likely to be open. Also working against the middle-aged worker was that he was sometimes "unable, and more often unwilling, to learn new ways." His term of service would also be short, compared with that of a young man. That caused the editor to place an even odder spin on age discrimination when he declared: "Not many employers, nowadays, fail to recognize some sort and degree of obligation to take care of faithful employes after their working days are over, and it is this sense of responsibility, so new and so commendable, that makes the old man's search for a salaried position perhaps a little longer than it used to be." This was about the last heard of Osler and Oslerism, but the problem itself continued.[19]

When the American Federation of Labor (AFL) executive Arthur Holder appeared in Washington before the Employers' Liability Commission in 1911, he told the panel that the man over 40 with a few gray hairs could not get a new position if he lost his job, but he could hold on if he had a place. That would tend to be true right through to the present time. That is, many firms would openly refuse to hire new employees over a certain age—openly when it was not illegal—but happily keep on people well past the age cut-off, people hired when they were younger than the cut-off. The irony of that situation would not be lost on many future commentators on the issue. Holder went on to state that the situation of the over-40 worker was the same in England, Germany, and the remainder of the Continent, as it was in the United States. He thought it was the result of economic conditions and arose from a determination to get the greatest possible product out of people employed by others.[20]

In a largely sympathetic article about the problem in 1910, the unnamed reporter mentioned the increasing army of involuntarily "Oslerized" men of 45 and over. He wrote: "There is no more pathetic figure than the man of 45 hunting a position, and finding door after door closed to him for no other reason than that in the modern commercial and industrial world the demand is for young men and not for those who have begun to show the gray at the temples." The reporter spoke to an unnamed executive who employed a lot of men. That manager asserted: "A man who has failed to make good at 45 is not wanted to-day; he never will make good. We can't afford to bother with him. The fact that he's hunting a job shows he's a failure." Pointing out that half or more of the job-seekers were not dropped or discharged for incompetency but because of the changing conditions of economic life, this reporter added that the consolidation or reorganization of a company often played havoc with the older employees, and many of them, if not discharged outright, were demoted to minor posts. He felt this waste of good material was too enormous for the economical exploitation of labor. A second unnamed manager, this one in charge of a large corporate office employing 500 people, gleefully remarked, with respect to hard economic times referred to as the panic of 1908: "One good thing the panic did for us, it gave us an opportunity to get rid of all our old men. No dead wood here. Every man is under thirty-five." While it has been, and remains, generally true that firms which have exercised age discrimination regarding new hires have also kept on employees well past that age, there have been exceptions. In periods of economic depression, companies have sometimes used that as an excuse to deliberately get rid of older workers, purely because of age. The case mentioned above appears to be one. Examples also exist from the late 1920s—a period of merger mania—and in the 1980s and 1990s— a period combing bad times with feverish merger activity.[21]

Investigating further, the reporter interviewed half a dozen clerks, all in their late forties, who had been thrown out of work in that panic some two years earlier. None of them got jobs comparable to the ones they had lost. Their only hope was to accept some minor position or take a clerk's job at about half their former salary in some office where older men were taken, on account of the reduced pay. At one such office the manager, who paid approximately half of the usual salary for clerks, explained that at those wages he could not get competent young men; so he employed men of 45 and over. To the question as to whether he was satisfied, the manager replied: "Yes, I suppose so. They're a cheap lot, but they do the work. It's all they're worth." A second experiment was being conducted by a businessman who was described as a sort of philanthropist. He paid regular wages to clerks and advertised for ones 45 and over. Swamped with applicants, he had his pick. He said: "I never had a better office force in my life, and from the first things went smoothly. There was no breaking in of green men; no carelessness; no idleness; no unruliness." Near the end of his lengthy article the journalist mentioned that a couple of the older clerks who had lost their jobs had gone into different areas—for example, one became a shopkeeper. But noting the impossibility of individuals always solving their problems, he concluded that "there must eventually be some concerted action to see what can be done for the jobless man of forty-five and over."[22]

Evidence of the common view of the issue, from both sides, could be found in letters to the editor, several of which appeared in 1915. One was from a woman who signed herself "Personally interested." She wanted the newspaper to open its columns to the discussion of employment for a woman of 50. She had been answering ads for some years but found that her age was always the drawback. She wanted to know why. Believing there should be some way for a middle-aged woman to make a living besides "keeping boarders and canvassing," she wanted to know what were the objections to a woman over 30 in the business world.[23]

On the other hand, Daniel Motley, the president of a small Christian college for ten years, first posed the question as to why people of middle age and beyond had trouble finding a job, and then answered it. Firstly, he thought, it was because they lacked the spirit of youth, second, they often had the "grouch," and third, they were not quick enough about doing a thing. In the fourth place, he concluded, while one might not object to having older people around, "yet it is more delightful to be surrounded by the young, with hopefulness, gladness, and outlook in their eyes."[24]

In response to this small flurry of letters on the issue the *Times* made an editorial reply. Specifically it was to a letter writer who suggested that the "common reluctance" to hire old workers had its explanation in the belief that if such a worker had given, and was still giving, competent and satisfactory service he would not now be seeking a new position. In response the editor said that such a theory was not without a certain plausibility, but then pointed out that many workers lost their positions due to business reorganizations: firms going out of business, the introduction of new machinery, and so forth. "These are the tragedies of trade, and they are so numerous as to make untrue as well as cruel, the placing on elderly seekers of employment, as a class, a general condemnation as convicted by their predicament of being unworthy or unpromising applicants." This was one of the first editorials from the *New York Times* which showed some understanding of the problem, and some sympathy for its victims. However, during this period it was a rare exception.[25]

Toward the end of 1916 a shortage of office boys in New York City was reported. A journalist attested to that by remarking on the number of "Boy wanted" signs he saw in hundreds of stores and businesses. Reasons given for the shortage were that more boys were staying in school and better economic times meant a greater variety of jobs to choose from. Of course, by then, the United States economy was on a war footing, which meant less unemployment. The unidentified head of one of the city's biggest printing and publishing houses couldn't find any office boys. Then he had the idea of advertising for active, elderly men to fill those positions. In reply to his ad he received 50 responses in the first mail, and hired three men. Enthusiastic about the results, the man declared his company would never go back to boys because those men performed the duties much more effectively; their understanding was better, and they were more reliable. Reportedly they were paid more money than were boys for the job. In conclusion he said: "Looked at from a humanitarian point of view—it is giving employment to men of 50 to 60; men who have been thrown into the discard. There are evidently thousands of such men in this city."[26]

When the story was picked up nationally in the *Literary Digest*, the reporter commented, "Middle-aged men, who have outlived their usefulness in other places, whose existence without work is a drain on the population, are now being given a chance to support themselves at easy work."[27]

In response to this development, the *Times* editorialized that it was a good situation for the boys since those jobs were dead end and it was good for the men because they got a job. However, against the aged office boy's sense of satisfaction at having his earning period extended would have to be counted "the almost inevitable humiliation he would feel as the result of a descent so obvious in the industrial scale. To necessity, however, all must yield, and resignation comes with wont." Also to be considered, mused the editor, was the general disinclination of employers to take on older workers. Such workers were sure, after no great time, to be unfit for further work of any kind, but modern sensibilities recoiled from turning such workers out in their helplessness. An alternative was some sort of pension, and that was more cheerfully given after long than short service. Thus, concluded the editorial, "that disinclination to hire older workers is actually a decent thing, proportional to the employer's kindness of heart."[28]

Some idea of the attitude toward older workers could also be seen in a 1917 article by B.C. Bean in *American Magazine*. He argued that if a man had not made himself a place in his profession, in a good business, or accumulated a competency by the time he was 40, he was fitted only for what the young man was much better fitted—the work of routine. As a result, wrote Bean, the man who stayed in competition with youth after he was 40 had no right to complain if the man with youth to market was able to underbid him.[29]

Specific age limits began to become commonplace in this period. The Pennsylvania Railroad would not hire anyone over the age of 45. It was a rule that was temporarily suspended during the World War I period. Cynics wondered why it was necessary to have a war in order that "old men shall be handed the boon of labor." And why didn't the government, at the federal, state and municipal levels, set the example?[30]

When a woman wrote a letter complaining that there was an age limit of 30 for filing and indexing positions, it produced a response from James N. McCord, who said he had placed over 5,000 graduates in such positions. McCord stated: "There is no age limit of 30 years in this profession, but there is an age limit for the beginner and, for reasons that are obvious, a business man would not want a middle-aged novice."[31]

A 1921 story revolved around a group of citizens worried about homeless and jobless men in the coming winter—that is, fear of a riot. Many of those men were ex-servicemen. Being hit for spare change by these young veterans prompted one woman to exclaim: "I am a woman over 50 years of age and three years ago I was left without any means of support. I was brought up in refinement, and now I have to go day after day looking for a position. Always the same thing. I am not young enough for the work! I am strong and willing to work, but I am having a heart-breaking time."[32]

A few years later, in 1925, another *New York Times* editorial revived the convoluted logic that older people had difficulty in finding work precisely because employers were more kindly, decent and caring than in the past. The editorial remarked that it was indeed a curious fact that out-of-work older people were then encountering more difficulty in getting employment than they did in the days, not so long ago, "when employers felt less of a responsibility for their employes than most of them do now. When a man could be used while he was worth using, and then turned off and forgotten, age did not count so much against him when he was out of a position as it does at present, for there is a natural inclination first to get services of some duration before the time comes for retirement with a pension of some kind or amount." There was much evidence to indicate that age discrimination in employment existed throughout the first quarter of the 20th century, and back before that. However, there is no good data which measures its extent, whether it was stable, whether it was increasing or decreasing. Certainly there is little evidence through this period that capitalist enterprises were behaving in markedly kinder and gentler ways toward their workers.[33]

Media attention to the problem of age discrimination in employment was relatively meager with somewhat heavier coverage in the 1905 to 1911 period. Most of the items dealt with male job-seekers only, with females receiving very minor mention. That women suffered from the double discrimination of both gender and age and that age discrimination against women began at an earlier age were also barely brought up. Other than an ineffectual Colorado law the government at all levels ignored the issue. In fact those governments practiced their own age discrimination in hiring, and would for some time to come. Also, corporations kept silent on the issue. But this was in an era before the corporate public relations arms would come to be prominent. What coverage the issue received got even sparser from the time of World War I until the mid 1920s, kept alive mostly by letters to the editor and editorial responses. However, the problem was perhaps increasing. That decade was marked by a merger fever among big business and a subsequent downsizing of the workforce, before the term was used. As an issue the problem of age discrimination in employment would explode in the media in 1927 and never leave again, not to the extent that it did in the decade prior to 1927. The reasons for this explosion of interest are unclear. Perhaps more and more people were feeling the effects of the discrimination. Perhaps more of its victims came from different classes of society, classes with more ability to have the problem brought out into the open. It would cause politicians and businesses to respond—no longer would they be able to ignore the issue. It all started in 1927, with the arrival of Mr. Action.

CHAPTER 2

Age Discrimination
Creates a Stir, 1927–1929

"40 is the dead-line when hiring new men."
—*Magazine of Business, 1929*

"There is another problem peculiar to the middle aged
who seek employment. Employers naturally prefer to
have young, good-looking women in their employ."
—*Helen Bradley, St. Barnabas House, 1928*

"There is, of course, the natural human element in favor
of youth."
—*American Vocational Exchange, 1927*

"The older men must share a part, at least, of the responsibility for the condition in which they find themselves."
—*Manchester, NH,* Union *editorial, 1929*

"Our concern does not take on discarded lumber from the
other man's cargo."
—*Anonymous executive, 1929*

Things started quietly enough in the summer of 1927 with a few
more letters to the editor of the *New York Times* on the topic, as happened
from time to time. One was from an S.L. Pinner who bemoaned the ever-

growing army of men over 40 condemned to idleness because of their advanced years, in the midst of American prosperity. A second missive came from T. Roberts who mentioned that the sentiments of Pinner appealed to him very strongly. Roberts invoked the name of Osler, although it was then over 20 years since that controversy, and commented that the callousness of the average employer toward age discrimination in employment was illustrated by the fact that only one had ever commented on the letters which had been published in regard to the problem. While government and business officials had been almost totally silent on the problem, that state would soon end as the issue would receive widespread media attention. Both would soon feel compelled to speak.[1]

A third letter appeared a couple of weeks later. Published on August 15, 1927, it seemed innocuous enough. The only signature it bore was the name "Action." Action observed that while contributions on the subject of finding jobs for middle-aged men appeared sporadically offering advice, he thought it was time for cooperative action. Concerted activity on behalf of those who now wasted their time job-hunting would bring relief to many very soon, he thought, and ultimately would solve the problem for most, if not all, of them. Action urged Pinner and the others to write to him at the Prospect Park branch of the YMCA in Brooklyn, with a view to arranging a meeting to start the ball rolling.[2]

It didn't take long with Action soon announcing that a meeting would be held on August 23. In a published interview a few days before the gathering, the reporter stated, "A strange gathering of men and women will assemble next Tuesday ... to discuss a subject nearly as strange." The aim of the meeting would be to initiate a drive against the practice of business of regarding people past 40 as too old to work. Adding further to media interest was Action refusing to reveal his name, saying only that he was successful in business and had no financial worries. Under his pseudonym he had criticized that "cruel" business practice in letters to various New York newspapers. During the interview he declared that in New York City there were thousands of efficient workers and skilled clerks who could not get jobs because they were 40 or 45. Many letters he had received in response to his proposed meeting, he said, were enthusiastic about the proposed organization, but they thought the task was hopeless because the prejudice against older employees beginning work again was too deep-rooted in the businessman's mind. Action's plan was to organize the members so they could help each other. There would be no fee charged, although a member who had obtained work through the group would be expected to deposit a small sum of money to aid other members.[3]

Some 200 to 250 men and women over the age of 40 attended that first meeting. Speakers that evening at the Brooklyn YMCA branch developed attacks against insurance companies, employment agencies, the YWCA, and even the YMCA itself. Group insurance for employees was objected to on the ground that companies refused to hire men over 50 because insurance firms would not issue policies for them. Employment agencies were criticized because virtually all were "order takers and not order fillers." Moving considerably off topic, the Ys were attacked because they charged more for older people to use their facilities. At the meeting Action tried to form a committee which would be charged with organizing a campaign for this new organization. While all those he approached said they would be glad to help, they also said their names must not be known, so they turned him down. Then Action got an idea. He promised to keep the names of committee members anonymous, at least for the moment. After that, the required 10 (five men, five women) were quickly lined up.[4]

It was a meeting that drew national coverage as well as editorial comments from around the nation. Full of fighting words, the meeting had been called to complain about "the callous dictum of business which adjudges men past forty as too old to keep pace with younger workers." People gathered that night to fight the prevalent idea "that on his fortieth birthday some awful change comes over a man to unfit him for new tasks." Much of the meeting was given over to men telling their stories. A former order department manager explained that he had walked the streets for nearly four solid months for a job, at any price. But, he concluded, "Business hires only youngsters today, telling them they have a future. In that way they secure workers at such cheap prices that a man with a family just can't compete. Business uses these youngsters up, and when they are forty they, in turn, will find that the future the business has for them is also out in the gutter to die."[5]

In the wake of the meeting most of the editorial coverage blamed the employees. The St. Paul, Minnesota, *Dispatch* declared that those over 40 must blame themselves for harboring the delusion that, having learned a trade, they had nothing more to learn and could live the rest of their days on the little they had learned as a kind of capital. Said the Cleveland, Ohio, *Plain Dealer*, "It is not hard to see that there is logic in the doubt of employers as to the habits, ability or character of middle-aged people who are out of work." Brooklyn's *Eagle* found it odd that the captains of industry were past 40 yet set rules that new hires had to be under 40. Yet it did not try to explain that seeming paradox, contenting itself with declaring "that the elderly person is indeed less pliable than youth; that he has not the nerve or energy of the young man." The *Eagle* did conclude that even at 60, keeping a job that was not beyond one's capacity was easy enough everywhere. But, "Getting a new place is altogether a different matter either in business or industry."[6]

Keeping media attention alive, Action came forward to ask the public to name his newly created organization, a group that he hoped would have enough power to force employers to accept the elderly and near-elderly for a job as quickly as they seemed to hire young workers. Soon thereafter, on August 30, the group held its second meeting, also at the Brooklyn YMCA. This time about 300 people were reported to be in attendance. Action announced that the group would be called the Cooperative Action Membership Corporation (CAMC). Dues were established and fixed at $6 a year with an initiation fee set at $1. Before 11 P.M. that evening 60 members were said to have paid their dues.[7]

For two or three weeks Action had kept up media attention as he parried questions as to his identity with responses such as, "My name is 'Action,' and that is what I mean to get. I will reveal my name when all is propitious." Apparently that time came early in September when he revealed himself as 48-year-old Clement Schwinges of Brooklyn, a graduate of the University of Bonn in Germany, a retired manufacturer, a student of international economics and a "benefactor of those who find their usefulness in a modern world decreasing in ratio to their increase in years." Confidently, he expected to start a revolt of age against youth. It was the younger generation he considered to be the tyrant, and not the elder. He hoped to break down the barrier he saw as having been erected between the employers and prospective employees over a certain age, regardless of ability or experience. "I want to prevent the waste of one of the nation's most valuable assets—experience—which one can only acquire with the passing years." In passing, Schwinges remarked that years earlier, when he lived in Germany, he had belonged to a group similar to the one he had just organized and incorporated in New York.[8]

A day later a female officer with CAMC (one of those anonymous ten) spoke out. She wanted her name to remain a secret because she didn't want any further obstacles thrown her way in looking for work, through publicity. One of her major complaints was that much was said about middle-aged men looking for work but little about middle-aged women, whose problem was equally great, if not greater. She said that employment agencies often advised middle-aged women to lie about their ages when applying for jobs. Showing some of the prejudice of the era herself, she stated that another hindrance was the number of young married women who continued to work after they married. As well, she blamed the "attractive blonde girl" who guarded the anteroom and seldom let a middle-aged woman get by her to see those that did the interviewing and hiring.[9]

Late in September 1927, Schwinges reported that his group had enrolled a little over 100 members, collected $300 in cash, and had several hundred applications from people looking for jobs. CAMC's office work was conducted entirely by volunteer assistants. Originally the intent was to make the association self-supporting, but Schwinges admitted the movement would not be immediately self-supporting and that CAMC would have to accept the offers of assistance from outsiders, which had already been made. He proposed then to start a campaign to obtain vacancies from employers, both small and large, who were willing to employ middle-aged people to fill those positions. He added that, "it seems that the extent of the unfortunate situation of the middle-aged unemployed is very little known among employers." This was hardly true as so many of them had open policies which precluded the hiring of people beyond a certain age.[10]

At an annual convention dinner of the National Employment Board, Schwinges was one of the speakers. He urged employment agencies to turn over to his group all vacancies they were unable to fill and let CAMC fill them with older workers. Urging them to do so for the feeling of satisfaction it would give them, rather than for profit, he noted that his group could afford to pay no fee.[11]

When CAMC held its first meeting in Manhattan, in November 1927, only 28 attended. A disappointed Schwinges blamed lack of cooperation on the part of the public and the press for the poor attendance.[12]

Then when the group held another meeting in Brooklyn, in May 1928, only 11 people turned up. When he formed the group he had expected to enlist the goodwill of employers on behalf of middle-aged applicants. By now, though, Schwinges admitted to being discouraged with the response given to CAMC. He told the meeting that he had concluded that it was impossible to interest the public in the plight of the middle-aged unemployed without making fools of them. He said one could not carry on a dignified publicity campaign such as CAMC was trying to do. The biggest mistake he made, he told the meeting, was in thinking that those who had jobs would contribute to the financial support of his group as a provision against the time they might find themselves out of work and turned away from an employment agency because they were over 40. Admitting CAMC had little money, Schwinges explained that most members could not pay the dues. Up until then they had 1,400 applicants but only 200 had been placed. One speaker at the meeting was Edwin F. Daley, chief mechanical engineer of the Morse Dry Dock company who, strangely, attacked older workers by contending that if a man over 40 was discriminated against by employers, it should be assigned to the mental stagnation that possessed the long-service employee. Daley explained that as both employee and employer, he had observed that the most stubborn obstacle an employer had to overcome in making the rapid changes so important to American industry was "the mental opposition of the old-time employe. He remains content to take a passive part in our industry, hoping that it will pull him up with it by some meeting."[13]

A few weeks after that poorly attended meeting, a man named Frank Egan suggested that as a remedy perhaps certain jobs and positions could be restricted to men over 50. An excellent beginning could be made, he believed, by restricting the position of doorman and usher in apartments, stores, theaters, and so on, to men over 50 years of age. Surely those were jobs, said Egan, that "younger men should not be permitted to take." However, Schwinges pointed out that the first qualification for doormen and ushers (male) in one of New York's modern movie theaters was an age limit of 27. Other necessary qualifications included perfectly straight legs, good teeth, and a marcel wave.[14]

Just two years after Action and his group were launched amid strong media coverage, the founder was even more discouraged. Pointing out his group was still not financially self-sufficient, he admitted that it was therefore not very effective. With its philosophy that service should be free to members and non-members alike, as well as employers, CAMC relied on donations, especially from those placed in a job; but most forgot the group as soon as they were placed. Claiming the association had placed several hundred people in permanent positions, Schwinges went on to observe they constituted only a small percentage of the thousands who had applied to CAMC for work. The best accomplishment of his group, he thought, was in the fact they had fully succeeded in the primary objective, which he then declared to have been to focus public attention on the problem of the middle-aged. Several other organizations similar to CAMC were said to have been formed in various parts of the nation, but not one had lasted more than a few months. All faced the same problem, lack of money. Schwinges concluded, in perhaps overly melodramatic fashion; "It will be forever the saddest memory of my life that I was unable to prevent several suicides, by some of those present at the first meetings, when they were disappointed in their last hope of getting a decent job soon." After this point Schwinges would appear once in a while as the writer of a letter to the editor, but essentially both he and CAMC faded into obscurity. It is impossible to say if Action was responsible for starting some of the media attention directed to the problem or whether his arrival was merely coincident with an already destined-to-arrive attention. Particularly strong from 1927 to 1929, that focus would wax and wane over the following decades but never entirely go away. In that sense Schwinges may have been more successful than he imagined.[15] Other similar organizations did attempt to form, in the wake of CAMC. Starting much like Action did, one William Henry Roberts had a letter published in the *Times* in which he urged those who had written other letters to the paper about the middle-aged employment problem, and others, to communicate with his organization, the National Association for the Benefit of Middle-Aged Employes. Roberts listed himself as the group's executive secretary.[16]

Six weeks later this group announced it was mailing a questionnaire to employers to obtain the view of the employer and his experience with young workers as compared to those aged 40 to 60. The Association noted that the practice of scrapping workers of 40 and over had created a problem of huge proportions and one of grave concern "to the leading economists, statesmen and philanthropists of our country ... it is creating an economic problem that is most serious in the eyes of the President, his cabinet, the Secretary of Labor, the Governors of our various States, as well as the great thinkers of our day." The problem had not then reached such lofty levels, but it was getting there. Roberts' group vanished from sight even more quickly than did CAMC.[17]

Media articles began to look at the problem. Journalist Walter Hiatt wrote a lengthy and sympathetic piece in which he pointed out that in a number of cases, federal and state civil service requirements had a 40-year age limit for new employees. Hiatt argued that, "Formerly—a generation ago, for instance—people of 40 received the preference. But a new industrial era has arisen; mass production has set in, new machinery has been devised, and there is now a call for 'pep,' which means youth." There was, of course, no preference for older workers 20 years earlier. Continuing, the report named William Osler as perhaps the unconscious spokesman for this so-called new era back in 1905, when he made his infamous remarks. After Osler, thought Hiatt, came the efficiency expert, and then, even in fiction, "youth was boomed at the expense of age." A couple of years after he made his comments, Osler was unrepentant: "The discussion which followed my remarks has not changed but has rather strengthened my belief that the real work of life is done before the fortieth year and that after the sixtieth year it would be best for the world and best for ourselves if men rested from their labors." Schwinges was cited as saying that people past 40 having trouble getting jobs was something that became "notably evident after the war" when a lot of them were thrown out of their positions and were never able to get work again. Behind that, said the CAMC head, was the delusion that had swept business circles that only the young man was fit. He also blamed, in part, efficiency experts. "Everywhere they go, posing as gods, they throw out older people; in order to sell themselves they must make changes." One person interviewed was Dr. H.S. Person, managing director of the Taylor Society, founded to promote the science of business management. According to him the over-40 problem had not yet been investigated by business. Person had two ideas regarding the prejudice of business toward employing older men "that has been conspicuous since the war." One was that the postwar period had been marked by an enormous advance in power machinery, and that equipment demanded energetic and alert young men to run it. Secondly, he thought that in the smaller plants, where skilled labor was demanded, the problem was less serious. President of the Psychological Corporation, the national association of industrial psychologists, W.V. Bingham remarked that modern industry had fewer places for the older white-collar workers to transfer to, if they sought to try a new business, than were available just a few years earlier. That was favorable for the employee on the inside, as long as his firm did well or it was "not swallowed up by a merger. Once out, he is in a worse position than ever before, and must begin to dye his hair." Bingham added that during the last five years thousands of men had gone into the hot dog stand business. He had just completed a study for the Boston Elevated Railway company with the results indicating that older men were safer workers than were younger employees.[18]

Writing in a business journal, Fred Colvin said there seemed to be another epidemic of "chloroform 'em at 40" starting in some manufacturing sections. Although industry was not yet starting to weed men out at 40, Colvin declared that employment people were receiving orders that "40 is the dead-line when hiring new men." Anybody over 39 looking for work was out of luck "as only in the case of war or other calamity is he likely to find a job better than a sweeper or night watchman."[19]

Stuart Chase reported in the August 1929 issue of *Harper's Magazine* that one of the cracks in the mirror of American prosperity was the apparently increasing difficulty with which men over 40 retained their jobs, and the even greater difficulty with which they found a new job once they had lost an old position. A machine shop factory manager from Indiana said he thought there was less opportunity for older men in industry now than there used to be. The main change he had seen in his plant was the speeding up of machines and the replacement of people by machines. Appearing before the United States Senate, the president of the Delaware and Hudson Railroad said his company hired no one over 40; Bethlehem Steel Company stated that their age cut-off was 45. Chase cautioned readers of his article not to become overly complacent because, "With mergers daily cracking about us like sky bombs, who is sure that his job is not one of the overhead costs which the merger is inaugurated in part to reduce? What we may be reasonably sure of is that the older man will be the chief sufferer when the selective process sets in." He also noted that as able employees lost their jobs through such processes, "the mark of failure goes with them. Whatever the facts, the general impression must henceforth be that they have been tried and found wanting."[20]

To illustrate the problem, Chase cited figures from the last Census of Occupations which showed that, of all active farmers in America, 8.8 percent were over 65, of all active bankers and brokers, 5.4 percent were over 65. But, of all active bookkeepers the number was just 1.2 percent; machinists, 1.7 percent; coal miners, 1.6 percent; clothing workers, 1.2 percent; printers, 1.3 percent; iron workers, 1.5 percent; and so on. In periods of unemployment he thought the old had been let out probably as often on average as had the young, possibly more often. "But never until the last few years, and in no other country save America, have age limits been set up—written or unwritten—in quantity lots; never have older men, often skilled and competent, had so much trouble in finding new work...—this is something new."[21]

The plight of female employees was investigated separately by an unbylined reporter who set out to find out if the charges of no office jobs for older women were true. It was all in response to the public statements made by the anonymous female officer from Schwinges' CAMC organization. The director of the American Vocational Exchange, a private employment agency, felt there was a definite downturn in opportunities as a result of the war, that the trained and experienced older female office worker stood a better chance of landing a job before World War I than she stood in 1927. Her reasoning was that the war brought many men into executive positions who otherwise would not have held them. That downward step was duplicated in the choice of women selected by them for positions in their departments. She added that there was no use in shutting one's eyes to the fact that youth and appearance were tremendous assets to the women seeking employment. "I do not quarrel with this attitude on the part of employers, for it is more or less natural; but it can occasionally be carried to an extreme." At her agency she was asked to supply a competent stenographer who was no older than 26. She sent a highly qualified woman who had turned 27 only a couple of days before the interview. Nonetheless she was rejected. At the American Vocational Exchange the question of age was said to have been emphasized very much by employers in recent years. Many of them insisted on women not more than 30, and during the previous few months it had been noticed that many of the finest secretarial jobs were for females not more than 26. The favorite age range from employers in calling her agency for stenographers was from 23 to 25. When asked what caused this change, the director brought up the reason of lack of adaptability by older workers, that very young girls worked for less money, and "Again, there is, of course, the natural human element in favor of youth." When she sent out two for a job interview—one pretty, young, not very experienced and one older, less attractive but far more experienced—she knew perfectly well "it will be the pretty and relatively inexperienced girl who will get the job." As an afterthought she added, "I am sorry to say that women have not the same pride of achievement as have men, and it is this lack that makes so many of them flotsam and jetsam of business offices."[22]

Harsher still was Helen Eldredge, director of the YWCA Central Branch's Employment Bureau, who spoke of getting a job as an aspect of survival of the fittest. For her, those who complained so loudly that they could no longer get jobs had enjoyed in their youth the same chance that the younger generation was then enjoying. If they had not made good she did not see how they could justly blame any one but themselves. Eldredge declared, "The plight of the jobless middle-aged is the best argument to parents so to train and educate their children that this situation is not likely to arise." In conclusion she said: "I consider that women should be content to do things within their capacity. It is no good for them to waste their time in attempting to do things entirely beyond their abilities and to fight to be where they cannot possibly get." That is, part of the problem of older women was that they were applying for jobs they had no business considering in the first place.[23]

The head worker at St. Barnabas House, a shelter for women and children in New York City, was Helen Romaine Bradley. She said, in 1928, that of all the problems brought to them none was more tragic than the middle-aged woman who had been thrown out of employment. Her shelter often received offers from housewives to feed and shelter those women, if they would do the housework without pay. However, St. Barnabas declined such offers, calling them unfair. Bradley felt most women would normally get a job, perhaps needing a little push, but that the unemployment situation had acted tragically upon middle-aged women. Such people might get a few days' work, then nothing, and so on. Bradley also remarked, "There is another problem, peculiar to the middle aged who seek employment. Employers naturally prefer to have young good-looking women in their employ...."[24]

With regard to age discrimination in specific occupations, Daisy Kugel undertook a 1929 study involving interviews, correspondence and questionnaires with employers of home economists in public schools, colleges, and extension work, and with employment agencies for teachers, dietitians and other professional workers. Employees in these fields were women. The 260 returned surveys came from 215 employers who had in their employ 5,668 home economists, living in 48 states and territories, and 93 cities. Kugel said her results showed the sentiment against older women in home economics was very general, at least in regard to teachers, extension workers, and hospital dietitians. From the study it was found that 58 percent of the college administrators, 56 percent of the city school employers, and 61 percent of the directors of extension followed a definite policy of age limits in the employment of new people. "In cases in which the upper age limit is fixed by law or school regulations, the mean is 44.5 years—a seemingly low limit to establish legally. The mean age limit as fixed by custom or opinion is 34.6 years." Objections to the older women, stated Kugel, were based on personality, fear of physical disability, and the belief that their professional ability was less than that of the younger women. The undesirable personal trait most frequently mentioned was lack of adaptability. Others often cited were "irritability and over-sensitiveness." However, Kugel noted that none of those objecting to older women presented facts or other scientific evidence in support of their expressed opinions.[25]

In an issue of *Printer's Ink*, Don Dickinson wrote about the plight of clerical men and technically educated men who were being thrown out of employment in great numbers, principally as the result of mergers. That caused Ernest McCullough to reply that he had made a personal investigation and knew that many employment agencies would not register men who admitted to being over 40, no matter how good their experience. Those agencies said that employers did not want men over 40. McCullough added that management no longer engaged in their former habit of laying off thousands of workers and reducing wages to save money. Rather, mergers were formed to reduce overhead with good paying positions formerly filled by middle-aged and over employees refilled with very young men at low wages, and seasoned executives at good pay were replaced by very young men who were their assistants at considerably lower salaries. He then argued that young men were hired because American employers followed the crowd and were "crazed with 'pep' and the gospel of pep and think that only young blood contains pep." However, his previous argument indicated that it was all about money—getting rid of older, more highly paid people for younger, lesser paid ones—and nothing to do with youthful pep. A last point made by McCullough was probably important in explaining why the problem got so much media attention in the last half of the 1920s, and relatively little in the quarter century prior to that. McCullough said, "Also, and this is important, the bar against middle-aged employes affects many whose education and social standing are far better than those of manual workers who chiefly were affected a generation or so ago. The people now affected are more articulate than the manual workers."[26]

Pronouncements on the issue came from prominent people from a variety of fields and walks of life. At a Miami meeting early in 1929 of the American Federation of Labor (AFL) it was decided to undertake a nationwide survey to determine the extent of the practice of fixing 40 or 45 as the age limit for employment and present the results to President Herbert Hoover. Nothing seems to have come from that resolution. That the situation was serious seemed apparent to the Columbus, Ohio, *Dispatch* from the anxiety manifested by "labor leaders and students of sociology the country over."[27]

In a 1929 Labor Day address in Baltimore by AFL president William Green, the labor leader declared that the practice of discrimination against workers of 40 or 45 years of age had grown to the point where it was causing grave concern and serious consideration. The organized labor movement protested against this practice, he said, because it was regarded as barbarous and inhuman. He added that if the public conscience could be sufficiently aroused to the dehumanizing effect of the discrimination it would protest so vigorously that large corporations and large employers would be compelled to discontinue it. It was inconceivable, he thought, that society would tolerate a practice of that kind, especially when it reached a serious stage. It was then the aim of the AFL to find a solution to the problem and to publicly proclaim it. When that point was reached, "we shall call upon all classes of people to support us in the application of the remedy and in such constructive action as may seem necessary," concluded Green.[28]

In a report prepared by the AFL for its annual convention, it was noted that studies of the subject indicated that the most frequent age limit for unskilled labor was 40, and for skilled labor 45. After referring to the effect of speed and mass production as a detriment to hiring older workers, the report declared that retirement pensions by the federal government and private employers were also factors adversely affecting the hiring of older people. Other causes mentioned were the introduction of group insurance and the employer's desire to keep the workmen's compensation rates low.[29]

That report, prepared by the Executive Council of the AFL, went on to allege that widespread discrimination against older employees existed in practically all industries and trades, as well as in federal, state and county governments. According to the report the railroad, oil, rubber, automobile, and steel industries each refused to employ workers who had reached age 45.[30]

When Green opened that Toronto, Ontario, convention he referred to the barring of men over 40 from new jobs in industry as a custom that was "inhuman, uncivilized and indefensible" from any point of view. Green pledged that, "It is the American Federation of Labor which will constantly protest against this policy and oppose it until public opinion and the public conscience is aroused and they call a halt to it."[31]

When New York State Governor Franklin Roosevelt's Commission on Old Age Security held hearings, one of those who made a presentation was Emmanuel Kovelski, a representative of the New York State Federation of Labor. Kovelski said that the worry about losing jobs due to age was such an obsession with American workers that they were even taking to dyeing their hair when the first streak of gray appeared.[32]

One federal official who spoke out against the discrimination was Secretary of Labor James J. Davis. In a speech at a banquet for its long-serving employees given by the Westinghouse company he said a person of 50 or 60 was just as capable a worker as he was at 30 and perhaps even more capable; the reason was that the years had brought the benefits of experience and added skill. In his own steel industry, where he once worked as a youth in a mill, Davis recalled that workers regularly lied about their age, never admitting to being more than 48; some darkened gray hair with soot from the furnace. Bosses willingly went along with such ruses because they wanted to keep good workers. Continuing, Davis said, "Now, it appears this arbitrary discharge of the worker, regardless of his fitness, at an age arbitrarily fixed, is becoming a general policy.... The tendency is to fix the age of retirement at a limit even progressively lower. By some employers it is placed as low as 40 years. It begins to be serious and alarming." In conclusion he stated: "I have said this practice of discharging workers for age is not a novelty; this popular resentment toward it is. I believe that if ever this public resentment reaches any volume, and acquires a voice, the custom is doomed to the extinction that it deserves. In the face of a public sufficiently aroused against it, the enlightened employer will abandon the practice of his own accord. The other kind will be driven from it."[33]

Taking a different approach was the Manchester, New Hampshire, *Union* which editorialized that the methods of industry had changed radically since the war and that older men had not shown themselves as amenable to change as their younger counterparts. Very often those older workers were said to have resisted the innovations made and conformed to them only in a half-hearted manner. That resistance and lack of cooperation hampered industry in the field of competition, and "in some instances it has led to a reorganization of the employment forces that has reacted against the older employees. The older men must share a part, at least, of the responsibility for the condition in which they now find themselves," concluded the paper.[34]

A trade group, the American Management Association, observed in a report that the reorganizations and mergers of companies often resulted in the release of older workers who were described as frequently slower, not so easily transferable, and higher salaried than younger ones. Also mentioned as drawbacks in the placing of older workers were their lack of adaptability and "personal peculiarities," although opinion on that point was reported to be not unanimous. That report made a number of recommendations to workers on how to improve their usefulness. Since it was pretty well agreed, believed the American Management Association, that the difficulties of older workers were due in no small part to their being set in their work habits and thought patterns, "not sufficiently adaptable nor teachable, not cooperative with associates, and above all not open-minded enough to new ideas and customs, it surely behooves them to watch out for these middle-aged tendencies."[35]

Reverend Dr. Charles Kendall Gilbert, secretary of the Social Service Commission, speaking at a church said that one of the greatest tragedies in industry was that of the middle-aged man with the man of 45 apparently too old for the industrial system. No one wanted him, thought Gilbert; "so at what should be the prime of his life he is discarded and the remorseless speeding up of our industrial machinery continues."[36]

Norman Thomas, then running as the Socialist candidate for Mayor of New York City, advocated the establishment of a municipal employment agency which would give special attention to placing men and women over the age of 45.[37]

Standard Oil Company of New York personnel manager C.R. Dooley urged an analysis of positions to find those which could be filled satisfactorily by older people be undertaken by every business organization. Places found to be suitable for older workers should be "reserved" for them as far as practical, to help solve the problem. However, he thought a modification of pension plans and other policies, which he thought had been largely responsible for the problem, would be necessary before the issue could be solved. He noted that some companies then allowed older applicants to waive pension rights. Dooley suggested that in searching for a new job the older worker would do well to apply first to the smaller firms since chances for work were usually better among small companies. To the middle-aged employee who found himself out of work because of a merger involving his company or through a reduction in the work force, Dooley warned against giving way to "panic."[38]

In a widely covered interview in the July 1929 issue of the *Ladies Home Journal*, automobile magnate Henry Ford declared that the rumors which surfaced from time to time that the Ford plants were refusing to hire anyone over 40 were untrue and that under no circumstances would he have a personnel policy of young men only. He added that he would prefer, if he could make the choice, to have all his employees between 35 and 60 years of age because then he would have a stable and experienced workforce. Ford didn't personally care how much over 60 the men were, as long as they could do the work. It was absolutely necessary, he said, in order to get the work done, to have a solid framework of older and more experienced men who knew exactly what they were doing: "The records of the employment department show that the work which calls for endurance is best served as a rule by men who are forty and over. Younger men seem to tire of jobs of this kind rather quickly and want to be transferred to lighter work." It was heavy praise indeed for older men workers from Ford. And it was for men only. Just a small fraction of the work was judged to be suitable for women. Of a total Ford workforce of 120,000 in and around Detroit, 710 were women. Furthermore, it was a Ford policy not to employ women who had no dependents.[39]

A problem with Ford's praise was that somebody bothered to check it against available plant data. No age data was available for the 120,000 then employed, but data did exist for just a short time earlier, when the workforce stood at 90,000. Employees 50 and over made up 7.3 percent of Ford employees, while that group was 22.5 percent of the American population; 30.1 percent of the workforce were 40 and over, compared to 39.3 percent of the total population. In the United States, as a percentage of "occupied persons" those aged 45 to 64 were 24.2 percent; those 65 and over were 4.1 percent, for a total of 28.3 percent. If half of Ford's 40- to 50-year-olds were assigned to the 45 to 50 group, then the proportion of Ford workers 45 and over would be about 18.7 percent, much lower than the 28.3 percent expected just to achieve the distribution found in the general population, never mind favoring the older worker. Since the number of men employed by age went steadily downward year by year after 40, putting the age 40 to 50 segment into two equal groups would overstate the 45 to 50 segment; the actual percentage would be something less than 18.7 percent, down perhaps a point or more.[40]

With all the media attention to the issue, business probably felt it had to respond in some way to take itself off the hook. One of the ways it did so was by a survey, done by its lobby group, the National Association of Manufacturers. That organization completed a survey in 1929 to determine the extent to which American manufacturers set maximum age limits for employment. They found that 70 percent of companies surveyed had no age limits; 30 percent did have a maximum hiring age, ranging from 25 to 70 years for unskilled and semiskilled positions, and from 35 to 70 years for skilled workers. Where maximums were in place, the most frequent limit for unskilled and semiskilled was 45; for skilled positions it was 50 years. Some 25 percent of the firms with limits used 45 as the limit; 50 percent set it higher, 25 percent put it lower. In firms with age limits, 22 percent of them said it was due to the physical condition of the workers or the work; 21 percent gave as a reason the difficulty of integrating older workers into company pension plans. The third most common reason, given by 19 percent, was "the tendency of older employes to slow up at their tasks." Fourteen percent gave as reasons the cost of workmen's compensation insurance, the liability of older employees to injuries "and added danger to other employes when working with older men." Eleven percent said it was due to the existence of group life insurance plans, since hiring older workers increased the cost of premiums. Reportedly, companies with age limits sometimes made exceptions to the age limits in the case of former employees who wished to return.[41]

While that survey's results were published in both the *New York*

Times and the *Monthly Labor Review*, neither one of them raised some obvious questions about the survey. Writing in *Harper's Magazine*, Stuart Chase addressed one of them. First he noted a survey in May 1929 by the Brooklyn Chamber of Commerce which showed 121 out of 400 firms with a maximum age policy, also 30 percent. Chase pointed out that in both surveys it was not stated what percentage of workers were employed by the discriminating 30 percent. There was reason to believe, he thought, that the companies which had a formal, written policy were usually the larger ones. He cited Abraham Epstein, executive secretary for the American Association for Old Age Security, as alleging that those 30 percent of the firms probably employed 90 percent of the workers. Concluded Chase, "It is in the great impersonal corporation that the lines are drawn; and certain it is that 30 percent of American corporations employ 90 percent of the workers or more."[42]

Another unraised question about the National Association of Manufacturers survey was answered indirectly in a paper presented by the American Management Association at its convention. That paper summarized the experience of 64 companies which answered this group's questionnaire. Only nine of the firms (14 percent) had definite written rules as to age at time of employment. However, the majority had "a tacit understanding that the employment office should not take on older men and women." One firm admitted such a tacit understanding had existed for about five years or more and was based on the assumption that after 50 there was in many individuals an increasing tendency to suffer accidents and one of decreasing efficiency. Another firm said it had a tacitly accepted age limit for employment of 45 years for men and 35 years for women. That one had been in effect for 10 years—"no written rule and subject to exceptions any time common sense dictates." Still another company had an unwritten rule, then in effect for two years, to hire no one over 45. A fourth enterprise had an unwritten rule to not hire anyone over 40.[43]

Referring to the companies with a written age limit, the American Management Association said where there was such a limit, it really "works out much lower than those established limits.... There were twelve times as many answers admitting that in practice the hiring age is much below the established age limit, as those taking the opposite view—rather conclusive proof of a real situation." One company said its effective hiring maximum was "slightly under 30 years," while another admitted that "actually very few people are employed who are over 35 years of age." In naming some of the reasons for setting age limits, the report mentioned: promotion from within—making positions at the bottom about the only

openings; and pension plans that required a certain length of service, usually 15 to 25 years. However, of the companies surveyed, nearly twice as
many did not have pension plans as had them. The article reporting this
survey concluded that there seemed to be no good reason why an arbitrary age limit should be established. People could be hired with the
understanding they would not qualify for a company pension due to lack
of service, "as was happening to some."[44]

Some prominent citizens blamed the problem on various causes. At
a conference on Old Age Security, Edward Lyman, director of the New
York Home for the Aged of the Protestant Episcopal Church, blamed the
machine age for casting middle-aged workers into the discard pile. He
felt the machine age was tending to make an increasing percentage of
people dependent, even before they had attained the beginning of old
age.[45]

Stuart Chase thought one of several reasons for the problem was
technological unemployment in which the total discharge rate was greater
than the total hiring rate. Then, when an older worker went to look for
a new job he ran into the other problems.[46]

Dr. Eugene Brandone was concerned about the release of middle-
aged managers from their jobs because of mergers, company reorganizations, and so on. One executive told him "Our concern does not take on
discarded lumber from the other man's cargo." Those types did not "fit
in" because they were experienced, had ideas of their own, and were "less
susceptible to the new order of things." When they entered the services
of a new concern they were "almost impossible to handle—they want to
do things in their way." This executive felt young workers could be made
to fit in, and thus his company preferred them. Brandone thought that in
general a company wouldn't take a chance with a man, no matter what
his successful experience had been "as against one failure." Acknowledging there were many extenuating circumstances which could have brought
about the job loss, he added, "but it, nevertheless, is a failure, and the busy
modern executive looks upon it as such without any thought of searching for the underlying causes." Brandone described business as a cruel and
relentless taskmaster, "and if you want to avoid the scrap pile, accumulate
a competence before you reach forty-five or more."[47]

Up until the mid–1920s there were no rational, sensible reasons
advanced for the refusal to hire older workers. Generally, vague reasons
such as lack of adaptability or "won't fit in" were given. They were reasons that had not been tested for validity, or in some cases could not be
tested at all. However, from around the mid–1920s reasons given started

to lean more to supposed rational causes, items that put up an employer's costs to the point that it made no economic sense to hire new workers over a certain age. Thus, business could argue that it was not discriminating against older workers at all, it was only making sound economic decisions. There was little truth in these reasons but, by using them, business hoped it could avoid looking like a villain. The Brooklyn *Eagle* newspaper found fault with the middle-aged because they were less pliable and had less energy, but it believed a more potent reason was found in the fact that workmen's compensation insurance laws, with premiums higher for age, offered an economic reason for preferring younger employees. Actually, those insurance premiums were based on the accident rate in a specific industry, not the age of the employees. It would only be a factor if older workers had more injury claims than younger ones.[48]

A study done which showed precisely that was done based on nearly 5,000 cases of industrial injury for which compensation was paid by the New York Bureau of Workmen's Compensation. For six of the seven injury categories studied there was a definite relationship between age and length of time off work. For example, in the category "cuts, punctures and lacerations" workers under 39 were off work for periods ranging from 2.5 to 3.5 weeks, while those over 40 were absent for 4.3 to 7.2 weeks. Overall, for those younger workers, 83 percent were able to return to work within four weeks; only 46.6 percent of the older workers did so. What remains true today is that for similar injuries sustained at work older workers will be off for longer periods than will younger ones. What this study did not look at was the rate of injury per age group. Later research would show consistently that older workers had less injuries than did younger ones. It meant it all came out about even in terms of costs. Workmen's compensation rates still vary enormously, but by the danger factor of the occupation. A steel mill pays much more per employee than does an insurance office. Using workers' compensation costs as a reason for not hiring older workers was always a weak one, one that didn't stand any investigation and was thus used less often than the other two prime reasons—group life insurance costs and the cost of pension plans.[49]

The New York *World* newspaper said that the increasingly popular policy of group insurance "unquestionably militates" against the older job seekers. In agreement with that sentiment was Stuart Chase who claimed that job discrimination against older applicants was something new and it resulted, in part, from an "excess of philanthropy" on the part of the companies. The first group insurance policy was written, said Chase, in 1913, but it was a benefit that didn't become important until after World

War I, around 1920. Some six million workers were said to be covered by 1929. Since premiums increased with age, Chase argued that when an employer hired a new person, other things being equal, he most likely picked the younger applicant.[50]

American Federation of Labor officials also felt the problem arose, in part, from the comparatively recent practice of insuring employees by group, something that worked against older applicants. Federation head William Green proposed his organization would find how much "untruth" there was in the assertion of some employers that social justice legislation was responsible for age discrimination in employment. "Here enters the question of State monopoly of workmen's compensation insurance, where the cost of administration is low and there is no profit, versus the system which permits private companies, operated for profit, to write such [life] insurance," he declared. "One way of erasing the 'forty-year dead line' may be in the general adoption of the former system." At least a few publications agreed with him. The New York *Journal of Commerce* said that if pension funds and group insurance were responsible for the situation "then changes in methods of pension and insurance administration are in order." Regarding the claim that the blame for age discrimination could be laid to insurance costs the Manchester, New Hampshire, *Union* offered the editorial opinion that, "This is doubtless true in isolated cases, but it can not be accepted as playing a prominent part in the growth of a tendency that has become so widespread."[51]

Abraham Epstein also thought that an additional factor compounding the problem had been introduced in the preceding decade—group insurance. Six million workers were covered, he said, and because premium rates depended on age, "The individual manufacturer is just as much a victim of this development as the 'fired' employe."[52]

In response to the claim that group life insurance plans worked against the hiring of older job applicants, Clement Schwinges told of a plan recently instituted by the General Electric Company. The employees had two policies, one given free by the company, the other paid entirely by the worker. On the company-paid plan the premium was inflexible, but the benefit decreased with the age of the insured at the time of the application. If the worker was 28 or less the face value was, say, $500; if he was 40 then it was only $440, and so on. Group insurance plans, said Schwinges, were only about 18 years old.[53]

Companies with private old-age pension plans then covered around four million workers, according to Stuart Chase. He gave the by-then standard company reason that if 25 years of service was required to receive benefits, a firm was reluctant to hire a 50-year-old who would retire in 15 years and get no pension. It made the company look bad in the eyes of the community, to the other workers, and so forth. Without comment Chase pointed out that other nations, particularly in Europe, had old-age pensions financed by the government. If he saw pension changes as a solution, he ignored the fact that age discrimination in employment also existed in Europe.[54]

One of the stronger advocates of pensions as a major part of the problem was Abraham Epstein, American Association for Old Age Security executive secretary. Unfortunately, he started off with a false assumption by saying, "The fact that arbitrary age limits, regardless of physical capacity, are unknown in industrial nations abroad indicates that the causes of the American developments are purely native." They resulted, he thought, from a unique and complete lack of social security for the worker and from placing that responsibility on the individual employer. Age discrimination in America was, in his view, to a large extent the outgrowth "of the entirely well-meaning and humanitarian desire on the part of many of our industrial leaders to protect" the worker in old age. He claimed the age barrier originated with the institution by American employers of private pension plans. More than 400 companies employing about four million workers were said to have adopted formal pension plans. Employers did not hire workers who were too old to work the 25 to 30 years necessary to qualify for a pension which was paid at age 65 or 70. "Many employers declare that were it not for the fear of being compelled to assume this moral responsibility, they would feel freer in employing workers regardless of age."[55]

For Epstein the burden of supporting old age had to be removed from employers and placed in the hands of the state. A government old-age pension would eliminate those employer fears of hiring older people then being burdened by old and incapable employees who had not worked long enough to qualify. Such a government plan, said Epstein, "would unquestionably result in the abolition of age qualifications for employment."[56]

Setting aside its usual hostility, the *New York Times* devoted an editorial to the "paradox" that the middle-aged worker was, in part at least, the victim of a general improvement in the status of the wage earner. Regarding the idea that insurance and pension plans conspired against older workers, the newspaper editorialized that there should be some way of shaping those rates and charges so that the middle-aged group was not separated from the main body of workers.[57]

American legislators stayed away from any attempt to enact laws in this period that affected age discrimination in employment. Nothing was on the books except the old 1903 Colorado statute which barred employers from discharging workers solely on the grounds of age. That law was never enforced. Farther afield a bill was presented in 1929 to the Uruguayan Chamber of Deputies that would require all public service corporations and all public works companies presenting bids for government work to submit evidence that at least ten percent of their total workforce was older than 45. Reportedly, many firms had been refusing to employ people over the age of 45. The bill did not become law.[58]

During this short period age discrimination in employment received a large amount of media attention. It is impossible to tell if it became a little worse, a lot worse, or if its incidence was unchanged but just got more attention. Prominent citizens and politicians weighed in with opinions, possible solutions, and so forth. Companies began to fashion "rational" reasons, such as insurance and pension plan costs, to explain what were often blatant and open age limits. It was an attempt to come out of the controversy as less than villains. Already some were aiding capitalist concerns with the bizarre explanation that workers were actually victims not of discrimination, but of company kindness, generosity and benevolence. That is, firms didn't hire older people who wouldn't work long enough to qualify for a pension because they were too decent to then have to turn them out at 65, pensionless. Some people seemed to believe it.

CHAPTER 3

The Problem Becomes Entrenched, 1930–1946

"It would be safe to say that a very large percentage of the [47- to 55-year-old] men who come into my office every day are not employable."
— *C. R. Dooley, personnel manager, Standard Oil of New York, 1931*

"The older job-seeker is definitely barred from 59 percent of the available jobs and is discriminated against in 89 percent of them."
— *New York State Commission on Old Age Security, 1932*

"Older people as a general rule are not interested in civil service.... Older people are not particularly interested in taking promotion exams."
— *New York City Mayor Fiorello La Guardia, 1937*

"[T]his problem has been developing steadily for fifteen years until it is now a menace and terror to thousands of family breadwinners when they reach the age of 45 or 50."
— *Secretary of Labor Frances Perkins, 1937*

"The problem of the middle-aged worker on the scrap
heap has always been much exaggerated."
                                —New York Times *editorial, 1937*

"We can't be forced 'to take on another fellow's discarded
workers.'"
                    —*Mark Daly, general secretary of the Associated
                              Industries of Buffalo, 1938*

With the onset of the Depression at the start of this period, unemployment in general soared to unheard-of levels. It was a problem that
was not fully solved until the American economy went on a war footing
at the end of the 1930s. Despite unemployment being outrageously high
in general, the problem of joblessness among older workers was not lost
in the more widespread despair. The issue continued to draw steady media
interest. For the first time laws designed to be at least partly successful
were enacted.

When Frank Hill wrote a 1934 article sympathetic to working beyond
age 65—that is, no compulsory retirement—he said it was generally
acknowledged that because of the attitude of industrial and business executives women of 40 or older and men of 45 and over found "difficulty in
getting new positions.... Too old!" Arguing that cry had always been
uttered, Hill thought that perhaps never before in history had there
been a tendency not just to set an arbitrary limit upon service measured
by number of years, "but also to put a definite penalty on the mere passing of youth."[1]

In early 1930 *Business Week* reported data from firms employing in
total over three million workers. Forty-two percent of those firms, employing 26 percent of the personnel, had no age limit; 40 percent of the firms,
employing 61 percent of the workers, barred all new hires over a certain
age. In 18 percent of the companies employing 13 percent of the people,
there was no age limit, but pensions were not granted to people hired after
a certain age.[2]

When one article pointed out that half the people on federal relief
had reached or passed the age of 40, it went on to remind readers that
even in the boom days want ads were cruelly explicit as to age limits.
Waitresses were said to have been too old at 26; applicants for clerical
jobs were out of luck if they were over 30. One company advertised for a
man of wide experience, managerial ability, a forceful type of executive—
yet he could be not more than 35 to 40 years old. According to this
account, critics of age discrimination blamed exaggeration and distortion

of observations by the then late surgeon William Osler. It was then more than 30 years since Osler had made his infamous utterances, yet they still were not forgotten. Osler's remarks were distorted to the point that the late doctor was misquoted as having said "a man should be chloroformed at sixty."[3]

Reporter Benjamin Colby observed in 1936 that no one knew just what percentage of the unemployed was, say, age 45 and over. Estimates were rooted in the unemployment census of 1930. In that earlier year unemployment among people past 45 was about 25 percent higher, proportionately, than among those 30 to 40 years of age. For Colby the problem of increasing unemployment among middle-aged and older men had been growing with the declining importance of skilled hand trades and the increasing mechanization of industry. That was recognized during the Twenties, he wrote, when different surveys showed a substantial proportion of business firms had a stated or an informal hiring deadline, around age 45 to 50, sometimes as low as 40. He added that the handicap of age was greatest among unskilled workers whose chief value to employers was usually their physical strength and ability. Next hardest affected were the semiskilled.[4]

When Colby looked at studies of workers on relief in March 1935, he found the number of older workers relative to the total labor force in about the same proportion as the older unemployed bore to the total unemployed in that 1930 census. Although from that it could be inferred that the position of older workers without work got no worse during the Depression Colby thought the number of workers on the relief rolls didn't tell the whole story. A WPA (Works Progress Administration) study of 198,157 workers on relief in 79 cities in May 1934 showed that people who had been out of work a long time were largely past 45 or 50. The ones who had been unemployed only a year or two were generally in the under-40 age brackets. Male workers on relief who had been jobless less than a year were mainly younger men, their median age being 32.2 years. At the other end of the scale, those without work for 10 years or more had a median age of 50.5 years. Between those two groups, the median age ranged upward consistently with the lengthening of the period of unemployment. The same trend was true for female workers who were, however, younger in all groups.[5]

That WPA study continued to track its people. Out of 416,082 workers on relief in 13 cities during the last quarter of 1935, an average of 2.5 percent found employment each month. For men between 25 and 34, the rate was 4.1 percent; for those between 35 and 44, it was 3.1 percent; for those 45 to 54, just 1.9 percent found work each month.[6]

Data from the United States Employment Service, drawn from seven states in 1937, looked at the placement ratio per hundred registrants, in the active file, by age and occupation. Results showed a very marked falling off in rates of placement in the older age groups. Among men the decline started in the 40s; among women, in the 50s for service workers, and in the 30s for white-collar women workers.[7]

At a 1930 gathering of 500 women at the American Woman's Association in New York three speakers discussed the problem of what to do with American women who were "fair, fit and forty." All of them agreed that women over 40 did not get anything like the same opportunity for employment that men that age did.[8]

Social service groups in Philadelphia conducted a 1933 study on women without work. The group totaled 1,654 females living on their own, the majority of those receiving unemployment relief in Philadelphia. Divided by age, 27.3 percent of them were over 60, 49.8 percent were over 50, and 74.3 percent were 40 and older. The average age of the women was 49.2 years; it was 46.6 years for the 749 Black women, 50.8 years for the native-born whites, and 56.2 years for the 281 foreign-born whites. Most of these women had been unemployed for long periods with lows of between 2.5 to 3.5 years, ranging up to 8.5 years. To determine as definitely as possible the employability of the group, representatives of the United States Women's Bureau interviewed a selected sample of 277 women, all under 60 years of age. Results were tabulated as follows: definitely employable, 37.1 percent of whites, 56 percent of Blacks; employable with limitations, 24.7 percent of whites, 5.5 percent of Blacks; employability doubtful, 14.5 percent of whites, 9.9 percent of Blacks; definitely unemployable, 23.7 percent of whites, 28.6 percent of Blacks. Those diagnosed as being employable with limitations had handicaps of age or mental or physical disabilities which, while not sufficient to prevent them from obtaining work, still limited their possibilities. One conclusion drawn from this study was that "age was considered less a deterrent to reemployment for colored workers than for the white women, because in the common occupation of the colored—domestic service—age does not constitute a handicap to the same extent as in clerical work or manufacture."[9]

Ollie Randall was head of the women's division of the Emergency Work Bureau in 1930. Some years later, in 1938, she was assistant director of welfare for the Association for Improving the Condition of the Poor. In that latter year she commented, "Not many years ago forty was a hazardous age for a woman to seek re-employment. Employers have lowered this standard now to an age limit of 35 years, which is considered the maximum age for re-employment today. In some classes of work, such as secretarial jobs, 28 years is the absolute top with the personnel directors." She added that most of the women who were thrown out of work in 1930, between the ages of 35 and 40, were still then, in 1938, out of work.[10]

Age bars were found in all types of occupations. At one of its 1930 meetings, the American Engineering Council declared the plight of the professional engineer being at the age of 40 was one of the chief problems confronting him. Arthur Berresford, managing director of the National Electrical Manufacturers' Association as well as president of the American Engineering Council, stated that the 40-year age bar was a very real problem. He found it unbelievable that a trained man of 40, an age when, as an engineer, experience had brought him to his real producing value, "should find difficulty in making a new connection because of his age." The bringing of those conditions into public attention by the Engineering Council, thought Berresford, "will be no small service to society."[11]

A study by a carpenter's union in upstate New York showed the average time without work during the previous 12 months by those under 45 was about six weeks, while those 45 to 54 were idle on average for six months. The 55 to 70 age group was without work for nine months out of 12; those over 70 were unemployed for the entire year.[12]

As Chief of the Personnel Division of the American Library Association, Hazel Timmerman reported on the plight of librarians in 1940 by noting "the ever narrowing employment opportunities in the profession for those over thirty-five years of age, WHATEVER THEIR QUALIFICATIONS" (emphasis in the original). Timmerman wrote of the administrative policy that excluded the professionally qualified candidate nearing 40 from consideration for a position or for a change of position after that age. She felt that very few employers would spend more than a few moments on the record of an unusually well-qualified person who was over 40. In conclusion she warned librarians that every change of position which they made after the age of 30 "must be to a library in which they will be willing to stay until retirement."[13]

While politicians at various levels of government would get involved in urging firms to hire more older workers—and some jurisdictions would enact laws to meet that goal—the government remained in the forefront of employers who actively imposed age limits. Effective March 1, 1930, an order of the United States Civil Service Commission went into effect at the Brooklyn Navy Yard. It fixed 48 years as the age limit above which certain classes of workers could not be employed. Three groups of employees were mentioned: unskilled laborers, skilled laborers, and skilled artisans. Unnamed officials of the Yard noted that it was difficult to find a good ship artisan below that age.[14]

When the same Civil Service Commission issued regulations, in 1933, to make 40 the maximum age limit for candidates sitting examinations for certain vacancies in clerical work, it led to protests from members of both Houses of Congress and from many other sources. Secretary of Labor Frances Perkins called the age limit "short-sighted." In answer to those attacks Harry B. Mitchell, president of the Civil Service Commission, explained that the policy did not mean that "people are through at forty; it merely means that people are beginning at not over forty." Commented a reporter, "The practice, of course, is one that has been more or less prevalent in industry for a good while. But to have the Civil Service supporting the theory is a blow to every worker of whatever sort."[15]

One of those upset was Representative Cochran who expressed amazement over the announcement by the Commission that applicants for some civil service vacancies had to be under 45, and in some cases under 25. Cochran declared that "if the government rules that men and women over 45 cannot enter the service private industry will follow the government's example and decline to employ men who have reached their forty-fifth birthday."[16]

In 1938 it was reported that some announcements of United States Civil Service examinations for accountants, stenographers, and skilled office workers set age limits as low as 26.[17] At the start of the 1930s the age limit set for taking on new men in the United States Army was 42. At the same time the Massachusetts civil service put the age limit for policemen and firemen at 35 years of age; they were then considering lowering the bar to age 29.[18]

Early in 1937 it was reported that the New York City Municipal Civil Service Commission had just announced an examination for typists; the age limit was 29 years. A few weeks later Alderman James A. Burke of Queens demanded an investigation of what he considered unreasonable and discriminatory requirements of age for civil service positions. Burke introduced a resolution in the Board of Aldermen protesting that the Municipal Civil Service Commission had set a qualifying age limit of 39 years on many other civil service positions. His measure urged age limits be raised to within 10 years of retirement age, which was 70 for most city positions. Taking issue with the alderman's position was Mayor Fiorello La Guardia who said, "It is absolutely necessary and in keeping with the times to make the civil service an attraction for young people. Older people as a general rule are not interested in civil service, as it provides no particular advantages to them if they enter late in life, except that it furnishes employment for a short term of years." According to La Guardia, the young took promotion exams and had an opportunity to work their way up, while "older people are not particularly interested in taking promotion exams." The mayor found Burke's suggestion particularly impractical in relation to policemen, firemen, and sanitation workers where he felt younger men were needed "because of the kind of work they must perform."[19]

Burke's efforts went nowhere, for in April 1937 the Municipal Civil Service Commission announced that an examination would be held for the position of clerk, Grade 2. The age limit was set at 25. A journalist noted that there were hundreds of highly skilled clerks in New York who couldn't take the exam because they were too old. Given the size of that city the estimate of hundreds must have been a vast understatement.[20]

This time protestors took the issue to the state Supreme Court in an attempt to get people over 25 admitted to the clerk exams. For the city, Assistant Corporation Counsel Jeremiah Evarts argued in court that the Civil Service Commission restricted age to 25 because it wanted flexibility in city employees who would grow up with their departments. Evarts observed that many who qualified for appointment might not receive a position on the city payroll for another four years, when they would be nearing 30. He said that the Civil Service Commission had spent a great deal of time studying the question and urged the court not to substitute its judgment for that of the commission.[21]

In July 1937 Justice Louis A. Valente ruled that the commission lacked the power to exclude persons past 25 from competing for positions in the entering clerical grades. He noted that the idea of establishing a career service in the clerical branch of city service was praiseworthy but could not understand why one who had passed 25 should be deprived of the opportunity of embarking on such a career. Valente added that the salary range of $1,200 to almost $1,800 made the positions attractive to many who were above the maximum age. The case was brought by Florence Ryan, 27 years of age, for a peremptory writ of mandamus directing the commission to cancel its plan for proceeding with the exam, to formulate new requirements for applicants and to extend the age limits. The court granted those terms.[22]

Within days the Commission appealed to the Appellate Division of the state Supreme Court for the suspension, pending a formal appeal, of the injunction order restraining it from proceeding with the exam for clerk. At the same time, however, since the exam remained scheduled for July 23 as originally planned, Civil Service Commission president James E. Finegan was cited for contempt of court for failing to observe the injunction. When the order granting mandamus was first issued by Valente, Finegan announced the exam would go ahead as set despite the mandamus.[23]

A day later Associate Justice Albert Cohn of the Appellate Division denied the commission's application for a stay of the restraining order. Immediately the commission announced it would ask Justice Valente for a modification of his order, so that 37,000 applicants between 18 and 25 could take the exam, set for a few days later. If Valente's order was upheld on formal appeal the commission said it would hold another exam for people over 25 in the following autumn, and successful candidates would be included in the civil service eligible list.[24]

On July 20 Supreme Court Justice Edward J. McGoldrick held Finegan and two other commission members in contempt of court. McGoldrick fixed no penalty but said they could purge themselves by putting into effect immediately the terms of the mandamus. As soon as he left the courtroom Finegan announced that the clerk exam would be postponed.[25]

During this period there was more activity in the establishment of clubs whose purpose was to organize and aid the older job-seekers. Clement Schwinges' group was gone but others tried to fill the void. The National Association for the Benefit of Middle-Aged Employes began on a temporary basis in November 1928. It was incorporated as a permanent organization in December 1929. Early in 1930 the group announced the start of a campaign, through churches, the press, clubs, charity organizations, political and social organizations, "and by direct appeal to larger employers and use of radio facilities for the purpose of offsetting the discrimination against mature employes now practiced to some extent by the government and in many industries."[26]

During their first public meeting to launch this public relations drive, executive director William Henry Roberts outlined the aims of the organization and suggested consideration of legislation to increase the age limit on all civic positions, at both the state and federal levels. Some 300 people attended. Within two months Roberts stated that his group received 250 to 500 applications each day from people aged from 35 to 50 or more who wanted a job. Appealing to employers to assist his group, he said that many of his members had been unable to obtain steady employment for between six months and two years. The National Association for the Benefit of Middle-Aged Employes then quickly disappeared from sight.[27]

A nationwide movement to combat prejudice against the employment of those past 40 years of age was launched at the start of 1937 with the announcement that papers had been filed for the incorporation of the American Citizen's League. The league's purpose was to change the attitude of American employers toward the employment of male and female citizens over the age of 40 and to use every effort to secure such persons legitimate employment. Fee for membership in the league was set at 25 cents per month with plans in the works to set up facilities to use to obtain employment for older workers. Organization president Peter A. Smith declared it was virtually impossible for those over 40 to get any kind of a legitimate job, once they had been thrown out of work. Smith said his group would fight for a no-age-limit civil service.[28]

At this group's first public meeting, held a few months later, about 100 people turned out to solve through public relations and legislation what it called "the greatest American tragedy." A score of those attending reportedly signed application blanks for membership, pledging themselves to pay a percentage of their salaries for its support, if and when they found paid work. However, the American Citizen's League promptly vanished from view.[29]

One national organization designed to fight age discrimination in employment that was formed during this period did manage to last. It was the Forty Plus Club, which had a somewhat narrow focus. Its origins went back to about March 1937 when Henry Simler, president of America's oldest typewriter company and chairman of the Employment Committee of the Sales Executives Club in New York City, persuaded the latter group to organize a special committee to fight "Fortyphobia."[30]

Simler was still with his group in the summer of 1938, then called the "40-Plus Committee." It was said to include people and groups attached to sales executives clubs, chambers of commerce, Rotary and Kiwanis clubs, and similar civic groups throughout the United States. Women reportedly joined the movement through female groups such as the Soroptimist Club in Los Angeles, the Altrusa clubs (similar to Rotary groups) and other associations.[31]

That summer of 1938 a new club was formed in Boston by Ronald Darling—the Forty Plus Club. You could not join unless you were out of work and over 40, unless you had earned from $4,000 to $14,000 a year as a business executive, unless you were fully capable of holding such a job again, and unless you were a male. The name was adopted with the blessing of the Sales Executives Club of New York and Henry Simler, who both faded from sight. Whereas the latter fought in general against age discrimination in employment, the Forty Plus Club organized to try and get jobs for each other. Every member called on employers and other contacts and tried to obtain a job for another club member. By the fall of 1938 the club had already expanded, in just a few months, with chapters launched in both Brocton and Salem, Massachusetts.[32]

By the spring of 1939 Forty Plus had 40 branches organized, or in process, in the United States, as well as six in Europe. The New York City branch formed in January 1939, and two months later it had 107 members and 50 applications for membership pending. That branch planned to get in touch with 200 firms a week in its quest for jobs. Forty Plus continued to operate without initiation fees or dues.[33]

Two years later Forty Plus reportedly had 35 branches in as many cities. If it was a real drop, as opposed to a mixup in numbers, it may have been due to the economic turnaround with World War II then underway. The New York City branch then had only 70 active members (a low point) as against the 200 (a self-imposed maximum) it had had at some point in its two-year history. In addition to the other conditions, prospective members also had to be American citizens.[34]

Bessie Mott complained in May 1940 that while much cognizance was taken of the problem of the unemployed man over 40, little attention had been paid to the unemployed woman over 35. Two months earlier Mott had founded the Executive Woman's Association of New York. Its aim was to help women over 35 who had executive experience and had earned $2,000 a year or more to find jobs by seeking cooperatively for them. Modeled on the Forty Plus Club the association was an outgrowth of the Soroptimist Clubs of New York, San Francisco, and Philadelphia. Mott said prejudice among employers against women over 35 was as widespread as the reluctance to hire men over 40. Mott added that the employer was the loser because practice and experience were what counted. "You cannot get these things in a very young person. Young women come and go. Most of them marry. The young woman usually falls in love with a man. The more mature woman falls in love with her job." This group also quickly vanished.[35]

At least a couple of other groups tried to emerge, apparently without success, during this period. One was formed in 1937 when several Washington, D.C., area women's groups banded together to form the Foundation for Americans of Mature Age, Inc., said to be active in six states. Its purpose was to aid older women in getting training, jobs, and so forth. Existing around the same time was The Over Forty Project, a group formed to better conditions for those over 40. Claiming to have a national membership of almost 100,000 it was said to be working for, among other things, a change in the Civil Service law to raise the age limits and to change the attitude of business and industry toward the older job seeker.[36]

Only the Forty Plus Club would survive, after a brief dormant period. With the coming of World War II and its relatively booming economy it became much easier for people of any description to get jobs. Most of those Forty Plus Clubs suspended their activity during this period. Typical was the original one—in Boston. However, founder Ronald Darling announced in April 1946 that his group had resumed its activities. This decision by Darling came after conferring with a considerable number of older men who got work, but were unemployed by this date. After talking to many men who had been unemployed in 1938 and who took war jobs which had by then terminated, Darling said the general opinion of those men was that "there is more opposition to the employment of older men with executive experience than before the war." During the late pre-war days there were an estimated 38 Forty Plus Clubs in operation. After the start of defense activities and especially after the attack on Pearl Harbor that number dwindled to about 13 branches known to be in active existence as of October 1945. Expenses of those clubs continued to be met exclusively by members' voluntary contributions. Each member pledged the equivalent of 2½ days a week to doing club work. There were no paid staff. They sprang back to life in the immediate postwar period because, as one reporter commented, "Many older workers are realizing that in the serious readjustment of the reconversion period their foothold in the wage-earning world will be precarious."[37]

Opinion-makers were regularly heard from during the period. In an editorial in early 1931 the *New York Times* declared that "discrimination against the man over 40 has been perhaps exaggerated, but it attained sufficient dimensions to constitute a problem." Explaining it away as something recent, the editorial continued: "Business has its fads, like other walks of life, and the bar raised against middle-aged men was one of them.... Employers permitted themselves to be hypnotized by the idea of speed and efficiency into exaggerated worship of the stop-watch method. There must have been employers who thought they were not being modern and progressive if they had elderly men about them without looking into the service such men were rendering."[38]

Later that same year a second editorial about age discrimination in employment spoke of the "legend" that had won a degree of popularity "altogether out of proportion to the kernel of fact it contains."[39]

Edward Rybicki, director of New York City's Free Employment Agency, announced in 1930 that the city's Department of Public Welfare officials would soon confer with 30 of the city's leading industrialists to study the problem of finding work for people over 40, who were "swamping" his agency and for whose services there was "little or no demand." He described the unemployment situation facing those over 40 as "shocking." Most middle-aged applicants at his agency were skilled workers whom Rybicki felt were superseded by both youth and machinery.[40]

Two years later Rybicki had a letter published in the *New York Times* about the plight of older workers. That prompted an editorial which started by stating Rybicki's letter was a challenge to the view set forth in earlier editorials "that the 40-year deadline and scrap-heap are largely a myth." As evidence that it was a myth the newspaper noted that in the 1930 census, men of 45 and over constituted 34 percent of all men in gainful employment; in 1920 they were 32 percent. As far as the editor was concerned, "This shows that the middle-aged man is not being driven out of employment." In reality, those numbers proved nothing since, among other shortcomings, they took no account of the percentage of all people in each age group. However, having proved to his satisfaction that age discrimination in employment was indeed a myth, the editor went on to wonder how people like Rybicki, and others in close touch with the unemployed, could speak of discrimination against older workers as "very real." The answer perhaps lay, in part, said the editor; "not in the callousness of employers and personnel directors, but, on the contrary, in a wish to be considerate." The editor concluded, "In discharging an incompetent employe, it is kinder to tell him that the business needs a younger man than to tell him that he is not up to his work. So, in hiring, it is a bit easier to tell a man that he is too old than he is unfit."[41]

Auto magnate Henry Ford made himself heard again, this time in a July 1933 issue of *Good Housekeeping*. Ford asserted that the United States would be rescued from its difficulties (that is, the Depression) by men over 40. He added that he had never known men under 40 who were "worth much" and that youth would not take the lead in rehabilitation.[42]

The New York Council on Economics asked the State of New York to launch a Congressional investigation of discrimination by private employers against job-seekers over 35. Its letter to state legislators complained that to hold the idea that people between 35 and 50 were unfit for further employment constituted a serious indictment of the American economic system. In the past, continued the plea, people in that age group were looked on as the very backbone of the country but "now, because they cannot work as cheaply as youngsters of 19 and 20, industry and business have decided to scrap them." According to the letter, a recent WPA study done in upstate New York revealed that out of 9,000 people on the federal relief rolls, 62 percent were 35 years of age or older.[43]

New York City Commissioner of Public Welfare Frank J. Taylor declared that more and more men of 50 and over were entering the "unemployable group." He based his statement on data from the Municipal Lodging House, compiled in a report by Joseph A. Mannix, superintendent of that institution. The report said that those men of 50 and over would experience real difficulty in ever obtaining regular employment. Younger homeless men averaged 10 nights per month per man at the Lodging House, while those over 50 averaged 18 nights a month.[44]

A view from an ordinary citizen was presented by Frances Henry, who told of a female friend of 35 who was well qualified for an executive position but the most frequent answer she got was, "We really want a young person." She was interviewed by the executive vice president of one of Manhattan's largest banks for a position of advertising and public relations director. This man, who was about 45, told Henry's friend that she was too old. Henry added, "I am told that most employment agencies refuse to accept applications for positions from those over 30 years of age."[45]

Novelist Channing Pollock wrote, in 1937, about how hard it was to get a job after 40, describing the situation as becoming one of the most acute and tragic problems in America. Calling the idea inhumanly cruel and economically unsound he went on to state, "Throughout 50 centuries the 'counsel of graybeards' has been the sought and respected counsel ... Even now, it is safe to say that very little of the 'important' work is being done by people under 40." Here he borrowed shamelessly from Osler, without mentioning the doctor. One factor he blamed was the "cult of youth" with America's books, plays, movies and general interests all being concerned, he thought, with adolescence. Pollock concluded that whatever cheerful, best-selling books were written on the subject "in this land of opportunity and this era of government-planned security, it is not life but death that begins at 40."[46]

One of those cheerful books Pollock referred to was likely *Careers After Forty* by Walter B. Pitkin, a prominent author of the time. Overall, the tone of the book was optimistic. However, it contained many warnings for those over 40. He wrote, "My argument is simple and unshaken. People seeking careers after forty should sedulously avoid the high-energy enterprises such as running governments, armies, political parties, or billion-dollar corporations." Pitkin listed a number of jobs "mostly without glamour" where age could compete with youth: watchmen, inspectors, crane operators, gardeners, markers, guides, and cashiers. Readily admitting it was not a prepossessing range, he declared it a step in the right direction. When the average person of 40 hears that polite, "We're sorry, but we think the job calls for someone younger," Pitkin said, "It's usually the time to forget all about that field." A special warning was given to some over-40 female job hunters: "Married women should look for careers outside business and industry."[47]

Frances Maule wrote an article supposedly designed to help female job seekers. It was published in *Independent Woman*, a popular but serious woman's magazine geared to the working females. Maule cited a boss as saying he was not against older people because of age but because of old-age habits. She then went on to list the standard complaints against older workers which were then in vogue, such as they were stuck in a rut, set in their ways, their brains had ossified, their ideas had stiffened with their joints, they were narrow-minded, and they resisted change, new ideas and new methods. As well, they shirked effort, they evaded responsibility, they were intolerant and they lacked initiative. Older female workers had all these faults plus a few restricted to them; they were trouble-makers, bossy, cranky, cantankerous or else touchy, hypersensitive, or ready to burst into tears at the slightest hint of criticism. And, "they are likely either to give up trying to look well, or else do entirely too much in the wrong way." The way to beat the employment deadline, therefore, said Maule, was "to check or root out the traits, habits and tendencies." As for specific bad habits, Maule advised, "If you find yourself settling down into a rut, pull yourself out of it if only by adopting a new hair-do, or moving all the furniture about in your home."[48]

Similar quality advice appeared in the same magazine, a year later, in 1941. This second article summarized the advice of Helen Trimpe, who ran a guidance service in New York called Careers for Women, which seemed to be some sort of career counseling for rich females. The first two weeks of her 10-week course consisted of self-study in which a "glamorous expert" was called in and went over items such as hair, make-up, wardrobe, and so on. Those two weeks of study "point out to older women the folly of typing courses, modeling courses and other unsuitable occupational training they may have had in mind." Trimpe was also co-host of an NBC radio program called Pin Money Party. Reporter Helen Stetson warned that "the older woman must stop trying to enter fields where she is in competition with men and young girls."[49]

As would be expected, much of the prominent opinion that appeared came from management or those that supported a management–type view. That view, of course, was that there was no problem. Journalist Antoinette Gilman said she set out in 1933 to investigate the problem of the older woman looking for work. She said that not so long ago the arrival of the first gray hair in a business woman's head was regarded as a supreme tragedy; "Self-respecting employers would not tolerate gray-haired women in their employ, at least in the outer offices or in any other capacity where they came in contact with the public." However, all that was over. Gilman claimed to have found all kinds of jobs and to have received all kinds of employment offers. In investigating vacancies, she said she was regularly told, "Oh we can't use anyone under thirty, preferably over thirty-five or forty." According to Gilman, "The older woman is leading the field in business to-day."[50]

Similar advice came from Clara Belle Thompson and Margaret Lukes Wise. Together they authored the book *We Are Forty and We Did Get Jobs*. Driving around seven states to find work, they asserted, "We landed all manner of jobs in widely varying fields. Not important, high-salaried positions, but with sufficient pay to keep the wolf from the door and hope in the heart." In a separate article they claimed to have discovered three recurring reasons that many shy, excellently equipped women over 40 did not get jobs. For one thing they carried a bitter attitude coupled with their own troubles to the employer; they failed to take stock of their possibilities and to adapt past experience to present demands. Thirdly, they overwhelmed the employer with their past importance instead of concentrating on the needs of the job at hand.[51]

Writing in the scholarly *American Journal of Sociology* in 1944, Otto Pollak also downplayed the problem by arguing that complaints about discrimination against older workers, while over a century old, had culminated in the belief that modern industry scrapped the workers at the age of 40. He suggested the size of the problem had been greatly overstated. Also, he felt that some of the reasons advanced for differential treatment of older workers were valid. Overstatement of the problem was explained by the zeal of reformers who painted the situation of middle-aged workers darker than reality justified. Acceptance of those overstatements was due, he argued, to a culturally based preference for youth and fear of old age. Since both management and labor were said to accept the

profit motive as primary, therefore, if it should be found that older workers gave the employer a smaller profit than he could reach by employing
younger workers, the existence of discrimination would have to be denied.
Pollak said that reasons advanced for not hiring older workers mostly fell
into two groups: the higher costs of employing older workers, and smaller
returns from their work. Included in the first area were such items as
group insurance, workers' compensation and pension plans. Surprisingly,
Pollak did not agree with that, saying, "However, historical analysis shows
that age hiring limits were established and complained about before any
one of these factors came into existence; and we may well assume, therefore, that they represent rationalizations on the part of those who pro-
pose them for purposes of justification."[52]

While Pollak had no statistical evidence that middle-aged workers
produced less, he felt it was likely to be true—that lesser productivity
could not be ruled out. He argued that the problem of the older worker
in industry only became an independent issue "fairly recently." Before that
it was always part of something else, such as organized labor's fight for
the 8-hour day, and so on. Actually, organized labor had raised the specific
issue of age discrimination some 20 years earlier than when Pollak was
writing. In conclusion he declared "that discrimination against older workers in industry, if it exists at all, is very small indeed."[53]

At an employment security conference, the industrial relations advi-
sor of the Associated Industries of Massachusetts declared that "it was
too difficult to teach old minds and old muscles new tricks." Employment
opportunity was neither increased nor decreased due to age limits "when
such limits are reasonably related to the efficiency and safety of the occupation." He felt older workers could be kept in employment much longer
"if the salvage point of view dominates our labor policy." That meant that
as workers aged they had to be "adjusted" medically and socially to their
work and to their decreasing ease of performance. Having a hiring-age
limit was an aid in the administration of labor policy along those lines
because "it reduces the competition of older workers for the few positions
which can be held by the less efficient in the particular organization." An
additional benefit was that it increased the likelihood a worker would stay
at his job since he would see the "barrier to re-employment" if he should
try and change his job after a certain age. At the same conference a representative of the Industrial Relations Counselors (a private New York
company) stated that hiring-age limits were fixed primarily "because of
the fact that various jobs had exacting requirements which could not be
met by older persons."[54]

C.R. Dooley, personnel manager of Standard Oil Company of New York, offered his thoughts in 1931. First he emphasized the loyalty of the large corporation to its employees, arguing that it was doing many things to take care of them, "in many instances letting his pay roll suffer; he is letting his cost of production go up where it is at all possible." Addressing the issue directly, Dooley admitted the older worker looking for work had a hard time, but "I personally believe that the arbitrary limit of forty-five will sooner or later be abolished." As to pension plans being the main stumbling block, he noted two firms had modified their plans to the extent that they "have practically abolished the maximum age limit as an employment policy." A second factor against the older job seeker was promotion policy, said Dooley, although he did not elaborate.[55]

However, Dooley devoted most of his article to the third factor in the problem, the personal qualifications of job applicants: "It would be safe to say that a very large percentage of the men who come into my office every day are not employable…. How many of their problems they lay to their wives and families! They are not adaptable." He was complaining about many of those job seekers wanting to choose their work, about some being discourteous; about some refusing to go to another town where they might get work, because they had always lived in one place and their wives would not want to go. Going on, Dooley related that almost every day he had at least one and frequently more cases of men 47 to 55 "who have neuritis or bad hearts or kidneys going bad or stomachs needing special foods—men and women not sick unto death, not in a condition requiring a hospital, but past their prime of production, and almost through in this competitive life." With their minds out of the habit of study and their bodies neglected or abused, "they face the balance of life as best they can, having to take whatever they can get." Dooley concluded by saying that young people had to have impressed on them that they should not expect society to take care of them if they ruined their health, neglected their mental training and failed to appreciate their responsibility for their own future. He added that "people who are looking for jobs ought to be adaptable and willing to fit into anything they can get." That a 50-year-old worker's health may have been damaged by decades of industrial employment was left unmentioned by the personnel man.[56]

Many surveys of the problem were carried out. Most showed an appalling degree of age discrimination in employment. One that did not was a 1930 industrial survey done by the Associated Industries of Massachusetts. They reported their data "disproved" statements to the effect that men over 40 were not wanted in industry. In conclusion they claimed

there were no data to show general discrimination against older workers—that most employers were earnestly trying to find ways to "lessen the
difficulty" of older workers in finding employment. Public pensions were
disapproved of by this group's researcher.[57]

A report from the Rochester office of the division of employment of
the New York Department of Labor called attention to the difficulty that
office was having in placing middle-aged workers. Stating that one of its
greatest problems was the person past 50 who was out of a job but men-
tally and physically fit, the report said, "The most regrettable feature is
that even with an intensive and persistent appeal for these people we are
able to place only a small percentage of them." Out of 370 such applicants, that office found jobs for only 140 of them, and even then "the
placement of this number required special efforts." In many cases the
applicant was accompanied to the job site by a representative of the
employment office "where the man labeled unfit at 50 is given permanent
or temporary employment (more often temporary than permanent) out
of consideration for the employment bureau appeal rather than the mer-
its of the applicant." Employers interviewed by the Rochester office admitted that when they hired new men, other things being equal, "they choose
young men." In Rochester's experience the age limit for skilled workers
was 50 years, 45 for unskilled workers.[58]

The California State Department of Industrial Relations published
a series of bulletins on the general subject of the older worker in industry after it concluded, "The arbitrary discharge of workers because of age,
and regardless of their fitness, is becoming a general policy." It also determined that the refusal to hire or retain employees 45 and older would
affect, roughly, "the economic interests of over one-fourth of gainfully
employed persons in California."[59]

During the spring of 1930 the Maryland Commissioner of Labor &
Statistics conducted a survey in which questionnaires were received from
858 large firms in that state, employing a total of 17,724 people. Of those
companies, 772 (employing 65.3 percent of the total) set no age limit; 32
firms (4.3 percent) had no definite age limit but admitted a tendency or
preference toward employing younger workers; 54 companies (with 30.3
percent of the employees) had definite age limits. Public utilities and railroads led the way in setting age bars, with the most frequently used age
limit for men and women being 45. A total of 19 companies had differential age limits for the sexes; in 17 cases the limit was lower for women; it
was lower for men in the other two cases. Lowest age limit given for
men was 23; for women it was 30. Reasons given by the companies for

3. The Problem Becomes Entrenched, 1930–1946   57

refusing to employ older workers fell into four general categories: the nature of the work to be done; the lesser desirability of the older worker; the maintenance of benefit plans; organization policies such as promotion from within, the desire for new blood, and so forth. Employers who cited the second category viewed older workers as less active, less adaptable, that their employment slowed down production and tended to increase the accident rate, that they were less efficient than younger employees "and that the consideration which their age renders necessary is often burdensome."[60]

This study then looked at the age distribution of workers in manufacturing industries and retail department stores. For the group between 45 and 64, the percentage of store employees was less than half that of either the general population or of those gainfully employed. When the comparison was with those employed in manufacturing, the study found the disproportion was not as great, but was "still strikingly large." Overall, the study concluded that in addition to the conscious and deliberate setting of hiring age limits there was at work a definite tendency to choose the younger worker at a time—during the Depression—when choice was easy "and that this is perhaps even more widely effective than the acknowledged placing of limits." In other words, even companies which claimed to have no fixed hiring age limits did, in fact, discriminate against the older people. The study felt this was demonstrated by the age analysis of manufacturing employees which revealed that older workers were highly underrepresented, when compared to the general population and to those gainfully employed. That age data came from 79 manufacturing establishments in Maryland, of which 64 said they had no specific maximum age limits for employment.[61]

A study done around the same time by the California Department of Labor received data from 2,098 manufacturing firms and 710 nonmanufacturing companies in reply to questionnaires. Some 290,000 workers were employed by the manufacturing firms, 245,000 in nonmanufacturing. Employers with maximum age limits numbered 306 (11 percent of the firms employing 39 percent of the workers) while 2,502 firms had no such limits. While nine percent of manufacturing firms and 17 percent of nonmanufacturing concerns had limits, 18 percent of employees in manufacturing and 64 percent in nonmanufacturing were employed in firms having such limits. Public utilities had the worst record. Of 71 such companies, 28 had age limits (39 percent of the companies, 94 percent of the employees). Next were transportation concerns wherein 11 had age bars (30 percent of the 37 companies, 73 percent of the employees).

Apparently there was a direct relationship between the size of a firm and the adoption of age bars. Overall the average number of employees per company was 190; for firms with age limits it was 683, while enterprises with no such limits averaged 130 employees. In the public utilities group the average number of workers overall was 1,923; those with age limits averaged 4,603, those without had 179 workers. The most common age limits used by these companies were 45 and 50, although the age limit ranged from 30 through 60. Of the 2,808 firms, 783 had group insurance or pension plans or both. In this group 148 companies, 18.9 percent, had adopted age limits. Among the other 2,025 concerns 158, 7.8 percent, had age limits. Companies with both insurance and pension plans more frequently had age limits than those with group insurance only. This study determined that technological unemployment was "clearly one of the important causes of maximum hiring-age limits." Conceded was the fact that in periods of widespread unemployment it was more difficult for middle-aged workers to find work than for younger persons. As well the study found that "a considerable part of the difficulty, however, is ascribed to sheer prejudice against the older worker." Both the Maryland and California studies agreed in finding "the adoption of maximum age limits for hiring is sufficiently common to create a social and economic problem of the first magnitude."[62]

Yet another study was conducted that year by the New York State Commission on Old Age Security which looked at data from 2,100 manufacturing firms in that state. The report declared that "the older jobseeker is definitely barred from 59 per cent of the available jobs and is discriminated against in 89 per cent of them." Results indicated that the older men were most secure from discharge, but because of the low survival rates for employees and the high mortality rates of business firms, "no large proportion of older persons are in a position to enjoy such security." Said commission member Solomon Barkin, "The studies suggest very definitely that the older person is handicapped in most industries and most areas." The study found that age first became a handicap in obtaining employment after 35 for men and after 30 for women. Men from 35 to 39 were 13 percent handicapped in their job hunting, and from age 50 to 54 the handicap rate was 66 percent; there was an 83 percent handicap rate of those aged 60 to 64. Barkin observed that older people were not among the first to be laid off, except when they attained old age. Most of the weeding out of employees took place among the younger people, particularly those under 40. The survivors became more secure until the oldest age, 65 for males, 55 for females. For workers trying to get another job with a former employer, age was not a handicap until after 45 for both men and women.[63]

A few years later that same New York State Commission on Old Age Security released another report based on a two-year study of the older worker in industry in which 2,500 manufacturing firms cooperated. Additionally, a canvass of more than one-third of the employees in the manufacturing industries was conducted. The report declared that people past the age of 40 presented a "real industrial problem." It called on the state and private industry to develop more effective and extensive provisions for the economic security of this age group.[64]

When the National Conference Board conducted a 1937 survey of 405 industrial companies it reported that maximum age limits had not been set by 75 percent of the firms, although it made no mention of percentage of employees involved. Wherever age limits had been set, the age restrictions were lower for women. Almost 75 percent of the companies with limits set the maximum hiring age for women at 45 or less, while only about 40 percent of the firms with limits fixed them that low for men. Referring to the three-quarters of the concerns with no fixed age limit, the Conference Board noted that did not necessarily mean that age had no bearing on the hiring of new workers. "While these companies have no definite policy forbidding the hiring of workers beyond a given age, it is probable that, all other factors being equal, the employment manager or foreman generally accepts the younger applicant."[65]

Novelist Channing Pollock and the magazine *The Forum* sent out a questionnaire to 18 of the largest employment agencies in New York; 13 replied. Among other things, it asked the agencies what was the average age limit set by employers when seeking clerical workers. Commonest answer was: men 25 to 30, women 23 to 25. An overall average gave a range of 22.6 to 31.4 years. Only one agency reported a demand for men up to 40, and not one for men beyond that age. Average age limit for executives sought was from 30.2 to 40.7 years. Three of the 13 agencies found executives employable "up to 45" but 10 answered "always under 40." Also asked was a two-part question: What reason did the employer give for the age discrimination? What, in your opinion, was the real reason? Most common response to the first part was that older men lacked adaptability and "flexibility of thinking." Also mentioned were pension plans and group insurance. Regarding the second part of the question, replies included "the youth cult," "party looks," "Older women are not as attractive as young girls," "younger people will work for less money," and so forth. One agency said that in those cases where the employers were not "primarily concerned with the appearance of the applicant, we believe that they do not employ older people because the salaries now being paid are too low to offer to people of experience and training." Pollock concluded that "there can be no doubt that an appalling number of us must remain jobless after 40—perhaps even after 35. The statistical proof is overwhelming."[66]

Massachusetts gathered data in 1937 to study the problem of age discrimination in employment in that state. Acknowledging that complaints of discrimination in employment against workers over the age of 45 were common long before the Depression, the demands for legislation which gave birth to the study began in 1934. In fact, Massachusetts wage earners had complained bitterly about the problem faced by people aged 45 to 64 and had called upon the General Court at its sessions of 1934, 1935, 1936 and 1937 to find remedies. Repeated charges that discrimination was promoted by the demands made by insurance companies carrying workmen's compensation were refuted by J.W. Downs, counsel for the Insurance Federation of Massachusetts, who pointed out that premiums were adjusted to the hazards of the industries without regard to employees' ages. The Secretary of the Boston Retail Trade Board, and employment manager of one of the largest department stores, told of generous treatment given older workers by Boston mercantile concerns. "However, it was admitted that the chain stores gave work to very few older employees." Also determined by the study was that charges made that private pension plans and group insurance benefits were causes of discrimination "were not verified."[67]

Beginning at the age of 45, said the study, the chances of reemployment in Massachusetts factories were less than one in four for men and one in 10 for women, and "The deadline for rehiring was drawn even more drastically in establishments other than factories." Variations in employment during the Depression were found to have made possible the rapid elimination of older workers by a policy of selective rehiring "from the great army of cheaper, younger workers, after the frequent lay-offs or shutdowns made necessary by fluctuating markets. Age discrimination in hiring is evident at an earlier age than in rehiring." Another conclusion drawn was that "employers prefer to hire males under 30 and females under 25 years of age." Thus, only five percent of the hiring of females and 15 percent of those of men took place in the age groups over 45 in which, however, were found 20 percent of the employable women and 36 percent of the men. In January 1934 in Massachusetts the unemployment rate for men between 25 and 45 ranged from 20.7 percent to 25 percent, depending on specific age groups, while for men over 45 the range was 22.8 to 31.2 percent. For women under 45 the unemployment rate ranged from 13.7 to 16.7 percent; for women 45 and over it was 19 to 21.7 percent. Reporter Lucile Evans declared, "The existence of discrimination in employment against older workers in Massachusetts was fully established by this investigation."[68]

After a study by New York University issued the advice that women over 30 should not be encouraged to prepare for clerical work, a director of one of the largest single government agencies in New York made the statement that 25 was the maximum age at which she would consider clerical workers. When the United States Department of Labor made a survey of industries it found that 31.7 percent of the plants reported a definite age limit. In a few cases it was under 40; most had limits between 40 and 45. This all caused journalist Helen Welshimer to state that "forty marks an economic twilight for job hunters." She found that in many instances the deadline for employment for women was being pushed steadily forward, then standing at around 30. Even that could be a ripe old age for clerical work. The New York State Labor Department advised women who were getting into their late 20s, and needed to acquire a means of livelihood, to avoid stenographic courses.[69]

A 1938 survey by the New York State League of Economics found the average maximum age at which employers in the state would hire new workers was 35. In only three occupational areas, of 25 listed, was the maximum age as high as 45; one of them was road construction. All the other categories were lower, with two listed as low as 20: department store waitresses, and jobs in some large New York City banks. Those figures were based on interviews with 403 employers. In the white-collar division, under the heading of experienced male office worker, the survey revealed that 35 was the maximum age for new employees.[70]

Reports from the United States Employment Service in 1940 indicated that although about 42 percent of the registered applicants for jobs were over 40, only about 30 percent of the jobs went to them. And the rate of placement in permanent jobs was only about half as high for men over 40 as for younger men; many of them got only temporary employment. A government survey of 3,781 industrial plants in Massachusetts found 230 plants which had no employees over 45 and 767 firms in which less than 20 percent of the workers were over 45. Yet the 1930 Census showed that 43 percent of the United States working population was between 40 and 70 years of age. When the National Association of Manufacturers surveyed 750 member companies, it found that about

33 percent of their 2.5 million workers were over 40. A 1939 analysis of people on the WPA rolls revealed nearly half of those engaged in relief projects for the WPA in New York City were over 40; in upstate New York the percentage rose to 57.[71]

Still, a few positive changes were happening. Generally the civil service at the federal, state and municipal levels had clung to inflexible age deadlines. New York State broke with that tradition in April 1938 by abolishing civil service age limits which previously had set up bars against stenographers over 27, laborers over 32, stationary engineers over 35, and so on. Thirty-five had been the average New York State civil service age deadline for applicants.[72]

Conditions for older workers in countries around the world mirrored those found in America. During February 1935 in London, England, a small group of women got together and organized the Over Thirty Association, to assist older unemployed women. With only 10 members to start, it had reportedly grown to 4,032 in June 1937. The focus of the group was to help unemployed women receive training, find jobs, and so forth. When those women complained about the situation to female members of Parliament, the latter also could not find jobs for the women, "but they are seeing that jobless spinsters get their old age pensions at fifty-five instead of sixty."[73]

When Canada's federal National Employment Commission surveyed 7,725 firms in 1937, it found that 928 (12 percent) had specific maximum hiring ages; 83.3 percent stated they had no such limits while 4.7 percent did not report on that point. Those 928 companies employed 302,379 people, or 29.4 percent of the 1,028,756 employees of the 7,725 concerns.[74]

In Belgium in 1936 the average duration of unemployment was 7.75 months for those under 20, rising steadily in each age group until it reached 28.5 months for those between 60 and 65. An inquiry found that in some firms, although no maximum age limit was specified, it was the practice to reject older workers; in others the age limit was 55 or even 60 for skilled workers but 50 for unskilled and semiskilled; in still other concerns the limit was as low as 45, 40, 35, or even 30. German data showed the situation for older workers became less favorable in 1936, compared to 1933, in spite of a general improvement in the employment situation. In November 1936 unemployed male German workers over 40 made up 50.3 percent of the total unemployed; those over 40 who were placed in jobs formed only 31.9 percent of all workers who found jobs in the previous month. The hiring age limit of salaried employees was generally set by companies at 35 years. At least it was until an order was issued on

November 7, 1936, by the Commissioner of the Four-Year-Plan which obliged companies with more than 10 salaried workers to engage a certain proportion of employees above the age of 40. That followed an earlier decree requiring that preference be given to heads of families and providing for the gradual replacement of young persons under 25 by men over 40, preferably married men.[75]

Statistics from the United Kingdom for the unemployment rate in four different years from 1927 to 1938 revealed the rate was fairly uniform for males between the ages of 21 and 44, but that it increased for each five-year age group thereafter; the rates for women showed a general tendency to increase from the age of 21 onward. A 1931 UK study covering males in 14 industries in two main age groups (18 to 44, 45 to 64) found the percentage of unemployment was higher in all of them for the older group. Similar data for women (age groups 18 to 34, 35 to 64) yielded the same results. After analyzing the results of several studies in England, William Beveridge concluded that the risk of losing one's job did not increase with advancing years, but the risk connected with being out of a job did increase materially. Switzerland also had higher rates of unemployment for men and women over 50, as measured in 1936, 1937 and 1938. One Swiss study showed that older workers had fewer on-the-job injuries but took longer to recuperate. The two factors balanced. However, if employers believed older people were more prone to accidents, whether fact or fiction, such a belief could result in discrimination against the middle-aged. Overall, those who looked at the European situation concluded that older workers were no more likely to lose their jobs than younger workers, but if they did become unemployed they had much more difficulty in obtaining new positions. "The effect of age upon opportunity for employment begins to appear at about age 45, although it varies from country to country and as between men and women."[76]

When it came to the reasons advanced in this period in the United States for the refusal to hire older people, they tended to follow those of the previous period. These were, of course, the supposedly logical and rational reasons for engaging in age discrimination in employment. Cost of workmen's compensation insurance was still raised, albeit infrequently, since it was the easiest to disprove. The New York State Legislative Committee on Discrimination in Employment of the Middle-Aged dismissed in strong terms the charge that older workers cost more in terms of workmen's compensation, calling the charge "a prejudice without foundation ... [which] must be exposed by the widest sort of publicity." A further recommendation from the committee was that employers everywhere make a serious effort to reflect in their employee rolls the actual age proportions among the employables in their particular communities.[77]

A survey conducted in Massachusetts which involved over 100 firms there employing over 25,000 workers came to the conclusion that "some companies may find a general age limitation necessary because their very existence is threatened by an expensive pension system." Some nine years later, in 1939, another study in Massachusetts, this time of mostly large employers, concluded, about the pension issue, "When industrialists feel, as they seem to in New England, that needy older workers cannot be laid off without some kind of pension, there appears to be a strong case for hiring younger men for those job vacancies which occur."[78]

Abraham Epstein was still Executive Secretary of the American Association for Old Age Security in the early 1930s, and he was still making similar statements about the issue as those in the past. He blamed standardized production for greatly eliminating the need for skill and experience, the sole assets of the older employee within the handicraft system. Epstein also cited Henry Ford as having recently said that the man with no experience at all was the best person when it came to fitting him into a new type of production scheme—he had no bad habits. The introduction of new inventions and specialized machinery involved the replacing of men and workers who wore out sooner under the swifter pace of modern production. When Epstein looked at conditions in "Middletown" he called them typical. Among males in the entire city, 12 percent were between the ages of 20 and 24. However, in two of the city's leading machine shops their percentage was 19 and 27. On the other hand, men between 45 and 64 comprised 27 percent of the city's population but were only 17 and 12 percent in the two shops. Epstein felt older workers were still hanging on in areas such as agriculture, in small business and in the professions but had been practically eliminated from all the major industrial occupations. Still, his major point remained that the age bar against employment became a serious problem when American employers adopted private industrial pension plans. In order to avoid the assumption of responsibility for older workers who had not worked long enough to get pensions, "Employers were forced to adopt the simplest way out, i.e., to deny employment to any one who might become old and incapacitated before the passing of the number of years which would entitle him to retire under the pension plans." He said that over 400 firms employing four million workers had such plans. Yet his argument that older workers had all but vanished from industrial work was based on 1920 census data, when the pension plans covered even fewer employees.[79]

Joseph McAfee, community service director of New York City's The Community Church, observed that because of mergers and bankruptcies white-collar workers were in as much peril as were blue-collar employees. He believed the problem of the middle-aged unemployed was no passing phase; the Depression had not created it, and the passing of that crisis would not cure it. Strict efficiency meant that workers and executives who were closest to being superannuated would be the ones most likely to lose their positions. For McAfee, a review of the situation led him to conclude there were six causes of economic insecurity for older workers: (1) the introduction of pension and group insurance plans; (2) the cost of workmen's compensation insurance; (3) the increasing demands of industry for physical fitness and mental adaptability; (4) the lower wage cost of younger workers; (5) the policy of promotion from within the company; (6) the displacing of workers by machine. As for ways to change the system, he suggested adult education and community plans.[80]

New York State struck a joint legislative committee in the late 1930s to investigate the subject. It declared that discrimination against the employment of middle-aged workers existed in practically all of the industry areas found in the state. From its investigation the committee put together an exhaustive list of 21 alleged causes of that discrimination, along with its own comments on those points: (1) increased rates of workers' compensation insurance—found to be false; (2) higher accident rate—false, lower but slower to recuperate; (3) greater susceptibility to occupational diseases—true; (4) insurance companies urging employment of younger men—not enough evidence to comment; (5) increased rates of group insurance—no comment; (6) increased rates for employers under their own pension plans—too complex to comment on, portability recommended; (7) physical unfitness in middle age and (8) refusal of employers to hire men with minor disabilities because of greater compensation/insurance hazard—some truth; (9) the speed-up in industry and (10) displacement of middle-aged workers by modern machinery—true; (11) industry's preference for younger men who can be hired more cheaply and trained more readily and (12) middle-aged workers' lesser efficiency than younger men and (13) public demand for younger people in certain occupations—some truth in each; (14) lack of educational qualifications and requirements—some truth; (15) loss of skill during lay-off in the Depression and (16) lack of skilled workers among middle-aged—some truth but older workers are easily retrainable; (17) skilled workers eliminated by changes in methods and (18) by industries going out of business—obviously true; (19) industry's failure to train employees for middle-aged usefulness—true; (20) discrimination practiced by municipal, state and federal civil services—many such cases of age discrimination were brought to the attention of the committee; (21) discrimination against persons on relief—no evidence to support that idea.[81]

When the Massachusetts Department of Labor and Industries made a survey in that state with regard to older workers, it found that a large number of employers explicitly reported that they used no maximum hiring-age limit, "whereas further investigation showed that many of them actually did have such limits."[82]

A solution to the problem was proposed by at least two different sources during World War II years. Anton Carlson agreed that older workers should not be thrown on the scrap heap but felt they should get less money for doing the same job. He proposed three specific groups: (1) younger workers, (2) adult workers, (3) older workers, and argued that groups 1 and 3 should each get less money since each gave less than an adult performance. Carlson did not specify the ages assigned to each category.[83]

Presenting a similar position was Howard Meyerhoff, a management executive of a hosiery company whose workers belonged to the American Federation of Hosiery Workers. According to him, that labor organization made provision for reduced salaries for older workers and he had in one of his mills two women "who are receiving less than the minimum wage for the job performed, though more than would compensate them for the work which they perform. We apply the privilege of placing people in the group of sub-standard workers very cautiously, and thus far we have received Union endorsement and backing whenever we have taken this step. It is the humane and sensible thing to do."[84]

Studies, both formal and informal, conducted during this period, generally favored the older worker. A report by the Boston Elevated Railway showed that workers between 36 and 40 had the largest number of injuries, but also had the largest number of workers. From the perspective of accident frequency per 1,000 employees, the largest number of injuries occurred in the age group of 25 and under, containing the new and inexperienced employees. Except for a slight rise for the age group 45 to 50 years, a steady decrease in accident rates took place with an increase in age, up to 56 years, after which there was a small increase. Data from the Industrial Commission of Wisconsin showed a lessening trend for injuries causing temporary disability with an increase in age, while injuries causing permanent disability remained on practically the same level throughout all age groups from 18 to 65. Steel plant figures showed that new and inexperienced workers had the worst record. Workers with six months experience and less were charged with 37 injuries per one million hours of exposure; the rate was reduced but remained fairly high until after three years of service, when it dropped sharply and continued downward so that workers with 10 to 15 years experience were charged with only two injuries per one million hours. Statistics from both Wisconsin and New York showed that it took longer for older people to recover from injuries.[85]

Research by the New York State Joint Legislative Committee showed that older workers were not more liable to severe accidents than younger ones. It concluded not only that older workers did not cost employers more for compensation than younger ones, but indeed that the middle-aged worker was not as expensive to the employer as the younger one, from a compensation cost standpoint.[86]

According to a series of studies in leading department stores, undertaken by Charles Stech, specialist in employee relations surveys, retail sales figures showed that men and women in their 50s sold more merchandise than sales people in any other age group. For every $100 worth of goods sold by a sales person in their 20s, one in their 30s sold $102.04, in their 40s the figure was $107.38, and one above 50 sold $108.78 worth of merchandise.[87]

In a survey done by the National Association of Manufacturers, a questionnaire was sent to 2,485 industrial firms with a total of 2.33 million workers. With regard to employee work performance, 16.8 percent of the companies responding said that the frequency of illness of older workers was higher than it was for younger workers; 65.7 percent said it was the same; 17.5 percent said it was lower. Efficiency of older workers was rated as higher than that of younger workers by 33.7 percent of the firms, the same by 50.9 percent, and lower by 15.4 percent. The ability of the older worker was reported higher by 40.6 percent of the enterprises, the same by 51 percent, and lower by 8.4 percent. As for cooperation, 51.2 percent of the companies rated older workers better, 43.6 percent said the same, and 5.2 percent said they were worse than younger employees. Degree of accident risk for older workers, compared to younger ones, was reported as higher by 13.8 percent of the firms, the same by 55.9 percent, and lower by 30.3 percent.[88]

Over the months of March and April 1932 the Massachusetts Commission on the Stabilization of Employment made a study of the employment of older workers in Springfield department stores. Three large stores in the city were selected with all employees over 45 being studied. Detailed interviews were held with 241. None of the managements would admit there was any age deadline of employability and, in fact, the proportion of older workers was larger than would be found in any manufacturing firm. In each of the three stores staff over the age of 45 comprised 20 to 25 percent of the total. Women were in the majority in the total workforce of all the stores, but over half of the older workers in one store were men; in the other two they were 33 percent and 40 percent. From the detailed interviews it was learned that over half were hired for their current job before the age of 45, but 39 percent were taken on after their 45th birthday, and 13 of the 241 were hired after the age of 60. None of those stores had a pension plan system for their employees, but each of them was reportedly taking care of a number of former employees. In presenting the data, Amy Hewes observed that the employment policies that had been associated with the success of the older stores, in particular the policy of retaining the older workers, may not have been followed by stores whose relation to the community "was only a link in a wider organization." That reference was to chain stores which were then well established, although the three stores here were all single outlet, independent, and owned by someone who lived locally in Springfield. Hewes wrote that the conspicuous fact about the study "was not that the older employees had succeeded in building up claims to their jobs, but that their service was regarded as efficient, in spite of (and often because of) their age. This was emphasized many times by store superintendents and personnel managers." It led Hewes to conclude there were better prospects for older workers in retail, as compared to manufacturing industries, probably due in large part to the relatively smaller demands made by retailing upon their physique. Over the past 20 years there had been many technological changes such that a mechanic's experience acquired at the beginning of that period was no longer valuable. However, selling was selling.[89]

Among federal politicians speaking out on the problem none was more vocal than United States Secretary of Labor Frances Perkins. In her fifth annual Labor Day speech, in 1937, delivered over the CBS radio system she warned that industry's reluctance to hire the older worker, even though able-bodied and intelligent, "threatened our social structure." She remarked that while forward steps had been taken in other labor conditions, "this problem has been developing steadily for fifteen years until it is now a menace and terror to thousands of family breadwinners when they reach the age of 45 or 50." Perkins reported a study done in Massachusetts a year earlier which revealed that of 3,781 firms canvassed, 230 factories had no male employees 45 years or over. One hundred and thirty-seven had less than 10 percent; 434 companies had 10 percent or higher in that age range, but less than 20 percent. She added, "The problem was lost sight of during the depression when so many were out of work but it became more pressing than ever when recovery began and with the reopening of many plants older workers were not called back to their jobs, their places going to younger men and women."[90]

Two months later Perkins spoke about the problem again, saying that in some cases it was industrial policy to fix a hiring-age limit at 45 and in some instances it was down to 40, or even 35 years. She noted that a recent study of around 1,500 employees in seven cities revealed that the older men made the highest grades in terms of work and of quality. The older men tended to produce more than the younger men. That caused an editorial in the *New York Times* to question how that could be—why would profit-hungry employers refuse to hire the more productive people? Answering its own question, the editorial stated, "One explanation would be that the thing really isn't so. The problem of the middle-aged worker on the scrap heap has always been much exaggerated." Admitting that in a country as large as the United States with 50 million people there had to be employers who refused to hire, say, people over 40; "But such employers can only be rare exceptions."[91]

Early in 1938 Perkins appointed a national committee to study the problem of age discrimination in employment. Named to head the group was New York University Chancellor Chase, who said that men over 40 were at a disadvantage in seeking and keeping a job. In the last six months of 1937 the men of that age were 43 percent of all those seeking aid from the United States Employment Service, but they got only 30 percent of the jobs.[92]

A lengthy and sympathetic article, under Perkins' name, was published in the *New York Times Magazine* in March 1938, wherein she presented some of the problems faced by middle-aged workers. She wrote about a Massachusetts study which looked at the workers' situation. The evidence showed that nonresidents were hired in the Lawrence textile mills while older, local workers were still unemployed. A union secretary remarked that "in no other place have I ever encountered so much discrimination against older workers. There is a general feeling of fear among the people." Workers who had been employed for years in those mills, sometimes 25 years or more, were laid off during slack periods but not rehired when work at the mills picked up again. By this time those textile plants were running at full capacity and there was no room for those older workers, said the secretary, because workers had flocked there from

New Hampshire, Vermont and Rhode Island. He added, "I also wish to mention that mill workers refuse to give their right ages in Lawrence. In every mill except one textile workers never pass the age of 55." An official of the National Leather Workers Union told of a firm in Lynn which had existed for 75 years. Hard times led to layoffs and finally to the plant closure. When it closed, the plant had 100 men over the age of 50. After several years, 60 of those men were on welfare or had been at one time. With an economic pickup the plant started up again, but less than five of those 100 men were taken back.[93]

A union official in Fall River described the situation there by noting there were 4,000 women employed in the mills with more than half of them being under 21. "I find that a special effort is made to employ younger men," he explained. He felt that preference was due, first of all, to the tension and speed under which garment workers toiled. When women got to be 30 or 40 it was difficult to get them back to work, "because they are told they are slower than the younger people." Perkins told of a study conducted over the preceding 18 months by the United States Employment Service, which declared, "Men and women beyond the middle forties, who have fallen out of work, have on the whole regained a place in industry less easily than younger workers. This statement holds good for workers in all types of occupations." Another report made to the Labor Department indicated that in a certain city employment in the prevailing industry was back to normal, after the worst of the Depression. At the same time a report showed that just as many people were unemployed there as in the depths of the Depression and that 90 percent of those people on relief had once worked in that prevailing industry. Both reports turned out to be correct because the industry had not taken back the laid-off men but employed new and younger workers.[94]

Another politician who spoke out was James Mead, a Congressman from New York. In a speech broadcast on CBS in January 1938 he called the problem of the older worker one that was becoming increasingly a subject of national concern. If the social system was to continue, Mead felt something had to be done to ensure employment for workers over the age of 45 "who find it difficult to locate employment because of the policy of government and industry ... We all know that private industry is setting up age limits and that the government offends in the same direction. We know the older worker has suffered keenly from this discrimination." Mead related that when someone checked the hiring policies as to age limits of principal Minneapolis and St. Paul companies it was revealed that none of the firms would hire people who were over 40. Some would not take those over 35. Others set their limit at 25. Said Mead, "There is apprehension in the hearts of our people who are now approaching thirty years of age. By the time they are thirty-five, the apprehension will have become fear of the future. And by forty, in many cases their working life is over." At the time of Mead's speech a resolution had been introduced into the House of Representatives to bring about an immediate investigation of the problem.[95]

In a proclamation President Franklin D. Roosevelt declared the week of April 30, 1939, as Employment Week and April 30 itself as Employment Sunday "to the end that interest in the welfare of the older workers may be stimulated and employment opportunity afforded them." It was an initiative which FDR was said to have taken on his own volition, in the wake of Perkins' reports. Roosevelt challenged the nation to end "an unfounded prejudice based on age alone," which prevented people past 40 from sharing along with other groups in the revival of employment. He urged all employers to reexamine their policies to determine whether middle-aged workers were receiving a fair opportunity to qualify for jobs. Especially mentioned by FDR were World War I veterans, who then had an average age of 46.[96]

One year later FDR designated the first week in May as National Employment Week and again made a special appeal for the employment of those over 40. Once again he asked specifically for consideration for World War veterans. He urged all of society to observe the week "to the end that interest in the welfare of all the unemployed, and especially the worker over 40, may be stimulated and employment be extended to them." Regarding the first such week, held in 1939, FDR said it was a success because in that month a third more jobs were filled than during the same month of 1938.[97]

Roosevelt returned a year later to declare the week of May 4, 1941, as National Employment Week. His proclamation pointed out that notwithstanding the enormous number of placements resulting from the defense program, numerous older workers were still in the ranks of the unemployed. The rest of his message was similar to the two prior calls, calling upon employers to give special attention to the employment of older workers and citing World War I vets.[98]

Governments were also busy during this period in issuing reports and holding hearings. The Joint Legislative Committee on Unemployment of New York State delivered a report to the legislature in January 1933, a report titled the Older Worker in Industry. Presented in the study was a summary of the history of the development of public realization that the older worker had a special difficulty to face. Until the coming of the modern factory system, advancing years were not taken seriously into account in estimating a worker's chances of employment. Under the guild system he was likely to gain status as he grew older, and under the domestic system he was part of the family and as such was employed no matter what his productive capacity. With the introduction of the factory system, labor was employed to make a profit for the employer and the relative superiority of a worker determined whether he or someone else would be hired. Under those circumstances, said the report, age naturally became a handicap, "but comparatively little attention was paid to the subject until the present century." Since then the position of the older person in the labor market had passed through three stages; the first preceded World War I, when the situation of the man aged 45 and over was rendered more difficult by the utilization of new sources of labor supply, the changes in industry methods, and the business depressions of the first decade. Next came the war itself when many young men were drafted and the older worker "was eagerly welcomed back into industry." The third stage came after 1920 when the earlier attitude again became apparent. Workers discharged from one firm sought openings in another, "and the older employees, once displaced, found it hard to gain a foothold elsewhere. The situation was noted and public concern was raised."[99]

The Joint Committee found similar results in California, Maryland and elsewhere; "the existence of discrimination was clearly shown." In New York State one in every five manufacturing firms had adopted age limits in hiring; they employed 40 percent of the employees. Of those with limits 29 percent had formal rules, 71 percent informal. Commonest age limit set for men was 45 years. Age limits set for women were regularly lower; "forty years or less appears to be the general rule." Large companies were more likely than small firms to have age limits "and to enforce them rigidly." Another conclusion from the report was that not only were increasingly larger proportions of older workers considered unemployable by private firms, but those who were still considered employable experienced greater amounts of unemployment than the average employable person. Unemployment rates for older workers rose consistently through all of the older age groups. Along with the methods of distributing work opportunities went modern industrial hiring and separation policies with the result that they imposed "an unusually heavy economic burden upon the older persons." Agreeing that older employees with long service were not the first to be fired, the report noted that the chances for reemployment of the older unemployed person "are comparatively small, particularly if unemployment is widespread. When the amount of employment increases, they will be among the last to enjoy its advantages."[100]

Looking at ways to combat the problem, the Joint Committee found that several states had undertaken special work to aid the middle-aged in securing work. Departments of Labor in California and Pennsylvania had conducted campaigns to secure lists of companies that would not refuse to hire men solely on account of age. In both states a number of firms registered, but critics said that few of the important larger companies were to be found on those lists. One recommendation made was that strong public employment bureaus were needed, calling the history of the development in the United States of such exchanges as "a history of decadence rather than achievement ... The more advanced and efficient the employment exchange, the greater will be its possibilities for convincing employers that their age prejudice is unwarranted."[101]

Many years later, in January 1938, a public hearing was held by New York State's Joint Legislative Committee on Discrimination in Employment of the Middle-Aged (formed around September 1937). One who testified was Abraham Epstein, still executive secretary of the American Association for Social Security. He declared the problem to be part and parcel of the industrial profit system. With no particular solution in mind, he suggested "encouraging public opinion to have employers take a certain percentage of older workers and to resent unnecessary discharge of middle-aged employes." As in the past, Epstein also argued that pension systems set up by firms and group insurance plans militated against hiring older people. He added, "You cannot enforce any legislation forbidding discrimination against middle-aged workers." More adamant on that point was Merwin Hart, president of the New York State Economic Council, who asserted, "Don't pass any more laws restricting business ... Private enterprise is crushed by taxation, burdened to death by new and costly regulation." Continuing on he declared, "Don't pass another law telling employers what to do. Try an experiment of passing a resolution calling upon the employers of the State to do what you think they ought to do. Employers are patriotic. You will probably get 90 per cent of all you would get anyway by this method." Mark Daly, the general secretary of the Associated Industries of Buffalo said, without explanation, "The problem has existed since 1876 and no special care need be taken of it." Also, he insisted that neither himself nor any employer could be forced "to take on another fellow's discarded workers." Executives from many firms testified that their companies employed a fairly large percentage of people over 40 and that they did not discriminate. However, W.A. Griffin, assistant vice president of American Telephone and Telegraph company, admitted, in reply to a question, that his company would not take a woman over 40, except for a few special jobs, if younger and qualified women were available. Of 900 women hired by American Telephone and Telegraph in a recent period, he reported, only one was over the age of 40. Of the company's then current staff, 39 percent of the men were said to be over 40, 12 percent of the women.[102]

As the public hearing continued, evidence that drastic age limits were imposed by the New York City Municipal Civil Service Commission and by the New York State Civil Service Commission was given by many witnesses. Leopold Rossi, secretary of the Civil Service Association of the State of New York, read a long list of ads placed by the city commission giving age limits for applicants. Among those were: subway station agents, 34; highway engineer, 39; stenographer, 27; laborers, 32; stationary engineer, 35. Both Paul J. Kern, chairman of the municipal commission, and Grave Reavey, president of the state commission, denied that their bureaus discriminated against job seekers because of age, yet each admitted younger workers were "distinctly preferred" in the civil service. The idea that age had an effect on workmen's compensation insurance rates or that insurance carriers urged employers not to engage older workers because they cost more in pensions and accidents was called a fallacy by Leon Senior, manager of the State Compensation Rating Board, by Charles Smith, manager of the State Insurance Fund, and by C.J. Haugh, actuary of the National Bureau of Casualty and Surety Underwriters.[103]

Also appearing at the hearing was New York Mayor Fiorello La Guardia. When committee chairman James Wadsworth asked the mayor to comment on charges brought before the committee concerning drastic age limits for virtually all competitive jobs administered by the Municipal Civil Service Commission, La Guardia said, "I plead guilty to all the charges of age discrimination that have been made. We must have efficiency in the city government. You can't make us take all the employes private industry won't have." He reiterated that the policy was to get young people right out of high school and then advance them through the ranks in order to get 20 or 30 "of the best years of a man's life." La Guardia announced they were going to reduce the maximum age for entrance to the Police Department from 29 to 25 and that they might reduce further the maximum ages for both the Fire and Sanitation Departments. "If I were required by law to accept applicants older than our limit, I just wouldn't appoint," he declared. Mayor La Guardia warned the problem could not be dealt with locally and that he couldn't raise the limits even a little: "Suppose you did, every unemployed worker over 40 in the rest of the country would flock to New York."[104]

Two years later, in March 1940, that New York State Joint Legislative Committee on Discrimination in Employment of the Middle-Aged submitted its final report to the legislature. According to the report, the first requirement to successfully solve the problem was adequate employment opportunity which could not be had without expanding industrial activity. Calling the problem basically industrial rather than social, the study warned that "undue, top-heavy, or artificial pressure on behalf of the middle-aged would result in senseless discrimination against youth." Recommendations included the idea that the issue should be attacked on two major fronts: (a) employers must be ready to hire, (b) the jobless must be qualified to be hired. The report also concluded that employers in New York State were "rapidly" relaxing their previous prejudices against older workers, although no evidence was cited to support that claim.[105]

Federally, the Committee on Employment Problems of Older Workers (appointed by Secretary of Labor Frances Perkins in 1938 to look at the problems of those over 40) made its findings public in March 1939. It urged that age limits be abolished by the government and by private employers alike. Admitting the federal government had a higher proportion of older employees than did private employers, the report went on to say that age limits imposed by the government served as "an undesirable example" and urged they be lifted. One conclusion was that their exhaustive study gave "no evidence that would support, and much that would invalidate, a general prejudice against older workers on the score of age alone." Continuing on, the study declared that "an examination of actual data on productivity, accident, sickness, group insurance and pension plans has led ... to the conclusion that the prejudice against hiring older workers rests largely on inadequate and erroneous impressions, and that any policy, private or governmental, which arbitrarily discriminates against employees or applicants on the basis of a fixed age, is undesirable from the point of view of employees, employers and the public as a whole." Nevertheless, changes were recommended in private pension plans and/or Social Security to make it easier for middle-aged workers.[106]

Chaired by Harry Woodburn Chase, chancellor of New York University, the committee found that the 1937 United States unemployment rate was highest for the 20–24 group; after the age of 25 employment improved for a while, but some time after the age of 40 for men and 35 for women the trend turned downward. The unemployment of older workers was also likely to be a great deal more prolonged than that of workers in the younger age group. In Philadelphia the duration of unemployment was four times as long among men in the age group 40 to 44 as in the age group 20 to 24. With regard to accidents and cost, the study concluded older workers had less accidents, but those injuries cost more "so that the net cost is about the same throughout the age range." As for group insurance costs, the study declared that the employers' quota of the cost of group insurance was "so slight that ... it should not have been an influence on the fixing of hiring-age limits."[107]

Some unpublished material gathered by this Labor Department committee was released later in 1939 in a pamphlet published by the Public Affairs Committee. It said that the age at which men were most likely to be employed was in their early 30s. From the age of 35 onward the proportion of unemployed began to rise, at first gradually, then, after 45, more steeply. The skilled worker held his own until he was 45 or more, but the unskilled worker started to feel the handicap of age some 10 years earlier. Women were also affected earlier. For them the decline in employability set in at 30 instead of 35, and it increased much more rapidly. No fewer than 95 percent of large companies were found to confess to a more or less rigid hiring age. Even in firms that had no definite age limit, it was admitted that not many workers over 50 would be hired, that younger people would ordinarily be given preference. Government agencies, due to civil service regulations, were "often more discriminatory than private employers."[108]

Governments also became active in enacting legislation to deal with the problem. New Jersey enacted a law (Acts of 1930, ch. 104) permanently barring any discrimination against people of age 40 or over applying for employment in the service of the state or any county or municipality. However, the act did not apply to the police or fire departments of any county or municipality, nor did it apply to guards employed in any penal institutions. It was further provided that any person 40 or over accepting any employment with the state or any county or city would not be eligible to join any pension plan maintained by such a public body.[109]

Louisiana passed a law in 1934 (Act number 226) making it unlawful for an employer to fix an age limit of under 50 years in the employment of workers, "except in hazardous occupations or occupations requiring unusual skill and endurance." Also exempted were employers who provided a pension plan for their employees, if the plan had a required period of service of not more than 35 years and the pension payments were not less than $45 per quarter.[110]

With unemployment statistics for people in Delaware age 45 years and over standing 25 percent higher than for people in their 30s, State Representative David J. Lewis introduced the Lewis bill. It would have ensured employment to any man who proved himself competent. Under this bill, the worker 45 or over had to be hired by the employers' association of the industry in which he worked. If the industry was without opportunity for the man's services it was just too bad—the association would have to pay anyhow. The Lewis bill went nowhere.[111]

Massachusetts passed an act in August 1937 which stated that it was "against public policy to dismiss from employment any person between the ages of 45 and 65, or to refuse to employ him, because of his age." Penalties for violation of the act were puny, to say the least. The act allowed the state Labor Department to investigate any complaints and, if the firm stood guilty after due course, then the Labor Department had the power to publish the names of violators. There was no other penalty. One of the spurs to initiating this legislation was the result of a survey which showed that younger applicants were chosen for "the great majority of vacancies that occur in New England industry." When Roswell Phelps, director of statistics for the Massachusetts Labor Department, was explaining the act some five months after it became law, he noted that the penalty had not yet been imposed on any firm because employers had yielded to his department's "moral suasion" to keep a certain percentage of workers over age 40 on their payrolls. Phelps had found discrimination in Massachusetts beginning at around age 34 for men, 29 for women.[112]

During 1937 proposed legislation on the problem failed to pass in New York, Illinois, Pennsylvania, Minnesota and Texas. Because New York's Joint Legislative Committee agreed the government had little right to criticize private industry for discrimination unless the government set a good example, the committee itself originated a bill in the New York Legislature providing against such discrimination. Sponsored by committee chairman and Assemblyman James Wadsworth, the bill prohibited both the state or local civil service commissions from fixing arbitrary age limits for entrance into the civil service, except for positions requiring unusual physical ability such as those of fireman and policeman. In a memorandum sent to the legislature by Paul J. Kern, chairman of the New York City Municipal Civil Service Commission, he called the bill "a most vicious piece of legislation and a direct assault on the merit system." Nonetheless, it was passed in the legislature. Governor Herbert Lehman signed the bill into law in April 1938, saying it was time for the government to set an example for private companies. Soon after that sign-ing, Kern said removal of age restrictions would probably double the num-ber of applicants and would make New York State a refuge for people turned out by private industry because of age.[113]

Nothing indicated that the urging of President Roosevelt and Sec-retary Perkins or the enactment of legislation had much effect on the problem. What did turn things around was the coming of another World War. The urgent need for more employees in defense programs led to the lifting, in 1940, of age bars in taking on new employees in certain occu-pations in the War and Navy Departments. On June 3 that year the United States Civil Service Commission issued an order to all its district man-agers to extend the maximum age from 48 to 55 for any position in which, in their judgment, the existing maximum age of 48 would not produce enough qualified eligibles. On July 12, 1940, at the request of the Navy Department, those district managers were authorized to further extend the maximum age to 62 years, from 55, for certain trades and occupations in the Navy Yards.[114]

Newsweek magazine noted these changes a year later and also noted that one major firm doing critical defense work had raised its skilled labor age limit from 50 to 60. Figures from state employment offices for the third and fourth quarters of 1940 showed the largest group in placements was in the age 35 to 39 group, followed by those 40 to 44, and then by the 45 to 49 group. "Only on sales staffs, which are now being cut in con-sumer lines, and in the white-collar categories are advanced years still a handicap to employment."[115]

With respect to how the new situation affected women, journalist Dorothy Reid reported that a solution to the shortage of workers was coming from women, stating that young women first and preferably, then by degrees, older women had been hired. Regarding those older women Reid said that employers were still keeping their fingers crossed because, "Let's look at some of the evidence women have piled up against them-selves." One item was that they were said to lose more work days than men, particularly older women. Another complaint was that since young females entered the workplace only until they married, or in order to get married, female work attitude, at any age, was regarded as "lacking sta-bility."[116]

Edsel Ford, son of Henry, spoke of the gains being made by older workers in the River Rouge area in an article under his byline, titled, "Why We Employ Aged and Handicapped Workers." After outlining in some detail how many handicapped people he employed he went on to say, "Although more than 10 per cent of all men employed in the River Rouge industrial area are physically handicapped in some way, we have for many years been more concerned with a universal physical impairment—namely, old age." For Ford, old age began at 40. Perhaps some idea of general employer attitudes could be gained from Ford's definition of old age, its point of onset, his description of it as an impairment, and the combining of the terms aged and handicapped.[117]

As the war moved toward its conclusion, and the evidence showed the older worker to be competent, some observers believed that difficulties for older workers would more or less vanish when the war did end and a labor shortage was not dire. Reporter Ross Holman gave several examples of middle-aged workers doing well in factory work, which he termed "quite a revelation to many personnel managers that the man who used to be washed out at forty still has a great deal to offer at fifty, sixty and even seventy." Westinghouse had a "Middle-Aged Corps" (ages 40 to 67 or so) whose work had always before been done by young men. At the time this experiment started management insisted that workers of "advanced years" did not have the adaptability nor quick perception essential to learn anything as complicated as sealing radio and high-powered electronic tubes. After a few months management checked the records and found production just as good as with the younger workers. An added bonus was that the older men were absent only one-fourth as much as the young, they were late for work less often, and they had less than average turnover. Other surveys done at other firms yielded similar results. It all caused Holman to enthuse, "Such facts are bound to revolutionize future employment policies. The old practice of turning a cold shoulder to men and women over forty was both cruel and stupid. Industry was not alone in this regard." The other offender, and probably the biggest was, in Holman's view, the United States government wherein the civil service was set up to hire government employees largely on their qualifications for the job, "the chief test of fitness until the war was that the vast majority of them must not be over forty-five years of age and, for a great many positions, they must not be over thirty-five."[118]

Over the course of the period 1930 to 1946 the problem of age discrimination in employment became a public issue in ways it never had in the past. Survey after survey documented its widespread, pervasive existence. Politicians entered the discussion to a degree they never had before. Laws were enacted here and there, albeit with little impact. What a decade's worth of focus on the issue could not alter to any extent during the 1930s was altered dramatically with the coming of World War II.

People of all description who had prior difficulties in obtaining employment were suddenly in great demand. Not much attention was paid to the issue in the first half of the 1940s, nor was much written on the topic, for the obvious reason that it wasn't much of a problem. Self-help groups such as Forty Plus saw most of its branches disband or become dormant for the duration. Given that older workers acquitted themselves well during the war years, a set of expectations built up that perhaps the problem would disappear from the postwar world. Needless to say, those hopes were exaggerated, unfounded, and quickly dashed.

CHAPTER 4

States Enact Laws; Age Bias Remains Pervasive, 1947–1966

"Throughout the world, employers generally are not eager to hire older persons."
> —*Albert Abrams, New York State Joint Legislative Committee, 1952*

"[W]e cannot afford to squander our manpower through prejudice which obscures the values of maturity, responsibility and constancy found in older workers."
> —*President Dwight Eisenhower, 1955*

"If economic life becomes too hard for them [older people] they will form the most potent group this nation has known and force some kind of public program for their survival."
> —*Secretary of Labor James P. Mitchell, 1955*

"But discrimination in employment based solely on age is so widespread and freely admitted that free enterprise generally is to blame for its callous attitude toward the 40-plus worker."
> —*New York State Senator Thomas Desmond, 1956*

"The task of locating new employment for a man or woman past 30 gets increasingly difficult. By 45, the resistance, due solely to age, is very heavy."
—Office Management, *1958*

"[I]f [companies] agree to hire older workers 40 and over, they run the risk of upsetting their personnel structures far more seriously than if they stick to policies of Youngsters Only."
—Office Management, *1960*

"Studies show that the experience of the older, unemployed workers in the states with these [anti-age discrimination] laws does not vary significantly with the experience of those states without laws."
—*Robert Fjerstad, 1965*

World War II brought an economic upswing to the American economy to such an extent that almost no attention was given to the problem of age discrimination in employment until the war was over. Presumably, most people who wanted a job were able to find one. Since older workers acquitted themselves as well as the younger ones, in jobs they had not usually held and in companies that had not usually hired them, there was a hope that the problem would not resurface once the war ended. However, almost immediately after the war, it was business as usual for age discrimination in employment.

Federation Employment Service (FES), a non-profit, non-sectarian employment and vocational guidance agency, called in 1948 for a joint committee to assist "over-age" workers. It began a drive in April of that year to increase employment in New York City for those over 40. Over the next six months the FES placed 625 out of 7,000 job applicants over the age of 40. FES executive director Roland Baxt agreed that it seemed to be a small number but pointed out that compared with the pre-campaign placements by the agency, a "percentage increase running into the hundreds has been chalked up."[1]

That campaign drive by the FES, an affiliate of New York's Federation of Jewish philanthropies, involved a staff of 30: making phone calls; 35,000 letters sent out to employers; radio plugs, press publicity, car cards, and so forth. The theme of the drive was "Experience, Loyalty, Skill—Come With Age."[2]

What prompted that campaign was the situation in the immediate postwar period when, "At FES, we felt an immediate trend away from the employment of mature persons. Job orders without limitations fell sharply, while the number of older applicants rose sharply." Major trade associations as well as many prominent individuals were invited to endorse the drive and serve as honorary sponsors. Those accepting included New York Governor Thomas E. Dewey, New York City Mayor William O'Dwyer, New York State Senator Thomas C. Desmond, and more than 30 important trade organizations. Despite the resultant intensive media blitz and campaign, FES admitted that, "however, ten of our older applicants remained unemployed for each one placed, pointing up the difficulties of the situation." As an anticipated by-product of the campaign, FES was "immediately deluged with thousands of older job seekers, although all of our publicity had deliberately been directed toward employers." More than 70 percent of those applicants were between 45 and 55 years of age— not "aged" people.[3]

Also starting campaigns were some employers, although in a weak and ineffective manner. The National Association of Manufacturers along with the United States Chamber of Commerce announced in 1948 a campaign involving educational and promotional activities to find jobs for "older and physically handicapped workers." Perhaps revealing indirectly its view of older workers, a *New York Times* account of the drive carried the subhead, "Jobs for Aged and Crippled."[4]

Several months later it was announced that preliminary steps were being taken by various business groups to set up a New York State committee to coordinate "disjointed" efforts to find employment for older workers. However, the real reason was to be found in the position of many personnel men who felt that effective voluntary action by business had to be taken soon, to avert national and state legislation prohibiting discrimination against older workers. Said Bernard Fitzpatrick, personnel management bureau director of the Commerce and Industry Association of New York, "There is a bill pending in Congress—which nobody takes seriously as yet—to prohibit employers from hiring applicants for any job solely on the grounds of age." He also mentioned a New York State Joint Legislative group led by Thomas Desmond which had been studying the problem for two years, "and he may soon introduce legislation on the subject." Fitzpatrick said his group opposed any legislation because it felt business could solve the problem of the older worker more satisfactorily but admitted that "business can boast no impressive record on the matter so far."[5]

Speaking in 1948 Edward Rhatigan, former New York City welfare commissioner, disclosed that on the basis of experience in his city, economic old age came early. A woman over 30 and a man over 45 were seldom hired, he explained, because industry felt that they were too costly to be used in competitive production. A few months later a different group of speakers discussed the problem before a panel meeting of the Welfare Council, attended by 130 representatives of affiliated organizations. Irving Barshop, supervisor of placement with FES, said the problem was not confined to workers in their 50s and older, but that unemployment of women as young as 35 or men as young as 38 constituted a problem that most employers refused to face. He said employers most often paid little heed to qualifications and merely asked for someone "young." Another speaker there was Harriet Houghton, supervisor of the Adult Counseling Service in the commercial office of the New York State Employment Service. She said the employers were "open minded" and increasingly interested in the problem. However, she reported that in the 16 months since the counseling service had been established it had placed only 404 men and women over 50 years old, out of 5,400 interviewed.[6]

On January 14, 1951, an ad appeared in the *New York Times* which read: "Messenger, 40-hr., five-day, $34, steady. Prefer retired man bet. 45–65, G335 Times." Over 250 men in that age range answered this ad. Some of them even offered to work for $30 a week or less, some were college graduates, there were teachers, ministers, executives, and so on. A 52-year-old unemployed display manager wrote, in his reply, "I have won 18 national prizes but I am a has-been. I can't get a job despite my background. I'm over 45." Meanwhile, that ad also generated a lot of response from people who did not want the position. The *Times* received more than 100 calls and letters, ranging from offers of assistance to the surplus applicants to denunciations of anyone who would ask a man over 45 to work for $34 a week. One woman called for a state investigation. Her belief was that all the blame rested with employment agencies which, she said, screened all applicants and turned away the older ones.[7]

When the United States was once again on a war footing, in 1951 over Korea, William Kushnick, personnel division manager of the American Management Association, said there was a relaxing of standards for employee selection. Bars to the employment of older people were reported to be being let down slowly, but perceptively. However, it was all an illusion. The Korean conflict had no effect in slowing the course of age discrimination in employment.[8]

In 1956 the Packard Motor Company permanently closed its doors in Detroit. A study was conducted of displaced auto workers at the plant. Studied were 260 white, blue-collar workers. More than 90 percent were

40 years of age or older; about 35 percent were at least 60 years old. Almost half had over 26 years of service; five percent had worked at Packard since 1915. Interviews were held with the workers prior to the plant shutdown and then 27 months later. One item measured was months of unemployment: (1) never reemployed, average of 21.35 months of unemployment, 60 men; (2) reemployed but not working at the time of the second interview, 9.67 months, 82 men; (3) reemployed and still working, 5.13 months, 118 men.[9]

A second study at the Packard plant, which was carried out one year after the closure, showed no statistical difference in the success of whites and blacks in obtaining new jobs at the Big Three automakers. Older workers, however, were not as successful. Of those under 45, 58 percent were reemployed; for those 45 to 54 the reemployment rate was 30 percent; it was just 15 percent for those aged 55 to 64. Concluded the study, "Age was the most important factor in the number of months the respondent had gone without work; it was a more powerful predictor of the length of unemployment than either the respondent's education or skill level." One explanation put forth was that Michigan had a fair employment practice law, which prohibited discrimination on the basis of color, but not one against age.[10]

In a profile of the problem in 1955, the business magazine *U.S. News & World Report* explained that new jobs were becoming harder to get for a man after he reached the age of 45, or for a woman past 35. According to a government spot check, about 60 percent of help-wanted newspaper advertisements and jobs on offer in employment offices "were found to restrict hiring to these limits, or even to lower age brackets." The situation was worrisome to the magazine because, while the nation's total population had doubled since 1900, the age group 45 to 64 had tripled in size. It had the potential to become a large economic problem. In a recent month in America, workers 46 and older made up 29 percent of total unemployment but received only 18 percent of the job placements.[11]

Just six months later the same magazine was back to report that one of the first questions asked of a job hunter was, "How old are you?" President Dwight Eisenhower had just given a Labor Day message in which he told the country, "We cannot afford to squander our manpower through a prejudice which obscures the values of maturity, responsibility and constancy found in older workers." Labor Secretary James P. Mitchell was then campaigning to convince employers that people over 45 had many productive years ahead of them. Putting the problem in perspective, the magazine explained that in 1900 a male worker aged 60 could expect to

live 14 more years, of which 11 would be spent working, three in retirement. By 1950 that 60-year-old could expect to live 15 years longer, nine
working and six in retirement. Projected to 1975 the expected years equaled
17, eight on the job and nine retired. It was, therefore, a growing economic
problem—not just for those directly affected by age discrimination, but
for society as a whole, since those people had to be supported in some
fashion. What then was troubling Washington officials was that age was
a barrier to getting a job "at a time when many industries are in the market for more workers, and when business generally is booming." State
employment agencies reported that 66 percent of jobs that employers had
to offer contained age limits. Secretary Mitchell was also worried about
the economic implications: "If economic life becomes too hard for them
[older people] they will form the most potent group this nation has known
and force some kind of public program for their survival. This is a possibility industry must face immediately. Will it find places for older workers and make profits from their production, or be taxed much more heavily than now in order to sustain them as nonworkers?"[12]

Writing in *American Mercury* in 1959, reporter William Vassallo
declared that age barriers were going up all over America. He called this
"wanton" discrimination by corporations against the middle-age man a
"national disgrace." In San Francisco, he explained, seven of every ten
firms would not hire a man or woman of 50 or over; in the Southwest
conditions were worse. In New York City 75 percent of companies would
not hire a man at 55, while 80 percent barred a woman of 55. Seventy
percent of Houston firms would not consider men for office employment
if they had passed the age of 44; for women there the percentage was "dis-
couragingly higher." Also in Houston, 24 percent of companies barred
men at 35. In 90 percent of discriminating firms company policy did not
clearly spell out the restrictions; rather it was usually through verbal orders
"to favor younger men."[13]

When the Office Executives Association surveyed 121 companies in
1957, it found that the typical woman did not run into hiring trouble until
she was 35, compared with the male where age 30 was the marker. At 45
a female was considered too old to hire by about 25 percent of companies; after 50 she found 56 percent of the doors closed. For men, 42 percent of the businesses barred them outright at the age of 50.[14]

Toward the end of 1959, Margaret Gordon reported that there had
been widespread concern in the 1950s about the employment problems
of older workers, "but at no time has the concern been more evident than
in 1958–1959." Innumerable conferences had been held, state employment

agencies had expanded their special placement services for older workers, and more states were implementing laws banning age discrimination in hiring. Despite those widespread efforts of both public and private agencies to break down the barriers to the employment of older workers in recent years, Gordon declared, "there is little evidence that upper age limits in hiring are becoming less prevalent." Intensive interviews with representatives of 65 firms in the San Francisco area by the staff of the Institute of Industrial Relations, based at the University of California at Berkeley, were conducted from 1954 to 1956. Some of these representatives were reinterviewed in 1959. Interviews were also conducted in 1959 with representatives of 21 employment agencies. Results indicated that the great majority of firms in the sample of 65 reported that they had upper age limits in hiring, either through formal policies or through less formal practices. "There is little evidence of any appreciable change in employer hiring practices, as they related to the age of job applicants, in the area between 1954–56 and the spring of 1959." Management representatives who were reinterviewed related that their practices were much the same. Officials of the employment agencies likewise indicated that there had been little change. Another finding was that the older the company, the more likely it was to enforce relatively rigid upper age limits. Most of the firms without limits had relatively fluctuating employment along with relatively more union input to hiring, compared to those with age maximums, who had no union input and relatively stable employment. Also, the older the company, the more likely it was to have an age maximum. At one airline age limits were as follows: 27 for stewardesses, 35 for stewards, 27 for copilots, 31 for flight engineers, 55 for ground personnel. Gordon observed that reference to the influence of a pension plan ranked second in frequency among the reasons mentioned for age bias. However, she added, "There were an appreciable number of firms whose representatives specifically commented that the pension plan had no influence on the company's hiring policy of barring older job applicants, or if it did, that it was a consideration of relatively minor importance."[15]

If little headway was being made, part of the reason may have been in the practices of the government itself. The New York State Civil Service Commission chairman Alexander Falk explained, in August 1958, that the agency set age limits for some jobs but only those that required "extraordinary physical efforts." A current posting of the commission sought applicants for the job of motor vehicle license examiner. It specified that applicants had to be at least 21 but not more than 40. A spokesman for the Motor Vehicle Bureau said that the duties of license examiners involved physical exertion for which men under 40 would be most suitable.[16]

When the situation for older women workers was looked at specifically during this period, the results usually showed that females faced an even bleaker situation than did men. In a 1950 speech before the Women's City Club, Ollie Randall of the Community Service Society said that commercial old age for women was 35 years. She said her statement was based on a recent study by the United States Employment Service of the diminishing number of jobs for women over 35 and for men over 45 years of age. "When these men and women go out looking for a new job," declared Randall, "they are not finding doors slammed in their faces, because doors aren't even being opened to them any more."[17]

That same year Mary Pirie looked at newspaper advertisements in the "help-wanted, female" columns and found that most of those ads stated, even in peak employment periods, rather plainly, "No one over thirty-five need apply."[18]

The United States Department of Labor announced, in 1956, a new project for helping older women get jobs. About 33 percent of the unemployed in America were in that category. One aspect of the project called for "Earning Opportunity Forums" which involved bringing together women seeking jobs, representatives of employers seeking workers, and community leaders. As well, the department had called in pension experts, and they had concluded that the argument that pension costs were higher for older workers need not stand in the way of hiring them. Pension plans, concluded the experts, were based on the length of time worked "and do not present any prohibitive cost for hiring older workers."[19]

A United Nations report on economic opportunities for older women workers studied conditions in Canada, the United States and Western Europe. Data was supplied by government sources, nonofficial publications, and the opinions of various influential women's organizations. That 1954 report emphasized that the traditional barriers against the employment of older women continued to be a stumbling block in most countries. The chief obstacle to be overcome was said to be undoubtedly the prejudice of the employer who stuck to the "too old at 40" argument. Solutions suggested included changes in compulsory retirement laws, changes in pension plans, and special legislation or "bonus" arrangements to induce employers to take on older help. Both France and West Germany had considered subsidies to persuade employers to hire older people. In both countries, however, the idea of legislation along those lines was opposed.[20]

A 1955 report submitted by the International Labour Organization stated that many factors made it harder for all older people to find work but, nevertheless, older women "come up against additional obstacles that complicate and aggravate the difficulties facing any older worker." Another conclusion was that older women were more subject to unemployment than men of the same age or younger workers of either sex. In Belgium in 1951 in the category of all wage earners, females under 50, 11.7 percent were unemployed; in the 50–64 group 20.4 percent were unemployed; for males under 50, 4.5 percent were unemployed; for 50- to 64-year-old males the figure was 12.7 percent. Two years later those rates in Belgium were as follows: females under 20, 4.8 percent; 20 to 30, 17.9 percent; 30 to 40, 18.5 percent; 40 to 50, 20.6 percent; 50 to 60, 26.6 percent; 60 to 65, 35.4 percent; for males under 20 the unemployment rate was 5.7 percent; 20 to 30, 7.6 percent; 30 to 40, 7.1 percent; 40 to 50, 8.9 percent; 50 to 60, 14.3 percent; 60 to 65, 27.9 percent. Older women were also usually out of work for longer periods than younger women, although there was no proof that in that respect their position was any worse than that of male workers. It was also felt there was probably more hidden unemployment among females. For example, a proportion of married women were not classed as unemployed, under some unemployment insurance schemes. The main reason for that higher unemployment among older workers was attributed in the study to "the preference of employers for youth." Formal restrictions in the form of specific age limits were also more frequently encountered by women than by men. Cited as examples by the International Labour Organization were Columbus, Ohio, and Houston, Texas, where 81 percent of job vacancies for women (at state employment centers) were subject to age restrictions, as compared with 64 percent for male vacancies. A West German inquiry found 51.5 percent of unemployed women and 41.5 percent of the unemployed men were idle for reasons of age discrimination. Also, that age barrier frequently struck earlier for women, often at 35, whereas for men it was more likely to be 40 or 45. Generally, the age limit for entry into the civil service was found to range, in the case of women, from 25 to 40, according to the country. In France that age was between 26 and 30; in Sweden it was 30; in Canada, it had been recently raised from 35 to 40. Stated the report, "In retailing, where great numbers of women are employed, appearance is so important that the loss of youth, looks and attractiveness is a serious handicap." Saleswomen in New York City were considered to be too old at 40. Big stores in city centers were said to be very rigid in imposing age limits, while small local shops were found to be more flexible.

Governments were urged to take the lead in bringing down age bars. One had already done so—certain branches of the British Civil Service had raised the entry age limit to 60 years for certain positions, such as typists and telephone operators, which were usually held by women.[21]

With regard to age bars in specific occupations, a group of airline stewardesses appeared in 1965 before a House Labor subcommittee considering the problem of older workers. They learned that four airlines had policies forcing stewardesses to resign at the age of 32 to 35. Asked why some airlines did that, Colleen Boland, president of the Air Line Stewards and Stewardesses, Local 550, referred to a newspaper article quoting an unnamed airline executive on the subject: "It's the sex thing. Put a dog on an airplane and 20 businessmen are sore for a month."[22]

Aute Carr was an official engaged in the placement of ministers. When he conducted a survey of 31 smaller churches offering a $4,000 salary and a parsonage, he found that less than 10 percent of them were willing to consider a man of 50 or over. Reasons given him were the usual ones such as older men got sick a lot, they were more prone to serious illness, they were off work a lot more, and so forth. Carr said that in the past when life moved at a slower pace and change was less frequent, elders of a community were sought out for their experience, skill, wisdom and counsel. Today, however, emphasis was on youth; "age has lost its prestige value," concluded Carr.[23]

The only club for older unemployed people which received any press coverage was the Forty Plus organization. In 1948 the Forty Plus Club of New England celebrated its tenth anniversary. No one could become a member unless: (1) he was an American citizen; (2) he had earned at least $4,000 a year at some time; (3) he was over 40 years of age; (4) he agreed to give the organization two days of his time each week until he was placed; (5) he attended weekly round-table meetings on Mondays; (6) he was unemployed through no fault of his own. New England newspaperman Ronald Darling founded Forty Plus of Boston in 1938—later its name was changed. Inspiration for the club came from the files of Henry Simler, of the American Writing & Adding Machine Company of New York. Darling wrote to Simler for permission to use the title "Forty Plus" (Simler had tried to organize a group under that name). He approved, became the group's first honorary member, and helped to promote the organization. After that the idea swept the nation, spread to Canada, England and several other foreign lands. Simler was never unemployed but decided to fight age discrimination. When Darling started his group he was 42 years old and unemployed. He met with several others informally the first time. Darling was not convinced that he could sell himself to an employer, but he felt he could sell somebody else. Thus came the idea that club members would contact potential employers to try and get them to hire one of the club's members, but not themselves. Those weekly round-table meetings took place at 11 A.M. Mondays. Absence from two meetings automatically resulted in dismissal from the club. Forty Plus was largely inactive during the World War II years. Members agreed to pay $1 a month into the club treasury in support of the group for two years after they were placed in jobs.[24]

A 1950 article about the club stated that an annual income of $5,000 was necessary for admission. It was said that only eight percent of applicants were accepted by Forty Plus. The new member paid $20 to join. Since the club was formed an estimated 2,400 men had been placed in jobs paying an average of $7,500 a year. The average salary of club members in their former jobs was $9,500. Four months was the average length of membership, with the current high being 16 months. Average age of club members was 52. The entire membership worked together on job solicitation and placement. Pledging 2½ days a week to the club, the new member made the rounds of companies. The members also did all the office work, paperwork, and so forth. Only through the club committee could a member apply for a job listed by Forty Plus. That committee decided who was qualified, sent out resumes, and arranged interviews.[25]

Six years later, in 1956, journalist Raymond Schuessler said about Forty Plus that it no longer gave a specific minimum dollar figure for admission, except to say the potential member "must have received substantial remuneration." Later he noted that prior salaries of members ranged from $5,000 to $50,000. Applicants who survived first and second interviews and subsequent investigation (also said here to be eight percent) were presented for election by the entire membership at the weekly meetings.[26]

Among those who expressed opinions on the topic was New York Welfare Commissioner Raymond Hilliard. In a 1950 report on his increasing workload, he observed there were then around 400,000 unemployed workers. His public assistance caseloads had risen for the fourteenth straight month as people exhausted their unemployment insurance benefits. Hilliard said that most of the younger workers were still able to find jobs before their unemployment claims were exhausted. "However, more and more of those over 45 are unsuccessful in their search for work. When their savings are spent, they must turn to the Welfare Department for help." Addressing employers, he added, "If business men would like to see a reduction of the public assistance tax burden, they must not discriminate either against the older worker or the qualified relief recipient."[27]

Canada's Labour Department assessed the situation over the last half of the 1940s. First though, putting the problem in context, the *Labour Gazette* said it was about 1910 that public recognition was first given to the special employment problems of older workers. One of the earliest expressions of public concern with the issue was a movement for reform and improvement in institutions for the aged and for old age pensions. That movement reached its peak in the first quarter of the 1900s and, in Canada, resulted in the establishment of a system of old age pensions in 1927. Regarding the last part of the 1940s, the report noted that a strong economy from 1946 to 1948 meant the problem of unemployed people over 45 did not occur in Canada. However, in bad times, such as during the Depression, and in both the United States and Canada, a poor economy showed the incidence of unemployment hit most heavily the younger and older workers.[28]

Trade unions agitated for laws against age discrimination in at least two states around 1950. In New York State a Joint Legislative Committee was warned by organized labor that unless employers curbed "arbitrary discrimination" against older job seekers it would demand that the legislature bar age limits in hiring, just as it had already barred bias on grounds of race, color, or creed. In Massachusetts the State Federation of Labor came out with two proposed bills. One would declare that it was "against public policy" to dismiss from employment any person between the ages of 45 and 65 or to refuse to hire him because of his age. It would provide violation penalties, including the possible loss of public contracts. The second proposed bill would amend the Massachusetts Fair Employment Act of 1946 to make it unlawful to discriminate against job seekers aged between 45 and 65. Under the proposal an employer could not ask the age of a job applicant, just as employers could then not ask the race or creed of applicants. Unions were said to see this need for legislation as stemming from three sources: (1) some employers might seek to discharge older workers to avoid the cost of pensioning them off; (2) where older workers were employed, industrial health programs, sickness benefits, sick-leave policies, and so forth, were going to cost employers more; "some insurance companies already are quietly advising against employment of older workers"; (3) employers had long held a deeply set opposition to hiring older applicants when younger ones were available in the labor market. Those arguments that older workers were less productive, less teachable, more likely to get hurt, and so forth were, despite their being false, "so habitual and traditional" that job safeguards for older workers would be needed even if pension and insurance problems had not come up. If job discrimination continued to spread, said *Business Week*, then the American Federation of Labor "stands to lose its best sales line: sound and secure job rights for veteran union members."[29]

Thomas Desmond was a state senator in New York as well as a long-time member of a joint legislative committee investigating the problems of older workers. At the beginning of the 1800s, he said, nine out of every 10 Americans were living on farms. As late as 1900 the population was still two-thirds rural. At the time Desmond was writing, 1952, less than 20 percent remained on farms. Life on the farm, either independently or with children, presented no retirement problems to the elderly. There was always enough for them to do. They could work as long as they wanted but begin to taper off when the time for a slowdown came. For older people trying to get along in the city in 1952, the story was quite the reverse. Desmond felt the age of usefulness, as far as employment went, was decided by the employer. Recent industrial development processes had militated against the older worker, for the emphasis was on speed, work that required little or no skill, set schedules of work and more exacting physical requirements. Out of 443 older people interviewed for employment during a two-month period at one New York State employment office, only 15 were placed in jobs. Even more discouraging, the office found that those few placements were rarely permanent. In western New York the Forty Plus Club, reported Desmond, said that the placement of older workers between 50 and 60 was possible by screening a large number of medium-sized industries. However, it was "just about impossible to place a man over 60."[30]

Also speaking out were some famous people. Financier Bernard Baruch came out in 1956 against any law that barred employers from discriminating against job applicants over 40. He contended that more could be done for the cause of the middle-aged by "education" than by compulsion. His views on the topic were solicited by Thomas Desmond, as chairman of that joint committee. Said the then 86-year-old Baruch, "You cannot legislate understanding. And it is not exhortation of industry that is required, but education of industry."[31]

Speaking to the 1950 annual meeting of the American Trade Association executives, Eric Johnston, president of Hollywood's lobby group, the Motion Picture Association of America, said that too often men over 45 were laid off and assigned "to a wickedly wasteful human scrap pile."

Employers, he added, had ignored that "American tragedy." Warning that the government would step in unless employers stopped discriminating, Johnston concluded, "The choice is clear. We'll have to grapple with the problem or there'll be more Government agents gumshoeing through out work shops."[32]

When H.L. Douse looked at the issue historically in the *International Labour Review*, he remarked that the twentieth century belonged to youth. Two world wars had placed emphasis upon the qualities of youth. Increased mechanization had quickened the pace of industrial life and given added importance to those same youthful qualities. "This glorification of the attributes of youth has been enhanced by contemporary authors and playwrights who almost invariably make their heroes and heroines young dynamic individuals, often bestowing upon them superior qualities quite incompatible with the inexperience of youth," he said. It all led to a lowered appreciation of the attributes of older people. For Douse it seemed natural that attitude would have spread to the labor market and created discrimination against older workers. Next he cited a special committee struck by Perkins in 1938 and which reported to the Labor Secretary a year later. After an examination of factual data on productivity, accidents, sickness, group insurance and pension plans, the committee concluded that "there is little significant relationship between age and costs, and that the prejudice against hiring older workers rests largely on inadequate and erroneous impressions. We urge that everything possible be done to dispel the idea that workers are through after 40." Douse concluded that age discrimination existed mainly because of prejudice and fallacious beliefs. Attitudes which arose from those causes were probably the core of the problem, but other contributing factors such as inflexible pension plans, overemphasis on promotions from within, and accelerated promotions for young people also played an important role.[33]

Presenting a management view, in 1960, was an anonymous article in the publication *Office Management* which agreed that many older workers—"usually with justification"—complained about management "prejudice" against hiring them. Arguing that management "reluctance" or management "policy" might be fairer words, the article added, "but the fact remains that the old (and even not-so-old) worker is barred from employment in many companies." Companies thus faced a dilemma—either refrain from hiring older workers and run the risk of violating laws, generating negative public opinion, and so on, or, "if they agree to hire older workers 40 and over, they run the risk of upsetting their personnel structures far more seriously than if they stick to policies of Youngsters Only."[34]

A few years later the magazine *Business Management* declared that despite all the recent talk about early retirement, "despite all the reports that companies won't hire people older than 45, American business looks with favor on the middle-aged employee." Based on its survey of 166 companies (each with 100 or more employees) it concluded that "all of the firms indicate they think well of the older employee." That survey asked mostly soft questions, nothing, for example, about specific age limits. The only relevant query was one that asked, "As a general rule, would your firm prefer to hire a young employee rather than one who is 45 or older?" Fifty-eight percent of the companies said yes, 27 percent no, five percent said it depended on circumstances, 10 percent gave no answer. "Most of the companies surveyed would prefer to hire younger men—other things being equal. But this preference wouldn't preclude them from hiring good older men," concluded the piece. That article set out to answer in the negative the question it posed in its own title: "Does business discriminate against employees above 45?" It did not succeed.[35]

It did not succeed because it could not. Age discrimination in employment had been well documented by many surveys in this period. One was conducted by the New York State Employment Service in 1948 in several upstate cities. In Schenectady, 49 percent of 2,400 registered job seekers could not qualify for listed positions because they were over 55 years old, and another 8.1 percent were ineligible because they were too young. The percentage of those too old and too young declined from that high of 57.1 percent (combined total) in Schenectady to a low of 29.6 percent in Utica.[36]

During December 1949 in New York State men over 45 made up 48.5 percent of all unemployment insurance claimants, although they made up only 36 percent of the insured male labor force. In that same month 64.1 percent of all men who had exhausted their benefits were over 45 years of age. An often unspoken worry for many was the rapid growth rate of the older population. Back in 1900 the 45- to 64-year group was 14 percent of the total United States population; four percent were 65 and over. By 1950 those two groups made up, respectively, 21 percent and eight percent of the population.[37]

The federal Bureau of Employment Security, collaborating with several state employment services, conducted studies of older (45 and up) workers in 1950 to shed some light on the what, why and how of the employment aspects of aging. Locales were Lancaster, Pennsylvania; Columbus, Ohio; Houston, Los Angeles, and New York. Local offices participating in the studies selected from among their older applicants a sample for the total applicants group; this was divided into control and experimental groups matched on age, sex, occupation, and length of unemployment. The control group received no services they would not have received under normal circumstances from the office. On the other hand, the experimental group received what was described as "intensive employment counseling and placement service exploiting every device within the knowledge and ingenuity of the most capable and thoroughly experienced counselors and placement interviewers available in the offices in which the studies were conducted." A total of 8,727 men were involved. It was accepted that the older worker, as compared with other workers, faced greater difficulties in finding new employment and that those difficulties existed in times of full employment or higher unemployment. Periods of unemployment for older people tended to be much longer than for younger ones, with unemployment of more than 20 weeks' duration not being unusual among workers age 45 and over who had failed to return to the workforce during the first four weeks of their unemployment. At one state office 23 percent of all those registered for clerical and sales jobs were over 45, yet that office had placed just two percent of the 454 registrants in that category. In the study itself the employment service placed 25 percent of the experimental group in jobs, as compared to 10 percent of the control group. One conclusion drawn was that, for older workers, the public employment service was of pivotal importance as a source of placement. "Traditional attitudes toward older people as workers are a major problem in their placement. Every local office participating in the study indicated that personnel workers, including employment service staff members, share and sometimes magnify these attitudes as they believe them to exist among employers and the public," said the study. Yet researchers believed those attitudes could be broken down with an individual approach. Among Pennsylvania employers who stated their policy was to not hire workers over 45, 4.4 percent of their actual hires were in that age group. However, among employers who stated they had no age restrictions in their hiring policy, just 3.9 percent of their actual hires were from the over-45 category.[38]

Welfare Commissioner Henry McCarthy, of New York City's Department of Welfare, said his department would meet with greater success in getting people off the welfare rolls if employers were to overcome their prejudice against hiring workers over 40. Department records showed that as they referred more and more people to private industry, the percentage of those remaining on the relief rolls who were over 40 increased, "because of the preference shown to the younger worker." On July 1, 1950,

50.1 percent of all employable people on the welfare rolls were over 40; three months later it was 58.6 percent; three months later still it was 64.4 percent; on April 1, 1951, the figure was 66.6 percent. It meant that within a period of nine months the number of employable people over 40 who were on the relief rolls had risen from one-half to two-thirds of the total.[39]

Commenting on several surveys was Albert Abrams, director of the New York State Joint Legislative Committee on Problems of the Aging. In his view there were two main barriers that hindered older job seek-ers—indirect and direct. Indirect barriers included industrial processes and techniques that excluded them, although not instituted primarily to do so. Examples included promotion from within systems, pensions, not validated medical and psychological tests, and certain union regulations. Indirect barriers were also found in the wider culture, which included industry and which had an impact on industry, such as the glorification of youth and a high-energy society. Direct bars were found in written rules excluding people over a certain age; unwritten rules; deficiencies of older workers, whether in training or preparation for job seeking; and lack of public or private counseling and placement services geared to older workers. Barriers against older people were not unique to the United States, observed Abrams: "There is evidence that they exist in underde-veloped and agrarian economies as well as in industrial societies, and in statist as well as democratic regimes ... throughout the world, employers generally are not eager to hire older persons."[40]

One postwar study cited by Abrams involved 38 companies in Rochester, New York, which employed 62,828 workers. Findings revealed that 29.5 percent of them had a specific maximum age above which new employees were not usually hired. A New York State survey disclosed that 39 percent of 172 firms admitted imposing formal age barriers. A nation-wide study by the National Association of Manufacturers (NAM) and the United States Chamber of Commerce in 1949 indicated that 26 percent of the enterprises "did not follow a practice" of hiring older people. Two decades earlier, in 1930, NAM did a similar survey and found that 28 per-cent of companies had maximum age limits. Another 1930 survey, in New York State, determined that in approximately 25 percent of the moder-ate and large companies (employing 40 percent of the state workforce) the older job seeker "would encounter an insurmountable hiring bar. His chances of being accepted would be practically zero." Data on job orders filled by public employment service agencies in 1950 showed that in Columbus, Ohio, of 3,925 jobs, 81 percent had age restrictions for women, 75 percent for men. Of 511 openings in Lancaster, Pennsylvania, 60 percent had age bars; in Birmingham, Alabama, the figure was 90 percent; 50 percent in Dallas; in New York State, 25 percent of the 3,500 job openings had age bars. Another measure of age bias was disclosed in the extent to which help-wanted ads contained such restrictions. One analysis of 3,474 job opportunities for males advertised in the *New York Times* showed that 38.2 percent included an age limit.[41]

Abrams pointed out that the pattern of barriers varied widely from industry to industry, from job to job, and from community to community. Advertising and public utility firms were said to be "notorious for rigid utilization of inflexible age requirements." New industries such as plastics and aviation were customarily worse than older industries. Age bars were not as numerous in the service industries or in service jobs in any industry. Also, there was a tendency to ignore age restrictions for jobs requiring a high degree of skill, such as tool and die maker. Large companies were more likely to impose age restrictions than were medium or small firms. Skilled cooks were hired in restraurants up to age 65, but waiters, waitresses and counter people encountered resistance at 50 or earlier. Hotel clerks hit the age deadline at 40. Professional nurses over 40 reportedly found difficulty obtaining jobs on hospital staffs but could be placed on private duty. In commercial offices the age limit was frequently 35 for women and 45 for men. A United States Employment Service survey disclosed that as unemployment increased, employer specifications with respect to age were tightened, and the percentage of older workers among the jobless increased; "and if not reemployed at their regular work [the older workers] are usually downgraded in skill and pay. Similar conclusions have been reached by studies in various foreign countries."[42]

In a more philosophical vein, Abrams mused that America's national heroes were not physicists or philosophers but 20-year-old baseball players and teen-age Hollywood stars. "Many respectable corporate fortunes are being made today by successfully conditioning the public to a dread of aging. The purveyors of face creams, liver pills, slenderizing mechanisms, and so forth hold before us the grim prospect of a wrinkled, obese, ill old age." He continued, "Youth, youth, youth! We idealize it. We crave it. We fear its loss." An additional factor he saw was the gradual disappearance of the kinship-oriented conjugal family. In bygone days working for relatives was quite common among older people. The family took care of the work needs of older people. However, in the current era the coupling of "older people" with "diminished capacity" was significant, as one of "the dominant stereotypes in industrial thinking is the linking of older workers with decreased production"—that, in spite of the fact that studies had shown there was no truth in the concept.[43]

When questionnaires were sent to companies in 1953 by the Washington, D.C.-based Bureau of National Affairs, it found that one-third of the firms had a maximum age restriction. The most frequently given maximum age for hiring both factory employees and white-collar staff was 45 years. Personnel executives of those surveyed companies "almost unanimously" opposed the idea of legislation that would force firms to ignore age as a factor in hiring. More than two-thirds of them also objected to proposals that tax reductions be given to employers who retained a certain percentage of older workers on their payroll.[44]

Professor H.C. Lehman of Ohio University reported in 1954 that his analysis of 3,474 jobs advertised in the help-wanted columns of the *New York Times* showed that 1,330 of them included age limits, 97 percent of which discriminated against men over the age of 45.[45]

The New York State Employment Service conducted a 1956 spot check in 10 different communities on the ages at which employers expressed reluctance to hire workers. Nine of the 10 communities had no call for women over 45 in retail specialty shops. In one city the top age for employment in those shops was as low as 25. Preferred age for experienced typists, male or female, was under 45, while an inexperienced retail shoe salesman could be no older than 30, with an edge given to those between 21 and 25. State Senator Thomas Desmond remarked that there appeared to be nothing inherent in the American system of free enterprise that made it impossible, unprofitable or unwise to hire and utilize older workers. However, he added, "But discrimination in employment based solely on age is so widespread and freely admitted that free enterprise generally is to blame for its callous attitude toward the 40-plus worker."[46]

The Community Council of Greater New York issued a report which said the problem of finding jobs for those over 45 years of age "is increasingly acute here." October 1956 unemployment figures revealed that more than 50 percent of applicants were over 45, yet only about 33 percent of total unemployables in the city were in that age group. Another finding by the Community Council, reinforcing others, was that most employers would retain a worker past 45, so long as he could "pull his weight." The problem arose when it came to finding new jobs for older workers when they lost their jobs.[47]

Another federal Labor Department study in seven major cities showed that workers 45 years of age and older represented an average of

22 percent of all people hired in a one-year period, yet they made up 40 percent of the job seekers at local employment offices in those cities. Companies without pension plans hired about 45 older workers per 100 employed, while firms with pension plans hired only about 17 per 100. That, despite an earlier Labor Department study which established that older workers hired later in life did not unduly raise pension costs under many private pension plans. In this current study it was also found that older people stayed unemployed for longer periods. Annual hiring rates for workers under 45 were 71 per 100 employed, compared with 38 per 100 older employees. The quit rate of older employees was 11 per 100, compared with 30 per 100 for workers under 45.[48]

That Labor Department study found that age limits varied greatly from occupation to occupation, from industry to industry. Some examples of upper age limits were: 30 for airline hostess, 45 for telephone linemen, and 65 for janitors. Detroit, Los Angeles, Miami, Seattle, Philadelphia, Minneapolis-St. Paul, and Worcester, Massachusetts were the seven cities in which the characteristics of job seekers and jobs were examined. Men age 45 and older comprised 24 percent of all hires in the one-year period yet were 43 percent of all male job seekers. Women in that age group represented 17.4 percent of all hires but were 34 percent of female job-seekers. For men the turning point came in the age range of 45 to 54; it was then that discrimination became a serious problem. It arrived earlier for women, between the ages of 35 and 44. One of the study authors, John Saks, said, "The conclusion seems clear that the more advanced in age beyond 45 that job seekers are, the less the possibility of their being hired as compared with younger job seekers." That was true even though older workers were less costly in the sense they were more stable, that is, they quit and were discharged at a much lower rate than those under 45 years of age.[49]

Besides looking at job seekers, this study examined 21,386 job openings listed with state employment offices in the seven cities listed above, in April 1956. In five of those seven cities over 50 percent of the job openings contained maximum hiring ages. The range was 73 to 79 percent in three communities, and 67 percent and 51 percent in the other two. Los Angeles had a rate of 34.5 percent, while in Worcester 23.5 percent of the lob listings had age limitations. Massachusetts then had a law in effect which prohibited discrimination in employment on the grounds of age. Despite that, Worcester still had almost one-quarter of its listings giving evidence of discrimination. That was because those listings indicated a "preferred" age, as employers under the law were still allowed to state an age preference.[50]

Of all job openings in Detroit, Miami, Philadelphia, Seattle and Minneapolis, 64 percent specified upper age limits of under 55, 49 percent under 45, and 25 percent under 35. In the seven cities combined, 58 percent of the openings had limits: 52 percent under age 55, 41 percent under 45, and 20 percent under 35. Job seekers began to encounter significant difficulty in seeking employment between the ages of 35 and 44 in four of seven occupational groups. That is, in sales, service, unskilled, and professional and managerial, 33 percent or more of the openings had maximum ages within or below the indicated age range of 35 to 44. A similar proportion of the job orders specified even lower maximum ages— between 25 and 34—for clerical jobs. Significant difficulty in obtaining employment apparently began to occur earlier for men than for women in a number of occupational fields—clerical, sales, and semiskilled. In the clerical field difficulty appeared to start between the ages of 25 and 34 for men, between 35 and 44 for women. In the sales and semiskilled fields the difficulty began between 35 and 44 for men and between 45 and 54 for women. Evidently the white-collar worker and the blue-collar employee over 45 without a specific skill faced the most difficult situation. Occupational groups with the most restrictive upper age limits were, in order, clerical, unskilled, professional and managerial, and sales. The larger industrial firms specified upper age limits most frequently and the smaller companies less frequently. Percentage of job openings with some age restriction increased progressively from the smallest to the largest establishment—from 52 percent in firms employing seven or fewer employees to 78 percent in companies employing 1,000 or more workers.[51]

Another part of this study involved sending questionnaires to the companies to find out the reasons which tended to limit the hiring of older people. Reasons most frequently listed were: "inability to meet production standard," "inability to meet physical requirements," "lack of flexibility to meet changing conditions," "pension and insurance costs." These types of reasons accounted for about 75 percent of those given and were predominant in each city. In exploring attitudes toward older workers, the study found that employers often hesitated to hire an older employee at a lower skill level than he had in his last employment, even though the applicant was interested in accepting such employment. That hesitancy served as an effective barrier to the older applicant since a large percentage of workers who got new jobs were willing to accept major occupational change and lower pay than they previously had received. Another part of the study involved two groups of job seekers: a control group who got the normal state employment office help, and a matched experimental group who got intensive help, counseling, and so forth. Overall, 48.4 percent of those in the experimental group got employment during the three-month period, compared to 41.3 percent of those in the control group. If applicants who returned to their former employer were not counted, the numbers were 39.2 percent for experimentals versus 14.6 percent for controls. Both sets of differences were statistically significant.[52]

A survey conducted by the Office Executives Association of New York (part of NOMA, the National Office Managers' Association) compared 1958 with 1957. It was shown that in 1958 both men and women faced resistance in hiring before the age of 30, whereas in 1957 resistance occurred after the age of 30. However, in both cases the resistance was slight, amounting to not more than two percent. Both surveys, though, pointed out that appreciable resistance developed at about age 45. For 1957 that age barrier of 45 covered nearly 21 percent of the firms, 20 percent in 1958. For women, in 1957, first resistance was felt at about age 35, while in 1958 it was below 30. A woman of 45 faced the age barrier in nearly 25 percent of companies in 1957, almost 30 percent in 1958. For both males and females the probability of being hired after the ages of 50 to 55 was found to be "almost impossible." As in 1957, the 1958 survey revealed that absenteeism and turnover rates of older workers were no worse than for younger employees. Older employees were just as reliable, just as productive and presented no special supervisory problems. A large majority of companies indicated age was not an important factor in jobs dealing with the public. Concluded the study, "The task of locating new employment for a man or woman past 30 gets increasingly difficult. By 45, the resistance, due solely to age, is very heavy."[53]

Later in 1958 that survey was extended from just New York City to include San Francisco and Houston. For males the percentage of firms imposing an age limit of 35 or lower was 7.0 percent in New York, 18.2 percent in San Francisco, and 24.4 percent in Houston. Companies imposing an age limit of 45 or lower on males were, respectively, 20.0, 44.0, and 73.1 percent. At age 50 the figures were 42.3, 69.5, and 82.9 percent. At age 55 for men the figures were 67.6, 80.5, and 85.3 percent. Firms with no maximum age limits numbered 13.0, 10.9, and 9.9 percent respectively in New York, San Francisco and Houston. For women, the percentage of companies imposing an age limit of 35 or lower was 9.1 percent in New York, 3.5 percent in San Francisco, and 26.8 percent in Houston. At age 45 the numbers were 28.9, 43.8, and 75.7 percent. By age 50 it was 56.8, 75.3, and 83.0 percent. At age 55 female job seekers found the door closed at 78.8 percent of firms in New York, 89.6 percent in San Francisco, and 92.8 percent in Houston. Companies with no maximum hiring ages for women were 10.2, 3.5, and 4.8 percent in the three cities, respectively.[54]

When the firms in the above survey sought employees through ads in newspaper help-wanted columns, 70 percent rarely, if ever, indicated a maximum age. By contrast, when they used an employment agency two of every three companies set an age limit more often than not. Less than three percent of the firms always mentioned an age limitation in newspapers; more than 15 percent always stated an age limit when going through an agency. Another 27 percent occasionally specified age in the newspaper, but a majority occasionally did so when they went through an employment agency. Only 11 percent said they never specified an age limit in newspaper ads; less than five percent said they never set an age limit when using an employment agency. For the 1958 survey companies with an age limit were asked if that restriction was a specifically stated company policy or an "understood routine." It was policy for 11.7 percent of the enterprises and routine for 88.3 percent.[55]

The Personnel Committee of the Minneapolis-St. Paul chapter of NOMA conducted a 1959 survey with responses from 109 member firms employing almost 20,000 office workers in Minneapolis-St. Paul. Men faced some resistance perhaps beginning around age 30. Appreciable resistance was encountered at around 45. By the age of 50 a man was barred from employment in over 53 percent of the surveyed companies. At age 55 a man was excluded from employment by nearly 68 percent of the enterprises, causing the study to declare that "it is practically impossible to find employment at the age of 55." Women first faced resistance around the age of 35, working up to the point where more than 69 percent of the companies would not hire a woman over 55. Those maximum age limits were adopted as official policy in only about 10 percent of the companies. However, about 83 percent followed the maximum ages as a routine procedure. That is, they were not written down. The overwhelming majority of the respondent companies did admit, though, that they found no real differences in attendance, turnover, or the reliability and productivity of older employees as compared to younger workers. When the companies sought employees through ads in newspapers, only 49 percent indicated an age maximum. In contrast, when using an employment agency about 73 percent of the firms always or occasionally set an age limitation. When the respondents were asked what was the maximum age at which their company would hire office workers, replies were as follows: 25 years, 0 percent for men (1.8 percent for women); 30 years, 5.5 (0.9); 35 years,

7.3 (7.3); 40 years, 7.3 (11.0); 45 years, 11.0 (16.5); 50 years, 22.0 (26.6); 55 years, 14.7 (12.8); 60 years, 4.6 (6.4); 65 years, 4.6 (1.8) percent. No maximum age was set for men in 14.7 percent of the firms, 13.8 percent for women. No answer was given to the question, with respect to males, by 8.3 percent of the companies, 1.8 percent for women.[56]

During the spring of 1965 a study was conducted by the federal Department of Labor to ascertain the hiring policies of selected employers in five metropolitan areas: Baltimore, Indianapolis, Memphis, Salt Lake City, and Kansas City. Represented in the poll were virtually all major nonagricultural industries. Only 8.6 percent of all new workers hired by surveyed firms during 1964 were 45 years of age or over—less than one-third of this age group's proportion among the unemployed. One out of every six firms had a policy of no age bar, but one in four imposed age limits for one or more occupational groups. "Moreover, some of these usually hired workers at much younger ages than their upper age limits permitted," said the study. Areas with the best record of hiring older people were: retail trade, hotels, personal and medical services, and government. Over 40 percent of the firms with no age bar were federal, state, or local government units. Federal establishments reported that 16 percent of their new workers were age 45 and older. In the private sector, however, almost 60 percent of the companies added older workers to their payrolls in below-average proportions, and a few limited all hiring to those under 45. Manufacturing industries, as a whole, hired few older workers. New hires of workers age 40 to 44 amounted to 7.6 percent of all new hires, about the same as their proportion among the unemployed nationally. New hires age 45 to 54 accounted for less than half the proportion of this age group among the unemployed and those 55 to 64, only 20 percent. Hires of employees 65 and over accounted for only 10 percent of their proportion.[57]

One finding from this study was that although employers rarely mentioned labor supply-and-demand relationships, it was apparent that those relationships influenced both the incidence of upper age limits and the age at which restrictions and preferences appeared. Some 60 percent of the companies said they made exceptions to their age bars. When asked under what conditions exceptions were made, respondents gave replies which convinced those conducting the survey that labor supply conditions outweighed any considerations which motivated the stipulation of upper age limits. Concluded the study, "When employers find it necessary or advantageous to hire workers who are over their specified age limits or their preferred ages for hiring, they will do so. Considerations of physical requirements, pension plans, work expectancy, adaptability, and other reasons which appeared to justify the upper age limits evaporate." Employers with age bars (and those with no bars but which did little or no hiring of older workers) were asked why. Reasons given were as follows: physical requirements, 34.2 percent (that was broken down into job requirements, 25.1 percent and company standards, 9.1 percent); promotion from within, 8.1 percent; earnings, 7.3 percent; pension plan costs and provisions, 6.7 percent; lack of skill and experience, 6.3 percent; limited work life expectancy, 5.1 percent; few applicants apply, 5.0 percent; educational requirements, 4.2 percent; adaptability, 3.1 percent; training too long and costly, 3.0 percent; inferior quality of work, 2.3 percent; slowness in attaining proficiency, 2.1 percent; need for balance of ages, 1.7 percent; undesirable personal characteristics, 1.7 percent; health insurance costs and provisions, 1.4 percent; life insurance costs and provisions, 1.2 percent; all other reasons, 6.8 percent.[58]

Age discrimination in employment was not limited to the United States. In 1955 the United Kingdom began to recruit men and women age 40 and over to the Civil Service. Special competitions were held regularly for established clerical posts. To start with, some 500 vacancies were filled in London and about 100 in Birmingham. It was a plan that was needed, as in June 1955 around 70,000 of the 113,500 men registered as unemployed were over 40; 24,000 of 64,000 women. Noting those figures, *The Economist* magazine called the government plan a "useful example." Among people over 40, clerical workers were one of the groups that found it particularly difficult to find work, although there was often a shortage of young clerical recruits. By abolishing a maximum age (other than the normal retiring age), noted the periodical, government might encourage other employers, notably local authorities and perhaps banks, to look to older workers. The Ministry of Labour had told an inquiry on the employment of older people that nearly half of the vacancies dealt with by agencies for professional, managerial and higher executive posts carried age limits for applicants, "many of the limits being under 40." While *The Economist* hoped the government example would encourage private employers, it worried that "unfortunately, however, not all private employers—since they are spending their own, instead of the taxpayers' money—may feel able to take such a generous view as the Government about the pension problem."[59]

Just two years later the UK government had moved even further. By then there were no upper age limits for recruitment to temporary posts in the Civil Service, and the age limit for many permanent posts had been raised. The Civil Service had also abandoned a fixed retirement age.[60]

A committee that advised the UK Ministry of Labour on the employment of older workers had, in its first report issued in 1953, argued against government action, such as enacting a special quota for older workers, or by setting up separate registers at employment exchanges, as that would give a special, undesirable aura to the employment of those people.[61]

Not long after the war, Canada's federal National Employment Service (NES) announced that the number of unplaced job applicants age 45 years and over had dropped in October 1947 to the lowest point since the end of the war. Nevertheless, the percentage of older people in the unemployed group had increased by October to the highest point since the end of the war. The basic problem, said the Labour Department in its publication, was that "employers' preference for younger workers was still with us." That reduction in the absolute number of the 45 and older group of unemployed people came "through intense placement activity by the NES, in cooperation with other groups." In October 1947 unplaced age-45-and-over registrants with NES numbered 27,466, about 12,000 fewer than in October 1946. At the same time unplaced males 45 and over were 36.6 percent of all unplaced male applicants, compared to 30 percent one year earlier. Labour Minister Humphrey Mitchell said the most promising feature of the older worker question was the great interest which had been aroused in the problem during 1947 throughout the country. Due to the combined efforts of the Department of Labour, the National Employment Service, the Department of Veterans Affairs (working on behalf of older veterans), employer organizations, and the cooperation of newspapers and national magazines, said Mitchell, "there is now general realization of the seriousness of the problem which must ultimately result in progress toward its solution."[62]

Around the same time, Canadian commentator Harold Hudson noted that employers had four main objections to hiring older people: alleged lowered productivity; increased accident frequency; lack of adaptability in learning new techniques; increased cost of group insurance and pension plans. An executive officer of a medium-sized Canadian firm told Hudson that many of the older people seeking jobs were drifters who went from job to job looking for, but apparently never finding, contentment. Similar sentiments were expressed in a letter to the editor; older workers were themselves blamed.[63]

Several years later a memorandum presented by the Information Branch of the Department of Labour to the federal National Advisory

Council on Manpower stated that in Canada one of the chief difficulties facing the National Employment Service in matching unplaced applicants with unfilled jobs was "the tendency on the part of employers to reject applicants over 40 (over 35 for women)." As in the United States, older Canadian workers who lost their jobs tended to remain unemployed longer than did younger people.[64]

A 1955 analysis of some 1,500 job openings in Toronto revealed that 74 percent of employers stipulated that applicants had to be under the age of 45. Commentator Sidney Katz proposed the idea of sheltered workshops for older people. Employees would set their own hours, rest whenever they wanted, and so forth. He gave as an example a sheltered workshop run by a charity which employed 45 "elderly women" between the ages of 50 and 90. They did needlework, sewed buttons on for bachelors, and helped housewives by remodeling drapes, among other work. Katz's idea, of course, ghettoized the participants.[65]

When a survey of Canada's help-wanted ads was conducted in 1957, it was found that 54 percent of all job vacancies stipulated a maximum age of 40 or less. A personnel manager in a firm with 6,000 employees said, "We'd like to hire men over 40, but there's no denying that after that age a man starts to slow down." Said a senior executive in a company that employed 3,500 people, "Older men shoot production costs sky-high. In any case we have an inflexible company rule about such hirings. I couldn't change things, even if I wanted to do so." Another comment came from the director of public relations in a 2,500-worker enterprise who said, "An older man just couldn't stand the pace." The manager of employee services in a firm with 4,000 employees stated, "Officially, we don't set any age limits, but it's more or less recognized by our personnel group that they look for the younger, rather than the older man … I expect we'd go for the under-35 applicant if we had a choice." Finally, an executive in a company with a 1,000-person workforce declared, "If we give older workers a job our competitors would step in and grab off all the young blood. We can't afford to take chances like that these days."[66]

Writing in a Canadian business journal in the mid–1960s, personnel administrator Winston Cameron remarked that the maximum employable age was slowly declining. A few years earlier the average job seeker had a reasonable opportunity for an employment interview even at the age of 50, he wrote. But the cutoff had slipped to 40, "and there is strong evidence that a further lowering of the age maximum to 35 years is becoming increasingly popular." Cameron noted that a quick review of the help-wanted ads in any metropolitan newspaper "blatantly reveals the practice since an increasing number of help wanted advertisements categorically state age limitations." Various personnel executives gave him reasons for the situation. Two of them were: "If a man is still unsatisfied and looking for a better job at the age of 40 chances are he is a social misfit"; and "We make a practice of not hiring another company's mistakes."[67]

During 1954 the Industrial Relations Committee of the Canadian Manufacturers Association appointed a subcommittee to survey its members on the issue of the aging worker. According to reporter George Harry, every employer recognized the desirability of retaining aging workers in their jobs and of hiring older applicants when vacancies occurred. However, some employers, while recognizing that desirability, "find that on occasion certain difficulties hinder its accomplishment." It was those difficulties that the survey, which brought replies from 750 firms, was meant to uncover. One question asked was what conditions or circumstances in their plant made it difficult to hire older workers? About 94 percent of the survey returns said there were difficulties in the way of hiring older workers. In order of importance they were as follows: job openings too heavy or hard; already employing too many older workers; because of a pension plan; too old to learn. In plants with over 2,000 workers the pension plan was the reason given most often, with "too heavy" second, and "too many older workers" in third place. Other fairly important difficulties given were the existence of a health insurance (or benefit) plan; company policy; lower learning ability; younger workers were more worth training because of longer prospective service; older people were not as alert, dextrous or sharp-eyed as were younger workers; and finally, that a union contract (seniority, wage and retirement conditions) militated against hiring older people. When asked, as part of this question, what steps should be taken to increase the hiring of older people, several firms suggested decreasing wages. Harry concluded, "The questionnaire seems to show that older workers are still finding it difficult to get jobs in industry. The problem is not getting better. It may be getting worse."[68]

Canada's federal government set its own example for other employers, in 1955, through its Civil Service Commission by eliminating age restrictions for veterans and by raising the entry age limits in many job categories. One prominent Canadian actuary who had made a study of the problem found that a company whose regular policy was to recruit up to the age of 59 would incur an extra cost of only about two percent of payroll as compared with the company which placed an age limitation on hiring at age 35.[69]

In 1959 Canadian business reporter Robert Majoribanks made the argument that pension plans were becoming more and more common in Canada, and, as their number grew, it became harder and harder to find jobs for workers between the ages of 35 and 45. He said that 30 percent of the workforce was enrolled in pension plans, yet then he went on to note that between 90 and 95 percent of orders placed with the federal employment agency specified an age limit. Employers felt it would be too costly to provide older people with an adequate pension by retirement age. As well, Majoribanks brought out an argument often used in America when he observed that if the older employee was retired on too low a pension it would reflect unfavorably on the company's reputation for fairness and generosity. Despite favoring the idea that pension plans bore a major responsibility for age discrimination in employment, Majoribanks did cite a 1957 federal government interdepartmental committee which said there was nothing inherent in the nature of a pension plan that made it impossible for an employer to hire an older worker or to retain him beyond normal retirement age: "The restrictive measures incorporated in some plans would appear to stem more from employment policy than from pension policy."[70]

During the 1960s two Canadian provinces enacted legislation dealing with the issue. British Columbia's Fair Employment Practices Act banned employers from refusing to hire or continue on the job any person between 45 and 65 and also prevented unions from excluding or expelling a member on similar grounds. Ontario passed legislation to ban discrimination in hiring on the grounds of age, applying it to those between 40 and 65. It expanded the province's Human Rights Code. Labour Minister Leslie Rowntree said that with the establishment of pension plan portability, employers would no longer be able to use the problem of enrolling older workers in pension plans as an excuse to prevent hiring beyond a certain age ceiling.[71]

One of the most exhaustive reports on the problem as it existed worldwide was published in 1964 by the United Nations agency, the International Labour Organization (ILO), in its publication. For the agency the problem of unemployment among older workers was not new. The economic recovery that followed the Depression years of 1930 to 1934 revealed clearly, noted the ILO, that a hard core of unemployment among older workers still persisted in national economies strained to the utmost by rearmament programs. The ILO turned its attention to the problem in 1938 but then shelved it due to the war, when older people did have a better chance of finding work. After the war, however, "notwithstanding the conclusive evidence of the occupational abilities" of these people, and in spite of the general aging of Western populations, employers again became "somewhat reluctant" to hire older workers. All that had led certain groups to recommend a policy of extending working life. Also noted by the report was the fact that in the United States the proportion of men employed beyond age 65 was lower in 1950 than in 1890 (41.6 percent versus 68.2 percent). It was a trend said to be common in most Western countries. In France the number of "idle" or retired men between the ages of 55 and 64 had gradually increased from 166 per thousand in 1896 to 186 per thousand in 1946.[72]

From the ILO's study of a number of reports from different nations on the older worker problem, the organization concluded that a study of unemployment statistics clearly revealed that there were "no exceptions to the rule that older people remain unemployed for longer periods than younger people and that unemployment is a more serious matter for older workers than for younger ones." In Belgium, 63.9 percent of unemployed men were over 40 and 43.6 percent were over 50. Norway's numbers disclosed that 27.9 percent of unemployed men were over 50; in Denmark, 41.9 percent of unemployed people were 45 and over; among unemployed men in the Netherlands, 46.7 percent were over 40. In the United Kingdom, of 175,620 unemployed men, 54,525 were between 40 and 55; 49,396 were over 55. That meant that 67 percent were aged 40 and over. In Switzerland, 40.4 percent of the unemployed were between 40 and 59; 70 percent were over 40. West German numbers revealed 41.6 percent of men without work were 45 and over, although that group contained only 32.5 percent of the male working population. Also noted by the study was that large numbers of older workers probably did not apply to their national employment services and that consequently "the figures probably understate the position in this age group." Not only were the older workers more likely to be without work, but they also remained unemployed for longer periods. In Belgium, duration of unemployment among workers between ages 50 and 60 averaged more than one year and was as much as 21 months for unemployed men age 60 and over. In the UK some 70 percent of all men remaining unemployed for more than 39 weeks were over 40, and 45 percent were 55 and over.[73]

Another conclusion drawn by the ILO was that it was clear from the data it studied "that the tendency to drive older workers off the employment market by dismissal or placing difficulties in the way of their re-employment on grounds of age has not perceptibly diminished in spite of the aging of the population, wartime experience of the employment of older workers and the existing tendency towards full employment and the utilization of all potential manpower available." Further noted was a study carried out in 1950–1951, which covered 69 nations and showed that discrimination was exercised against elderly workers in both industrial and nonindustrial countries, in North as well as in South America, and in both Asia and Africa.[74]

When the ILO asked itself what was the origin of the belief, above all in industrial nations, that a worker's value decreased as his age increased, it answered that it seemed to be a direct consequence of the industrial revolution and the changes that had taken place in industrial techniques. Formerly, the highly skilled craftsman was an irreplaceable element in all branches of production. However, he was becoming less and less essential. That gave rise, thought the ILO, to a gradual devaluation of age and experience as elements in the occupational skill required of a worker, while on the contrary, the importance of youth had increased in inverse proportion. Yet, reported the agency, the influence of age varied widely according to the occupation, the industry, and the place. For example, in most nations, there was a considerable surplus of labor for office jobs, and an applicant for employment in that area came up against discrimination at a relatively early age. In Belgium and Switzerland an office worker who lost his job at the age of 40 was unlikely to find another job for some time. The situation was the same in France, where discrimination on the grounds of age was applied vigorously to office workers and also affected older supervisory and managerial personnel. Yet that was the type of work where the onset of middle age had hardly any influence on the output and capacity of the worker. However, in the event of a labor shortage the age barrier was relaxed, even in occupations such as mining. Difficulties which arose from other factors were found in occupations "where the worker comes directly into contact with the customer."[75]

Looking at gender differences, the ILO stated that generally speaking it appeared that discrimination applied more to women than to men. In many cases a woman's age started to work against her at 35, while a man in the same situation would not be affected until he reached the age of 45. That tendency was observed everywhere, especially in office work and sales jobs in shops, and only disappeared in occupations where there were no young women at all (for instance, most domestic servants in the United States were elderly women).[76]

Studying characteristics of industries, the ILO found that industries employing a considerable proportion of skilled labor employed a higher proportion of older workers than other industries. Another factor was technology. The knitwear industry in France had recently modernized; a number of workers lost their jobs but were all found other jobs, with the exception of those who were over 50 years of age. Employers said that those workers had not been found other work because "their age rendered them unable to adapt themselves to the new processes." Size of firms also played a part. The larger the factory the more the employer tended to prefer young workers and to exclude older workers. Age of an industry also mattered. Relatively young industries employed more young workers.[77]

Regarding the reasons given by employers for not hiring older people, the ILO found little variation between the findings of different studies. Generally speaking, employers considered that the output of older workers was lower, that they were slower and less adaptable, and that their diminishing muscular strength and powers of resistance rendered them unsuitable for a number of tasks for which workers in full physical health were needed. They feared, as well, that older workers would have some difficulty in adapting themselves to the new rhythm of mass production and to the frequent changes in the organization of work made necessary by continuous progress in the techniques and equipment used. Another reason often given was that absenteeism, sickness and accidents were more common among older workers. Some employers also mentioned the "set characters" of older employees, particularly older women, while others pointed out that the other employees were unwilling to accept older workers in the factory. A further reason given by employers was the cost of social services for older people and the cost of pension plans. Lastly, particularly in office, administrative, and similar jobs where the wage usually increased according to the age of the worker, "some employers prefer younger workers because they can offer them lower wages." During the process wherein employers were asked about their reasons for not hiring older people "many employers were forced to admit that their assertions were based more on states of mind and prejudices than on actual experience."[78]

Regarding compulsory measures to aid the hiring of older people instituted in various nations, the ILO concluded that they had little effect. In certain states in the United States, said the agency, particularly Louisiana and Massachusetts, employment discrimination on the grounds of age had made offenders liable to penal sanctions since the 1930s, yet "in neither state has the law been even partially effective." Within most national legislation the agency found it difficult to find any suggestion of protection against discrimination on the basis of age. Compulsory employment of a certain percentage of older workers was suggested in France when several bills relating to older workers were submitted to the National

Assembly in 1951. Under one, 25 percent of all people hired by companies with more than five employees were to be over the age of 50. Similar proposals were studied in both Belgium and the Netherlands. Companies, of course, did not like such proposals. But organized labor was also generally opposed, being against any "coercive measures" in that field.[79]

In its conclusion the ILO declared that it was undesirable that in many countries there were insufficient opportunities for employment not only for aged workers, but even, in a number of occupations, for people of 40 or 45 years of age. Those difficulties faced were seen to be due to a number of economic and social factors and circumstances. "The prejudice against older workers increases these difficulties and raises new difficulties where there is no reason for them." However, no matter how the problem was considered, "one should not forget the danger that by drawing attention to the problem of the employment of older workers a false impression may develop, in the few branches of industry where recruitment policy has never been based on any standards other than those of occupational capacity, that older workers form a special category of wage earners. This would be exactly the opposite of what is desired."[80]

Some five years later Anna-Stina Ericson examined the policies and programs in that area in the following countries: Austria, Belgium, Canada, Denmark, France, Germany, Ireland, Italy, Luxembourg, the Netherlands, Norway, Sweden, Switzerland, and the United Kingdom. Both Great Britain and Canada were said to have reported declining prejudice among employers against hiring older workers as a result of official educational and publicity campaigns and of greater interest among business, women's, and social organizations. With one exception, however, the other countries studied had reported neither success nor failure from their efforts. Austria's Social Ministry reported in the winter of 1959 that, in spite of all its efforts, unemployment in the higher age groups failed to decline in the two preceding summers when other unemployment declined. Countries like Switzerland, Norway and the Netherlands, then with low unemployment rates of one to two percent, had no particular problem with respect to older workers. To promote hiring of people in the upper age ranges, governments used various tactics such as hiring from that group for the civil service, passing laws for special assistance to older people, and implementing educational campaigns. Among nations that actively pursued a policy of recruiting older people for government service were Canada, Germany, Sweden, the UK, and the Netherlands. In Canada age limits for recruitment into many of the civil service classifications were removed in 1953; in Sweden age maximums were removed as early as 1936. The Netherlands had no age limit on entry into government service, while the UK set no upper age limit in recruiting for temporary posts and had raised or removed the age limits for a number of permanent positions. None of the nations studied had legislation that actually prohibited discrimination against the employment of older workers. Ericson concluded, "Programs to promote the employment of older workers have been most successful where the educational efforts to this end have been most active."[81]

In America reasons put forward for age discrimination in employment revolved among the same old themes. J.W. Willard, a research executive with the Canadian Department of National Health and Welfare, cited the war experiences of older workers in the form of a survey sponsored by the United States National Association of Manufacturers. It revealed that about 17 percent of employers found the adjustment of older workers to new situations more difficult than in the case of younger workers, while about 50 percent reported there was no difference. However, 33 percent of those employers indicated that older workers adjusted themselves more readily than younger ones. Yet discrimination abounded after the war, with Willard stating that the downward path in employability for men began around the ages 40 to 45; for women it started five to 10 years earlier. He felt that the mechanization of industry and mass production techniques had led to increasing speed in industrial processes and, as a result, speed of reaction of the worker had become a prime consideration in many occupations of modern industry. That same industrial development had led in many cases to a dilution of skills through which many skilled trades had been converted to semiskilled or unskilled occupations. Since farm work did not raise the employment handicaps of age to the same extent as industry, the trend towards industrialization and urbanization had increased the employment problems of the middle-aged. Since many of the prejudices leading to age discrimination were unfounded, said Willard, educational efforts were needed. As part of an educational program the Canadian Department of Labour had appealed to employers on behalf of older workers through the radio, the press, and on the theater screen.[82]

A May 1957 article in the *New York Times* listed the eight reasons given by employers for not hiring older workers, reasons dismissed by the New York State Labor Department as myths with little basis in fact. Those reasons were: (1) older workers were less productive (surveys were cited to show such allegations were untrue); (2) they were frequently absent (a

1956 survey by the United States Labor Department showed older workers had a 20 percent better attendance record than younger ones); (3) they were involved in more accidents (the same survey found that workers 45 and over had 2.5 percent fewer disabling injuries and 25 percent fewer nondisabling injuries than those under 45); (4) they did not stay on the payroll long enough to justify the hiring expense (separation rates for older employees were much lower than for the younger ones); (5) it was too costly to provide them with adequate pensions (it often depended on the type of plan); (6) they caused major increases in employee group insurance plans (it depended on the nature of the plan); (7) they did not have the needed job skills (evidence was to the contrary); (8) they were inflexible and unimaginative and had trouble getting along with younger workers (a sweeping generalization with no supporting evidence).[83]

Writing in the September 1956 issue of *Science Digest*, L. Leonard observed that American employers were still set in their ways—"and dead set against taking on older workers." Actually, employment agencies told him, "The chances for being placed begin to diminish most noticeably at age 35 for both men and women, while for women alone, the age handicap is significant even at 30." Judith Decker of Atlanta, Georgia-based Capital Personnel Service added that a lot of companies were beginning to require men under 30. In a survey taken of private placement agencies across the United States, 87 percent of them termed the practice of age discrimination in employment unjustified. Reasons for the practice, as mentioned by employers, were: increased pension costs, 65 percent; hard to train, 40 percent; think they know too much, 33 percent; not enough pep or ambition, eight percent; poor job performance, three percent. Of the private employment agencies surveyed, 45 percent blamed short-sighted employers for the plight of middle-aged workers; 16 percent said the older workers had brought it on themselves; 19 percent said that they were equally to blame. Those who believed the workers were at least partly responsible mentioned reasons such as: being too choosy, over conscious of age, being unwilling to learn, having a discouraged attitude. This survey showed it took agencies three to 20 times longer to get a job for a worker past 40. Clerical jobs were the hardest to land, sales positions second, executive jobs third. Forty-one percent of agencies felt the situation for older workers was improving, 16 percent said there was no change, 33 percent said it was getting worse.[84]

As in past periods pension costs were mentioned more often than any other single reason as the supposed reason as to why older people had more difficulty in obtaining work than did their younger counterparts. A

1949 article in *Business Week* put almost all the blame on that factor, claiming that companies were shifting their hiring policies due to pension plans because "they aren't sure yet what new—or possible—pension plans labor contracts may bring forth." Cited as so-called evidence was the industrial state of Ohio where the Ohio State Employment Service said the number of jobless over age 45 was growing faster than the number in younger age groups. The situation was reportedly the same in New York State. Personnel managers were taking a new stand on older applicants: "They're saying: 'We don't know exactly where we stand yet on pensions. Until we do, we have to limit the number of older men and women we hire.'" Yet the article admitted few pension plans then being set up would make employment of an over-45 person more costly than one aged 20 to 35. Most pension plans tied the amount payable at retirement age to length of service. Given as an example was Ford's plan, retirement at 65 on full pension with 30 years' service, prorated for less service. Still, the article concluded, "But the fact remains that today the over 45 applicant is running into bars at the industrial hiring gate. And until companies know just where they stand on pensions, he is likely to be stuck there."[85]

Well-known business writer Peter Drucker also named pension plans as the chief culprit, in a 1950 *Harper's Magazine* article. He said that the recent steel-industry strike had indeed established the principle that industry was responsible for the support of the older worker: "In fact, the present pension contracts are bound greatly to increase the handicaps under which the older worker—the man over forty-five or fifty—already labors." As well, he thought that private pension plans, either pay-as-you-go, fully funded or a combination, would not work. "But there is nothing uncertain or hypothetical about the tremendous additional handicap the plans impose on the older worker and on his chances of finding a job and remaining in a job." Under the existing pension plans Drucker believed there was a very strong temptation to get rid of older employees before they reached the pension age, and that there were many ways for firms to keep the older worker out, without saying so, such as by imposing stricter physical tests. Thus, against such practices, a law forbidding age discrimination in employment as was sometimes mentioned, "would be utterly futile." However, that the demand for such a law was made, accompanied by the complaint that employers had already begun to "liquidate" older men wholesale, before any of the new pension plans had actually started to operate, "shows how seriously the older worker's employment opportunity is threatened by the very pension plan to which he looks for security." Drucker also did not like government pensions (over private plans) all that much. For him the crux of the problem was not of retiring the older worker but of keeping him productively employed. He concluded that retirement at 65 or 70 years of age would be politically unacceptable and impossible to impose in another 20 to 25 years (that is, by 1970 or 1975), no matter how liberal was the retirement pay. That would be due to future increases in the ratio of older to younger workers.[86]

When *U.S. News & World Report* blamed pensions, the article began by stating the number of unemployed people over age 40 had increased much faster than the average—the number of unemployed in that age group had nearly doubled. The article then declared: "Pensions definitely are beginning to influence employers' attitudes toward hiring of older workers. This is true even though under present plans the pension cost for newly hired older workers may be little if any greater than the cost incurred by adding younger workers." Admitted, however, was that the vast majority of pension plans gave a man with 15 years service a much smaller pension than given to a man with 40 years' service. Yet a conclusion drawn was that "fear of larger pension liabilities in the future is influencing employers from coast to coast against older workers." Another reason put forward for the existence of the problem was the "unwillingness of older workers to step down a grade, to take lower pay, [which] keeps many out of jobs longer than necessary." Pay cuts were said to be becoming the rule for older workers who got caught without a job and had to take what was offered. "But pay cuts are resisted as long as possible, and that adds to the employment problem." In conclusion, *U.S. New & World Report* observed that "if national unemployment develops on a big scale, workers over 40 will have more trouble than other groups."[87]

Even leaders of organized labor were capable of taking the position that pensions were the problem, despite the fact they fought so hard for them. A.R. Mosher, president of the Canadian Congress of Labour, stated in 1952, with regard to the problems of those 45 and over getting jobs, "Ironically, this practice is partly due to the adoption of pension plans."[88]

Business Week, in a May 1953 piece, noted that when pension plans first began spreading through mass-production industries in 1949, a lot of observers were wary of the effect those plans would have on the mobility of older workers. They believed pension plans would make it too costly to hire workers over 40 or 45 and expected many employers to set strict maximum limits on the age of new hires. "After four years of pensions, they seem to have been right." A pension "has become a big obstacle to older workers looking for new jobs," concluded a survey done by the Northwestern Mutual Life Insurance Company. The trouble, said the article, was that it cost companies about four times as much on average in pension contributions for a man they hire at 50 as for a 25-year-old, assuming each would retire at 65 with the same benefits. "As a result, employment agencies around the country report considerable reluctance on the part of companies with pension and welfare plans to hire older workers now." The trouble with this example was that no pension plan in operation paid the same benefit to people, at the same fixed age, who started employment with the company at different ages. *Business Week* then added another culprit when it said insurance loss increased with age and therefore firms tried to keep the average age of a workforce down to cut group benefit insurance. There was no truth in that statement. Finally, the article concluded that labor supply and demand still seemed to be the determining factor in setting age bars. In St. Louis, for example, the local employment office said that in the previous year almost no companies would touch men over 45 or women over 35. But defense industry expansion in the area had boosted demand for labor. The office then reported that many of those same companies were willing to take men up to 55 and women up to 50, if they were skilled.[89]

Pension consultant J. Coburn estimated that at least 40 percent of all job seekers, and possibly more, were 45 or older. In his view; "This high proportion is partly attributable to the wide incidence of pension plans." According to him the Canadian Manufacturers Association had just queried its members on the subject by asking them what circumstances or conditions made it difficult to hire older workers. Among plants with over 1,000 workers, the pension plans were said to be the main difficulty, while in smaller plants, pension plans were ranked third among causes. Coburn went on to state that with respect to pension costs associated with the hiring of older people, the majority of plans were so constructed that any factor tending to increase the average age of employees would, in itself, produce an eventual if not immediate increase in pension costs. Having said that he added, "The extent of such increases is easy to exaggerate, and the tendency to overestimate them is perhaps accentuated by the presence of provisions in many relatively long-established plans prohibiting the admission of new employees after some age such as 45." Coburn did argue that by introducing devices such as a flexible retirement age and graduated employee contributions, it should be possible to eliminate any problem of hiring older employees insofar as pension administration was concerned.[90]

Even President Dwight Eisenhower worried publicly that the growing popularity of pension plans might be affecting the structure of the national economy. He said that within the space of a few years over 12 million private business employees had come under private pension plans. While those plans "seem to be highly desirable" Eisenhower said they raised some questions. One was about the effect of those plans on the willingness of companies to hire older workers. A Labor Department study of employers' reluctance to hire workers over age 45 indicated that one factor was the relatively higher pension cost imposed on firms. A second worry for the President was what effect the plans would have on labor mobility. That is, workers covered by a pension plan would have a natural reluctance to switch jobs when the switch meant a loss of pension rights.[91]

U.S. News & World Report returned to attack pensions in the mid–1950s. This time it used figures. According to the article, to provide retirement pay of $100 a month at age 65: for a worker hired at age 30, the cost was $326 a year; age 40, $508; age 50, $939; age 55, $1,486. Even if the figures were accurate what was not pointed out by the article was the fact that no company had a pension plan in effect that worked like that.[92]

Those who cited pension plans as a major culprit in age discrimination in employment rarely cited any evidence. When they did cite numbers they were for types of plans which never had or never would exist. Secretary of Labor James P. Mitchell in 1956 appointed a committee of experts on employee welfare plans to study the problem. When they reported, they told Mitchell that pension costs were not a major obstacle to the employment of older people. Under most plans, benefits were related to length of service or earnings, or both, and formulas under those plans generally resulted in lower pensions for older employees because of their shorter work periods. Costs could sometimes be apparently lower for younger workers because there was more chance of them dying or becoming disabled, or otherwise terminating their employment. Any such advantage like that to a company disappeared as a greater proportion of contributions became vested, and as the vesting took place after a shorter number of years of employment.[93]

University of Michigan's Institute for Human Adjustment issued a report stating that pension plans need not deter the employment of older workers, because benefits could be varied in accordance with years of service, or short-term workers could be excluded from benefits. The Institute added that some group accident and health insurance cost plans could actually be less expensive for older workers because typically they had fewer dependents. Edwin C. McDonald, vice president of Metropolitan

Life Insurance company and a spokesman for the insurance industry, also denied that pension costs were a cause in making it harder for older people to get work. "I've watched this thing for many years. It is a question of the business cycle. If a lot of workers are available, employers tend to hire the younger ones. Long before pensions became popular, there was just as much reluctance to hire older workers as there is now. It has nothing to do with pensions costs," he explained.[94]

Burt Scanlan wrote a 1965 article for *Personnel Journal* about the assertion that pension plans reduced mobility and acted as a deterrent to the employment of anyone over 40. Reviewing the situation up to the time he was writing, Scanlan noted that studies had shown that employers "almost invariably cite higher pension costs … as reasons for not hiring older workers." A 1953 study found, in manufacturing, 18.2 percent of the companies (employing 45 percent of the workers in the sample) felt pension costs limited the feasibility of hiring older people. In total, 16.6 percent of the firms (33 percent of the total workforce) indicated that pension costs were a deterrent. Several other studies with similar conclusions were also cited. As far back as the 1920s, allegations appeared that the setting up of industrial pension plans, in an earlier period, was one of the chief factors in the adoption of hiring-age limits in American industry. From a 1932 study of industrial pension plans of the 1920s came the conclusion: "Hiring age limits have been adopted for various reasons. It appears unlikely that they are connected mainly with the inauguration of employee welfare schemes, for the data as are available indicate that age limits are about as prevalent in companies which do not have various types of employee benefit schemes as in those which have them. Moreover, in many, if not the majority of cases, the limits antedate the benefit schemes."[95]

Scanlan also pointed out that back in that earlier period the data revealed that maximum age limits were the rule in the railroads and public utilities, but still the exception in manufacturing concerns. From the time in which he was writing he cited a Bureau of Employment Security study which concluded there was no relationship between higher pension costs and older workers. From that he concluded that it seemed unlikely that employers were oblivious to the conclusions from the Bureau's study, "or that they are so sensitive to higher pension costs and the public reaction to lower or no pensions for workers hired later in life as they would have us believe. A more feasible possibility is that of all the possible excuses that can be made for not hiring older workers, higher pension costs is the least likely to draw criticism and correspondingly, if true, the most likely to be understood." Scanlan added that, in summary, there was little evidence to support the claim that pension plans were unduly restrictive in terms of reducing labor mobility or hindering the hiring of older workers. "Rather, it would seem that pension plans have become the scapegoat for other more significant factors. Also, on the surface they offer an easy explanation to problems whose solution is much more complicated." Scanlan felt the problem lay in swift technological change coupled with stereotypes of older workers being harder to train, and so forth. Back in the 1920s, he thought, the discrimination may have been due to the heavy physical demands of work, which might explain the higher prevalence of maximum hiring ages in industries such as railways and utilities.[96]

Reporter Alfred Zipser, Jr., conducted his own series of interviews in 1949 with personnel executives and representatives of a large insurance company. He said that all of them agreed with his conclusion that the higher costs of extending group insurance benefits including pension plans to older workers "are a negligible factor in employer reluctance to hire personnel over thirty-five." Employers declared that psychological drawbacks were far more important than the "infinitesimally higher inclusion costs" faced by hiring older employees. That was because even if the older worker understood he could not expect to receive as high a pension under the plan as a younger person who had participated longer, "he still resents it." The same was reported to be true for those older employees who had signed waivers on pension rights. Nonetheless, "many business organizations want no part of this unpleasant situation." Group life insurance costs were also reported by Zipser to make little difference. If the age distribution of the workforce was anywhere near normal, the average expense for the plan was "hardly affected unless a large number of applicants over 60 are hired." The strongest single reason for the failure of many companies to hire older workers, said one employer's spokesman, was the promotion-from-within policy. That meant that generally it left only one employment opportunity for older applicants—a starting job at beginners' wages. According to employers, the psychological disadvantages of taking on an older worker in a starting job were "too formidable" to permit widespread action in that direction. The employee's salary requirements could not be met, "his younger supervisors constitute a constant source of irritation to him, and the company is incurring the same training expense for him as for a younger worker who will probably more than make up for training costs by longer efficient service."[97]

Business writer Joseph Arkin looked more closely at the results obtained by that panel of experts appointed in 1956 by Secretary Mitchell.

Their general conclusion, after looking at pension costs, sickness and accident insurance, group life insurance and workers' compensation, was that age was not a cost factor. If maternity benefits were included, then the cost for older workers was actually less. Age was not a factor in workers' compensation costs, although they found that older people had few accidents. Pension costs, as mentioned above, were also not a factor. Regarding group life insurance, employee turnover tended to produce a fairly stable average age. Even on an individual basis, the difference in cost between a 35-year-old and a 55-year-old (for $3,500 coverage) was two cents per hour gross to the firm, a net differential of one cent per hour or less. Concluded the panel, "It is unlikely, therefore, that the cost of the fringe benefit package can be considered 'a real obstacle to the employment of older workers.'" The National Association of Manufacturers had stated that in any consideration of possible increased costs, "while it may be desirable to have a low insurance and pension rate, it is insignificant when one compares it with the costs involved in turnover, poor or indifferent performance, absenteeism, lack of job interest and application, and the fact that the company is cutting itself off from the services of able, mature employees."[98]

One proposal for a solution was put forward by the national Catholic weekly *America*. While the publication hoped that a recent appeal from President Eisenhower to hire more older workers would be successful, it noted that neither economic nor moral arguments had worked in the past. What it proposed was that the time had come to think about economic incentives. Perhaps the government could offer a tax deal to business that would render it profitable to hire older people. Until something like that was done, worried the editor, most companies would continue their policy of "hiring only younger men."[99]

Employment experts, to some extent, were placing their greatest hope in a different concept—special job counseling for workers past age 40. It was a strategy which had reportedly had some success in both the United States and Canada. Joe Nawn, special counselor to the 40-plus job seekers at the Newburgh, New York, state employment office commented that "persuading employers to drop their age bars is the toughest part of the counselor's job. It takes missionary zeal, diplomacy and sometimes a touch of honest guile."[100]

Besides the work which had been done to show that older workers were no more costly to employ than younger ones, other studies showed they were just as productive and efficient. Late in the 1940s State Senator Thomas C. Desmond, chairman of the New York State Joint Legislative

Committee on Problems of the Aging, stated that his committee had queried 1,000 employers, large and small. Findings included the fact that three of every four employers believed older workers produced as much as younger ones; only one of eight believed they produced less. Eighty percent believed older employees were as loyal and conscientious as younger ones; 17 percent believed the older ones were more loyal. Some 71 percent believed older workers were absent less, 17 percent said no difference, and seven percent reported higher rates of absenteeism for them. It all caused Desmond to conclude, erroneously, that industry was changing its mind about older workers, a good sign, perhaps due to positive war experiences, he thought.[101]

William Bowers was a social scientist whose study in 1952 involved a detailed appraisal of the personnel records of 3,164 workers between the ages of 18 and 76 (male and female) in a large organization. From 1900 until the time of this study the number of people aged between 45 and 64 had grown from 10.5 million to 31 million; those 65 and over had increased from three million to almost 12 million. Bowers found that men hired for the first time when over 45, and even when 60 and over, were given higher net appraisals than younger men being hired. He considered that to be a striking vindication of the older worker as being competent. The common business practice of refusing to hire a new worker over 45 seemed to be even contraindicated by the study, at least for some types of work. At all ages he found great individual differences. Bowers concluded that "older workers were mentioned somewhat more frequently than younger as not learning readily and as being slow; but the older workers were considered to be better in attendance, steadiness and conscientiousness. The remaining traits showed no consistent changes with age."[102]

A Bureau of Labor Statistics 1956 pilot study of age and on-the-job performance found that output per person-hour of both men and women piece workers showed only a slight variation up to age 54, and in no group did the average performance of workers 55 through 64 fall below 90 percent of the group aged 35 to 44. Variations in output of individuals in the same age group were large, generally larger than between age groups.[103]

Business writer Charles Odell summarized several studies showing older employees to be as productive as younger workers. Looking at surveys of firms on how they felt each group performed, he concluded that employers seemed to feel the older workers they already had were for the most part satisfactory, but they looked upon older people seeking new jobs as a poor employment risk. Asking himself if that was a justified conclusion, he replied, "The record would appear to indicate conclusively that it is not." Studies done by the Bureau of Employment Security indicated that on all factors considered important in the hiring process, except years of formal education, older job seekers compared favorably with younger ones. Asking himself why then there was a problem, he said, "The obvious answer is, of course, to level an accusing finger and say that this is simply a matter of prejudice or discrimination."[104]

An early 1960s study of female factory workers in a packing plant looked at age and absenteeism. The entire group of women employed for one year or more in that plant were investigated with the absence record of each reviewed for the period July 1, 1962, to June 30, 1963. Total mean number of days ill was 9.3; mean number for those under 45 was 10.2 days, for those 45 and over the mean number of days lost to illness was 7.9. Total mean number of times absent was 4.8; for women under 45, 5.6, for those 45 and up it was 3.6. Total mean number of days lost to "personal" absence was 2.1 days; 2.3 for those under 45, 1.8 days for those over 44. Mean number of visits to the first aid department was 1.4 for the total group; 1.7 for women under 45, 0.9 for those over that age. Concluded the article, "The results presented, by and large substantiate the bulk of evidence which indicates that the older worker is as good if not better in the matter of absenteeism and accidents than the younger worker."[105]

During this period, for the first time, psychological attitudes toward older workers were investigated. Jacob Tuckman and Irving Lorge developed a questionnaire of 51 items (statements) on the older worker. As they pointed out, although a body of opinion existed to indicate that older workers were unable to work under younger supervisors, resisted changes in work methods or the introduction of new machinery, were difficult to work with, and so forth, yet supporting evidence was not available. The questionnaire was given to 147 graduate students (92 men, 55 women) divided into two groups: under 30 years of age (46 men, 23 women) with a mean age of 24.6; and those over 30 (46 men, 32 women—the maximum age was 51) with a mean age of 36.5. Results indicated that responses did not vary by age. In comparing sex, there were seven statements with a difference that was statistically significant. A higher proportion of women agreed that older workers: failed to keep up with changing methods of work; were in a rut; could not supervise others well; could not concentrate; were not physically able to keep up with the work; were difficult to work with. A small proportion of women agreed with the statement that older workers got occupational diseases more often. For the respondents in total the percentage of agreement with the 51 items (all statements were answered yes or no) ranged from zero to 78 percent, with a mean percentage of agreement of 27 percent. From 70 to 78 percent of respondents subscribed to the beliefs that older workers: needed more time to learn new operations, took longer in getting over illness, and took longer in getting over injuries. From 63 to 68 percent subscribed to the beliefs that older employees: were slow, were more interested in security than advancement, and looked to the past. Respondents agreed more with statements covering resistance to new ideas, procedures, and physical changes than to statements covering interpersonal relationships and job shifting. Tuckman and Lorge concluded, "It is evident from the data that there is considerable acceptance of erroneous ideas about older workers. This is even more surprising when the educational level, previous training in psychology, and the interest of the group in the older adult ... are taken into consideration."[106]

Over the course of a year Tuckman gave his questionnaire to many groups differing in age, educational background and socioeconomic status. They included undergraduate students, graduate students, middle-aged nonprofessional workers and their wives, and retired men and women. The responses of all those groups, said Tuckman, "indicate a negative attitude toward the older worker. Both young and old subscribe to erroneous notions, although graduate students do not accept the beliefs as readily as the other groups studied."[107]

When a national meeting was called to discuss problems of the older worker, Tuckman attended with his survey. Participants included representatives of management, labor, government, medicine, social work, and universities. Only 35 of the 75 participants at the meeting agreed to fill out Tuckman's questionnaire. Results indicated that the respondents subscribed to fewer misconceptions about the older worker than did any of the other groups the researcher had surveyed. However, more than 30 percent of them exceeded the mean number of stereotypes subscribed to by graduate students. The number of stereotypes held by those representing the universities, government and labor was considerably below the mean for the total group, whereas the number accepted by those representing management, medicine, and social work was considerably above the mean. Tuckman felt the results suggested individuals generalized about older workers in terms of their own experience and orientation. Representatives from labor, government, and universities who, in their daily work, looked for and were impressed with the positive rather than the negative aspects of aging, subscribed less to the stereotyped opinions than the management, social work, and medical groups, which tended to see the negative rather than the positive aspects of aging. The labor representatives, whose orientation was in terms of job security and job protection, saw the older people as ones in need of protection. The social workers, who worked with individuals who had adjustment problems, saw them as people who were insecure, rigid, deteriorated, and difficult to get along with. Management representatives, concerned with production, saw older workers as ones with no ambition and who presented difficulties in supervision. The physician, whose orientation was in terms of pathology, viewed them as individuals who were slow, rigid and unproductive. Tuckman concluded, "The meager data from this study suggest the need for orienting experts about potential biases from their own experiences ... The experts seem to be in especial need of orientation."[108]

Researcher Wayne Kirchner, and others, gave a 27-item questionnaire (each item had a five-step agree/disagree scale) to a plant-wide sample of 46 rank-and-file employees and 16 supervisors and executives in a laundry to measure their attitudes toward the employment of older people. There was a statistically significant difference between employees and management in their responses. Mean score for management was 55.8. (A score of 54 was neutral, lower was unfavorable to older workers. The higher the score the more favorable the attitude.) Workers averaged a score of 65.1. Employees were broken into three age groups (each group gave a score which was statistically significant from the other two groups). Under-30-year-old workers had a mean score of 52.6; 30 to 49, 65.7; 50-and-over employees had a mean score of 74.0. Kirchner declared that it was clear that attitudes toward the older employee were a function of age itself; the younger the person, the less favorable was his attitude toward the older worker. No difference in attitude was found on the basis of sex or on the amount of formal education. Also, there was no difference between office workers and production workers, and no difference between union and nonunion people. That is, there was no difference between nonunion office workers and union production workers. Management's median age from their group was 44. If their attitudes reflected the age factor alone, Kirchner said he would have expected them to have a mean score of around 66 (the same as the 30-to-49 group), but it was closer to that of the under-30 group. That suggested a "conflict situation" for management. Kirchner then administered the same test to a small random sample of workers in a metal manufacturing plant. He found the same significant differences on the basis of age: under 30, 51.6 mean score; 30 to 49, 61.1; 50 and over, 69.3.[109]

When Temple University administered a questionnaire, it found that 31 percent of the industries polled expressed the belief that the work of older people tended to be poor. Paradoxically, the same survey showed that belief to be false because, in rating the work of their own employees over 50, some 80 percent of the respondents termed it as good as or better than that of their younger workers.[110]

Politicians continued to make public pronouncements on the problem, although they remained reluctant to take any concrete steps. Federal Secretary of Labor Maurice J. Tobin said, around the time of the Korean War, that a reluctance to hire older people was hampering the nation's efforts to achieve a full utilization of manpower in the defense program. He appealed for a more extensive use of workers in the age group over 45, while at the same time the Labor Department issued a handbook, "Selected Facts on the Employment and Economic Status of Older Men and Women."[111]

A few years later then Secretary of Labor James P. Mitchell, noting that the number of people aged 45 and over was increasing as a percentage of the population, said that half the nation's adult population might be jobless in 20 years unless prejudices about hiring older people were overcome: "Unless something is done to give them job opportunities, an estimated half of our adult population will be condemned to a life of economic uselessness." He observed that employers and labor unions often set up arbitrary barriers. If nothing was done those age 45 and over, worried Mitchell, "will form the most potent groups this nation has known and force some kind of public program for their survival. They will demand, and must get, sustenance, plus minimum attributes for agreeable living." Additionally, he noted that older workers no longer could retire comfortably to farms or depend on their children. The only solution, declared Mitchell, "is to hire the older worker and make a profit from his production."[112]

In trying to analyze why companies were reluctant to hire older people, Mitchell said the reasons were many and varied, but underlying all of them was "the national tendency to glorify the values of youth and minimize the values of maturity. This constant association of undesirability with age and desirability with youth tends to embed in our society a viewpoint that shunts the aged out of business, family and community life." The Labor Secretary also cited New York State Senator Thomas Desmond as having commented that "old" in our culture "is an epithet.... Too often it is an affliction, a penalty for survival, a yoke attached by the young and immature." Barriers facing older applicants, thought Mitchell, could be divided into three distinct types: (1) those resulting from cultural standards; (2) those erected by the older job seeker himself (the idea that the older person could not sell himself, and so forth); (3) those imposed by industry and labor unions; for example, that unions generally did not let members work for a lower wage with declining skills. However, Mitchell argued that the most serious obstacles the older worker encountered were usually those erected "by industry or labor unions—by the people who actually control the jobs."[113]

Mitchell also cited Department of Labor surveys as indicating there were two main issues involved in the problem. One involved the hiring policies of many firms that reflected a prejudice against workers over the age of 45, with some businesses even setting limits for women as low as 35. Even when the country was in an economic boom, there was still a wide restriction of employment on an age basis. One survey showed that although one-third of the applicants to local employment offices throughout the United States were over 45, that group received only 14 percent of the jobs. Nearly every local employment office reported, said Mitchell, that the majority of employers specified some restrictive age limits in their search for employees. The second big issue identified by the Secretary was that of old age pensions and retirement benefits, with department studies showing that the main reason given by employees for not hiring older people was the effect of such hiring on pension and insurance plans. In summary, Mitchell declared that departmental studies added up to these findings: (1) the odds were heavily against older people in competition for jobs; even in a tight labor market older job seekers experienced extreme difficulty in finding a new position; (2) ceilings on hiring ages were applied by the majority of employers; (3) limits were set at 35 to 45 years of age and even earlier—decades before the declines associated with senility were to be anticipated; (4) even when age limits were not deliberately established in actual practice, older workers were eliminated somewhere along the line; (5) personnel workers, taking their cues from employer attitudes, tended to anticipate and extend restrictive specifications; (6 & 7) although pension systems and resistance of older workers to downgrading and change were often mentioned as interfering in the placement of older workers, they were really secondary obstacles even though they loomed large in the thinking of employers; (8) the primary obstacles to the placement of older workers were "the unfounded assumptions and biases regarding the flexibility and capacity of older workers." Reasons for not hiring older people, cited by employers, most frequently fell into two categories: (1) decline in physical and mental capacity; (2) undesirable effects on pension systems. But, said Mitchell, "No investigation as yet has shown that these are real and significant factors in job performance or costs of operation."[114]

In a special Labor Day message in 1955, President Eisenhower hailed America's workers but urged the country not to overlook a growing problem facing a segment of the labor force—older people who could not find work. "This arbitrary bar to the full utilization of their abilities causes a waste of valuable skills and talents and must be eliminated."[115]

A 1957 letter signed by New York City Mayor Robert Wagner was sent to 15,000 business firms in the city asking them to cooperate with three vocational agencies to provide employment for older workers. Those agencies—Protestant, Jewish, and Roman Catholic—were trying to help 45- to 60-year-olds, under a grant issued 5 months earlier by the State Labor Department.[116]

Apparently this wasn't effective because later that same year New York State Governor Averell Harriman announced a plan to present certificates to employers who agreed not to discriminate against job seekers because of age. State Senator Desmond criticized the Harriman administration and accused it of engaging in "huff and puff" activity in an effort to promote the employment of older people. Said Desmond, "Public utilities, banks and large firms which do discriminate against older workers don't change their policies to get 'merit badges.'" In response, Harriman spokesman Philip Kaiser accused Desmond of attempting to discredit an "effort to break down prejudice against employment of older people."[117]

Politicians were also involved more formally in the problem in that some held hearings on the issue. Desmond was chairman of the Joint Legislative Committee on Problems of the Aging, in New York State. In that capacity he urged private industry to reconsider blind employment and pension plans that might work against older people, citing a previous survey of job opportunities in industry which revealed that more than one-third of the private companies questioned had formal rules with the maximum age ranging from 55 down to 35.[118]

At one of the public hearings of the Desmond committee in 1948, State Industrial Commissioner Edward Corsi said that employers considered the younger workers more desirable and better for business, while the middle-aged group of job seekers "has been conspicuously abandoned in the midst of the fullest employment we have ever known." At the same hearing Allen Dagget, vice president of the Forty Plus Executives of Western New York, described the refusal to hire men over 45 as "a crime" and "an economic blunder."[119]

At another public hearing of the Desmond committee one of those who appeared was Kenneth Kelley, legislative agent of the Massachusetts Federation of Labor. He suggested that a law against the practice be enacted and then described the recent adoption of such a law in his home state. That statute made discrimination for age subject to the same penalties as discrimination on the grounds of race, creed, color or origin. "Discrimination on the grounds of age is more cruel and common than the others," said Kelley.[120]

According to Desmond, the main reasons employers gave him and his committee for not hiring older people, over the course of many hearings, were: the cost of workmen's compensation; the elderly are more accident-prone, their reflexes have slowed down; they can't produce as much as younger workers; and "you can't teach an old dog new tricks."[121]

A decade later, at the federal level, hearings on the problem were held by the Senate Subcommittee on Problems of the Aged and Aging. At a stop in Detroit, the subcommittee heard from Max Horton, director of the Michigan Employment Security Commission, who testified that workers between ages 40 and 65 were the most in need of help—that one-third of the applicants for work at commission offices were in that category. He added that prejudice against hiring workers over 40 was "a very real thing."[122]

Later, in 1961, Secretary of Labor Arthur Goldberg told the subcommittee that five years earlier 58 percent of all job openings in five metro areas had restrictive age requirements. That had dropped to 39 percent in 1961, he said. Los Angeles saw its rate fall from 35 to 17 percent; in Miami it fell from 73 to 31 percent; Seattle's rate dropped from 51 to 22 percent; Minneapolis-St. Paul's number decreased from 75 to 70 percent. However, the fifth area, Detroit, had an increase, by an unstated amount.[123]

When it came to enacting laws to protect people from age discrimination in employment, lawmakers were almost as reticent to enact laws as they had been in earlier periods, although a few more jurisdictions did take action. In New York, State Senator Thomas Desmond ruled out any law to end age discrimination for the 1950 legislative session. He said he would delay presenting such a law until at least the next session, to start in January 1951, because his committee was well aware of the united opposition of business to any legal compulsion to hire older workers, and his committee was working on legislation that would not disrupt company personnel hiring and selection systems. The delay, it was hoped, would give business a final opportunity to voluntarily improve the situation.

Desmond said his legislation would not be patterned on the Massachu-setts laws, as he said those laws had proven to be unenforceable. By con-trast, he declared New York's law would definitely have teeth in it. The state then had about 13 million residents; more than four million were age 45 and over, and more than two million were 55 and over. In Decem-ber of 1949, 16.4 percent of all people in the state who had exhausted all their unemployment insurance were 45 to 55; 20 percent were 55 to 64; and 27.2 percent were 65 and over. In total, over 64 percent of all people in New York State who had been out of work long enough to exhaust their unemployment benefits were in the age group 45 and over.[124]

However, it was not until December 1951 that Desmond's Joint Leg-islative Committee on Aging went so far as to recommend the Legisla-ture take steps leading toward the adoption of a law barring age dis-crimination in employment. In its report, the committee said that while the immediate extension of the present antidiscrimination law to cover age seemed reasonable on the surface, "the weight of available evidence is that such a law would not be enforceable." The committee said that similar laws in other states had not been "even partially effective" because they could be evaded easily. It declared itself reluctant to recommend a law unless it was convinced it would not become just another "dead weight" or a law on the books which held forth false hopes for the older job seekers. All that the committee planned to do in the form of concrete steps was to keep a "close watch" on the law adopted in 1950 in Massa-chusetts and urge its adoption in New York State if there was any indi-cation that the Massachusetts law was bringing worthwhile results. Also recommended at this time by the committee was that the federal gov-ernment consider issuing a declaration of policy that older workers be utilized to the full in defense industries.[125]

Nothing more happened for years in New York until January 1957 when Governor Averell Harriman was urged to support a bill that would bar age discrimination in employment. It was a recommendation that came in a report submitted by Professor John A. Davis of the Depart-ment of Government at City College of New York. The Governor's office had requested that Davis undertake to study the problem. His report called for a new statue forbidding discrimination in hiring workers between the ages of 28 and 65. Also barred by the law would be any requirement that an applicant give his age in an interview or on a writ-ten form unless age had been established as a "bone fide" qualification for the job in question. Davis said that while the whole problem of unem-ployment of the older worker could not be solved by such a law, "the fundamental problem cannot be solved without it. The capable aging worker cannot receive fair employment without such a law." Such a law, he thought, should come under the oversight of the State Commission Against Discrimination—that is, that body would be responsible for enforcing the law. Davis was opposed to the idea that an end to age discrimination could be achieved by education rather than by law, because he believed the structure of the discrimination was "too great" to be broken by education alone.[126]

Almost a full year passed, until in December 1957 Harriman finally announced that he would not support legislation making it illegal for companies to discriminate against older people in their hiring policies. The Governor said he made his decision on the basis of united opposition to such a proposal by the chairmen of six regional committees on the employment problems of older people. Those chairmen felt education would be more pervasive in eliminating employer resistance to hiring the middle-aged. Harriman announced that, instead of a law, he would ask the 1958 legislature to approve an increase in the number of job counselors dealing with the problems of older workers. As well, the Governor reported that he had received 24,000 replies to requests he had sent out two months earlier, asking all employers to agree voluntarily not to discriminate on the basis of age. Harriman said the response to the 300,000 letters sent out was "gratifying beyond anything any of us expected."[127]

Nevertheless, a bill that would prohibit employers from discriminating against people age 45 to 65 in New York State because of their age was approved in April 1958 by Harriman, to take effect July 1, 1958. He called the bill a long step forward toward breaking down arbitrary and unrealistic barriers which prevented full employment opportunities to thousands of people who were able and anxious to work. That enthusiasm for the measure represented a recent change of heart by the Governor. New York thus became the fourth state to enact a modern age discrimination statute, after Massachusetts, Rhode Island, and Pennsylvania. Older laws with a similar intent were still on the books in Louisiana and Colorado, but they were not enforced. Also approved by the Governor was a bill giving the State Commission Against Discrimination (SCAD) $30,000 to meet the cost of investigating complaints under this new law. SCAD had estimated that the additional work would cost $150,000. Harriman commented, "I must point out that this shameful neglect to provide adequate funds will prevent SCAD from doing an adequate job of administering and enforcing this act."[128]

That New York State law consisted of two amendments to the existing law against discrimination, which were passed unanimously in the closing days of the legislative session. There were no public hearings or controversial debate on the bill to amend the law, with the result that relatively few people knew about the new prohibitions. The first amendment added the word "age" to the list of discriminations in employment already prohibited by law: race, creed, color, and national origin. Those prohibitions applied to employers, labor organizations, and employment agencies and concerned all hiring, discharge, pay and conditions of work. The second amendment added a new section to the law, by specifying that age referred to people between the ages of 45 and 65. In an editorial the *New York Times* declared that "we heartily approve of the intent of this legislation."[129]

Just weeks before the law took effect, SCAD held a series of public hearings in various cities wherein the agency attempted to set specific standards for how the new law would work. At these hearings representatives of business and social agencies generally spoke out against the measure. At the Rochester hearing W.C. Cameron Edey, vice president of a department store, said his company hired people of all ages but admitted that the firm considered age in choosing personnel for its training programs. Fred Schenk, assistant executive secretary of the Rochester Council of Social Agencies, agreed that age was important in training programs, saying, "I can see the employers' problems. It seems to me it is an employer's right to decide who can do the best job for him."[130]

When SCAD held a hearing at Syracuse, Stephen McNeil, an employment agency manager, told the panel that he thought the law should be held in abeyance as it was "virtually unenforceable except in flagrantly obvious cases." Thomas Ruck, industrial relations director for the Syracuse Manufacturers Association, said his group thought that no one should be discriminated against solely because of age. However, he also believed banning inquiries about age was unduly restrictive.[131]

Final rules on what questions employers and agencies would be permitted to ask of applicants on employment forms and in ads were announced at the end of June 1958 by SCAD chairman Charles Abrams. Help-wanted ads were not allowed to mention age nor were they allowed to use such code words as "young" man. One major change in regulations drawn up earlier by SCAD was related to the employment forms. While earlier regulations prohibited asking an applicant for his age on the form, the final regulations mandated that forms were required to say that state law prohibited discrimination because of age. However, the prospective employer was still permitted to request the age of the applicant.[132]

After the law had been in effect for about a year, a SCAD survey of 30,000 ads in six major newspapers in New York State found the use of verbal devices such as "recent graduate" or "state draft status" had dropped. In June 1958, just before the law went into effect, 17.2 percent of ads contained such references. During the month after the law went into effect, it rose to 21.6 percent. However, during the following eleven months the figure dropped to 11.6 percent. Prior to the law, 9.4 percent of ads contained outright age specifications, dropping a year later to 0.4 percent.[133]

When the law had been in force for 18 months, journalist Charles Grutzner took a long look at its effects. He concluded that "thousands of men and women are being denied employment because of their age despite the state law that prohibits such discrimination. Employment agencies continue to honor employers' requests to send them no applicants above specified ages." A 38-year-old woman answered an ad for stenographers and was told that only females in their 20s would be considered. She filed a complaint with SCAD. Despite the employer's denial of any age bar, the investigation showed that none of the dozen stenographers in the office pool had reached her thirtieth birthday and that the two hired as a result of the ad were 17 and 26 years of age. As a result of the complaint and investigation, the employer agreed to consider the complainant when the next vacancy occurred. As well, he agreed to inform subordinates that future discrimination would bring disciplinary action. SCAD declared they would check on this employer periodically. In the 18 months since the law came into effect, 200 people had complained to SCAD. That number was small, thought Grutzner, because some people were reluctant to become a party to controversy, others were not aware of their rights, and many more believed employers and agencies had ways of circumventing the law. Of 92 cases completed, 30 were dismissed for lack of jurisdiction, three were withdrawn by the complainants, in 29 cases no discrimination was found, in 15 cases SCAD obtained the employers' agreements to end discrimination, and in 15 the commission found no discrimination in the specific case in question but uncovered other discriminatory practices that the employers agreed to correct. Grutzner declared, "The main gain seems to have been this: Many job-seekers who formerly never got as far as an interview now get that opportunity. But many who get as far as the personnel interview don't get the job."[134]

SCAD chairman Elmer Carter described those first 18 months as an "initial educational period." The principal object, he explained, had been to reduce and regulate age specifications in newspaper ads and age specifications in job orders placed by employers with agencies. Still, observed

Grutzner, manufacturers had long been reluctant, and remained so, to hire women over 35, claiming older women weren't fast enough. Advertising agencies had in many cases refused to hire copywriters over 30 because they said they wanted men who "think young." Some retail stores drew the line at 40 for saleswomen, because older women "can't stand on their feet all day." Those, and other disbarments for age, were about to be questioned officially for the first time, said the reporter, meaning cases had been handled fairly gently to that point. Despite its fight against arbitrary age barriers, the New York State Employment Service—like most private agencies—complied with employers' requests to send no applicants above whatever age the employer specified. Grutzner thought there were two reasons for that situation: (1) lack of knowledge about the effect of age on abilities; (2) unwillingness on the part of agencies to antagonize employers who had fixed ideas about age limits.[135]

In April 1961 New York Governor Nelson Rockefeller approved a bill that would prohibit age discrimination in employment with respect to people between 40 and 45. That change and expansion of the law took effect on July 1, 1961.[136]

Another jurisdiction which adopted legislation was Massachusetts. Back in 1949 the Massachusetts State Federation of Labor was after the legislature to put teeth in the old law. In 1937 the state had gone part way by adding to its Labor Relations Act the pronouncement, "It is hereby declared to be against public policy to dismiss from employment any person between the ages of 45 and 65, or to refuse to employ him because of his age." That same law required firms to keep age records of workers and permitted the Commissioner of Labor and Industry to make investigations. The penalty for discrimination, following a hearing before the Commissioner, was the publication of his offense in the newspapers. In such instances the law protected the newspapers from libel suits. Needless to say, the Federation of Labor felt the law, which generally had been ignored, needed stronger teeth.[137]

Massachusetts did adopt a tougher measure in 1950, similar to the one that New York later adopted. During the first five years it was in effect, the Massachusetts Anti-Discrimination Commission handled over 300 cases of age discrimination. New York State Senator Thomas Desmond, speaking of those five years, said that some good had been accomplished. However, Desmond observed that evasion of such laws was easy enough and that antidiscrimination laws could not be expected to accomplish miracles, "but they can provide a clear statement of social policy." Desmond favored such laws noting that age discrimination was practiced especially by large firms that adopted broad, inflexible hiring policies. Major offenders tended to be the public utilities, banks, insurance companies, auto manufacturers, aviation, and other newer industries. New York State had then barred age discrimination in the hiring of public employees, and had for 22 years.[138]

Massachusetts thus became the first state to adopt an age discrimination measure in the modern, postwar era. It enacted its measure in 1950. Following with similar measures were Pennsylvania (1955), Rhode Island (1956), New York (1958), Connecticut, Oregon and Wisconsin (all in 1959). Louisiana had a statutory provision against age discrimination in hiring, but no commission was charged with enforcement as existed in all other states. Colorado still had its ancient 1903 law on the books, which barred the discharge of workers aged 18 to 60 based solely on age, but it had never been enforced.[139] A study of the Massachusetts law at the end of 1958 indicated that such legislation "is no guarantee that there will be a significant increase in jobs and job opportunities for older workers."[140]

When Desmond reviewed some of those laws, in 1962, Alaska had enacted a similar law. All of them declared that an employer could not discriminate against a person in obtaining employment, in their working conditions, or in work severance, solely because of age. In most cases those laws stipulated that help-wanted ads could not specify age preferences; prospective employers and employment agencies could not ask a person his age on application forms. There were some minor exceptions. The 1903 Colorado and 1934 Louisiana measures had long been unenforced and were, said Desmond, "dead letters." Since 1951 bills had been before Congress to make it unlawful to refuse to hire, discharge, and so forth, on the grounds of age. None, obviously, had succeeded in getting passed. Between 1950 and 1956 in Massachusetts, total placements by the Division of Employment increased 28.9 percent, but the placement of older people rose 71.2 percent (the state law was in effect throughout the period). During the same years in New York State the corresponding numbers were, respectively, 24.7 percent and 99.6 percent. No law was in effect. It was all due, thought Desmond, just to a change in labor supply and demand. "Significantly, not one agency or person of the many interviewed in Massachusetts," reported Desmond, "was able to show by concrete examples that the 1950 law had aided in the placement of older workers." They had a "feeling" that it had, or "hoped" that it had helped. Arguments for such legislation, said Desmond, included: removal of the sanction of discrimination as a legitimate employment practice; it forced unrealistic personnel practices to be reexamined; it provided an agency before which older workers could air grievances; it prevented compulsory retirement before 65; it served a useful educational purpose; it permitted job seekers to at least gain access to employment offices and personnel managers. Reasons against such legislation included: it was easily evaded; it did not wipe out prejudice about older workers; it did not strike at the fundamental problem of increased insurance and pension costs; it raised the hopes of older people without increasing their job opportunities; it drove business out of states by imposing additional burdens on employers.[141]

By early in 1965 some 14 states had passed laws barring discrimination on the basis of age in employment. Yet, as Robert Fjerstad observed, "Studies show that the experience of the older, unemployed workers in the states with these laws does not vary significantly with the experience of those states without laws." That was due to the ease of evading the laws. Even in the mid–1960s discrimination continued. A study in Minnesota revealed that workers age 45 and over represented 32 percent of all applicants for jobs registered by the Minnesota State Employment Service. However, they were securing only 15 percent of all job placements. As others before him, Fjerstad found it difficult to understand why employers who were so satisfied with their own older employees were reluctant when an older applicant came seeking work. In looking at two older studies (1939 and 1951) Fjerstad found that the percentage of companies saying older workers were equal or better than younger workers on work performance was 81.6 percent (1939), 92.7 percent (1951); on attendance 82.5 percent, 98.1 percent; on safety 86.2 percent, 97.4 percent; and on attitude toward work, 94.8 percent, 99.2 percent.[142]

Throughout this period more and more pressure was exerted on the federal government to enact legislation barring age discrimination in employment. In 1964 Congress passed the landmark Civil Rights Act which outlawed job barriers based on race, color, religion, and sex. It did nothing for the aging worker on the grounds that not enough was known about the problem. In passing that law in the summer of that year, Congress inserted a section instructing the Secretary of Labor to make a full study of age discrimination in the labor market and to report back to Congress no later than the end of June 1965. Whether or not Congress would amend the Civil Rights Act to bar age discrimination would depend, thought the publication *America*, on how quickly and efficiently the states tackled the problem. Thirty states then had no statute barring the practice. Up until then, said the magazine, "the record of local government in this field has been very spotty."[143]

One thing that did happen earlier in 1964 was that President Lyndon

Johnson, by executive order, declared a policy against discrimination in employment because of age. He ordered that ban be imposed in the federal service.[144]

When the Labor Department reported back to Congress in 1965, it advised Congress that a national law was needed to deal with the problem of discrimination against older workers. In his report, Secretary Willard Wirtz said there was "substantial evidence" of arbitrary discrimination. Their study showed that the setting of specific age limits "has become a characteristic practice in those states which do not prohibit such action." In those states without statutes more than half of all employers had such age limits, usually between 45 and 55. According to the report, about half of all job openings that developed in the private economy each year were closed to applicants over 55, and a quarter of them were closed to applicants over 45. Although state laws on the issue had been increasing (20 states then had them), some had not been implemented and "in most states resources were not adequate to assure compliance." Discrimination resulted, added the report, not from employer malice "but from the ruthless play of wholly impersonal forces."[145]

As the war ended, age discrimination in employment quickly resurfaced and just as quickly became as pervasive as it had been before the war. Survey after survey confirmed its existence; specific age limits were blatantly used, but more informal barriers were just as common. In the face of numerous studies which showed older workers to be just as productive and no more costly than younger ones, the stereotype of the middle-aged as less productive and more costly remained firmly in place. Social scientists found the negative image of the older worker in various groups of respondents. As pleas and public appeals had little effect in reducing the problem, states began to enact statutes which barred age discrimination in employment. These, too, had little effect. More and more pressure was exerted on the federal government to take steps.

CHAPTER 5

Getting Rid of the Gray, 1967-1999

"But the Volstead Act didn't end drinking, and this act isn't going to end age discrimination."
—Labor Department spokesman, 1968

"Age discrimination is rational..."
—Daniel Seligman, 1990

"Our findings indicate that all too often older job seekers fare barriers that are totally unrelated to their ability to do the job."
—Claudia Withers, Director, Fair Employment Council of Greater Washington, 1994

"[Companies] are finding more ways to get rid of them and the reason is because there is a lot of pure bias, of behaving toward older workers totally in the context of their age, not their ability."
—Michael Barth, Vice President, ICF, 1994

"Yet no evidence exists of widespread discrimination against these workers."
—Gary Becker, 1994

Although the federal government had declined to include age as one of the areas in which discrimination was prohibited in its Civil Rights Act of 1964, the problem did not go away. Pressure continued to be exerted on Congress to bring age under the protection of antidiscrimination legislation. Prior to 1958, except for a small number of relatively ineffective state laws, there was no age discrimination legislation. However, by 1968 the number of state laws dealing with the issue had increased to 23, with another state, Maryland, making age discrimination in employment a "harmful practice." Most of those laws applied to employers, labor unions and employment agencies; they typically covered people aged 40 to 65. Generally they tried to eliminate age discrimination by informal methods of conference, persuasion, and conciliation, and, if those methods failed, by the issuance of court orders. Meanwhile Congress and executive departments of the federal government had sought to bar discrimination in hiring because of age for a number of years. President John F. Kennedy issued a memorandum in March 1963 to his heads of executive departments and agencies, clearly stating his desire that they review their hiring practices and ensure that ability and not age was the basis used for evaluation. The following year, 1964, President Lyndon Johnson extended that policy beyond the departments and agencies of the federal government, to contractors and subcontractors of the federal government.[1]

Later, in the same year, the Civil Rights Act of 1964, which prohibited discrimination on the basis of religion, color, sex and national ancestry, also contained a direction to the Secretary of Labor to study the problem of age discrimination in employment. His report, issued in June 1965, said, in part, "The possibility of new nonstatutory means of dealing with such arbitrary discrimination has been explored. That area is barren ... A clear and implemented Federal policy ... would provide a foundation for a much-needed vigorous, nation-wide campaign to promote hiring without discrimination on the basis of age." When the Labor Department studied the effectiveness of those state laws banning age barriers, one conclusion was that those laws had created a greater opportunity for interviews and for consideration of older persons by potential employers. Specifically, the laws had resulted in an elimination of discriminatory age specifications in advertising job vacancies, an easing of specifications in employer orders made to the Employment Service, and an increase in referrals by the Service without regard to age. It all suggested that those state laws had eliminated the more obvious forms of age discrimination while doing little or nothing to eliminate the actual age discrimination.[2]

In 1965 the Senate included an amendment to the Fair Labor Standards Act prohibiting age discrimination, but that amendment was withdrawn in conference. During his January 1967 message to Congress, with regard to a program for older Americans, President Johnson called for the enactment of legislation that would prohibit "arbitrary and unjust discrimination in employment because of a person's age ... for workers 45 to 65 years old." Finally, in 1967, Congress enacted the Age Discrimination in Employment Act (ADEA). Congress' conception of the need for such a law could be seen in the following preamble: "Sec. 2(a) The Congress hereby finds and declares that: (1) in the face of rising productivity and affluence, older workers find themselves disadvantaged in their efforts to retain employment and especially regain employment... (2) the setting of arbitrary age limits ... has become a common practice... (3) the incidence of unemployment ... is, relative to younger ages, high among older workers." The statute protected people aged 40 to 65, making it unlawful for an employer or employment agency to fail or refuse to hire or refer for employment a person because of his age. Also prohibited by the law were any suggestions in help-wanted ads that people aged 40 to 65 were less favored than others. In that January 1967 message President Johnson declared: "Hundreds of thousands, not yet old, not yet voluntarily retired, find themselves jobless because of arbitrary age discrimination. Despite our present low rate of unemployment, there has been a persistent average of 850,000 people age 45 and over who are unemployed. Today more than three-quarters of the billion dollars in unemployment insurance is paid each year to workers who are 45 and over. They comprise 27 percent of all the unemployed, and 40 percent of the long-term unemployed."[3]

With regard to the studies done by the Labor Department in the area of age discrimination in employment, researcher Sumner Marcus observed that "they are uniform in their suggestion that the older job seeker is discriminated against." In 1967, for people aged 45 and over, the period of unemployment was, on average, twice as long as for those under 45. One year earlier, when that older age group represented 24.7 percent of the labor force, they made up 34.3 percent of the long-term unemployed. The proportion of long-term unemployed persons who were 45 and up leaped from 31.5 percent in 1961 to 49.2 percent in 1967. As well, a disproportionate number of older workers were employed in fields characterized by declining demand and relatively low earnings. For example, in the group aged under 45, self-employment accounted for less than 10 percent of their number, while it accounted for almost 20 percent of the men aged

45 to 64. Agriculture employed twice as many older men as it did younger ones.[4]

When Johnson signed the ADEA in December 1967, he termed it "humane and practical legislation." The program was to be administered by the Secretary of Labor, and up to $3 million a year in appropriations were to be authorized. If the government thought a job seeker had been discriminated against, then conciliation and persuasion would be attempted. However, the law also permitted court action. Going into effect on June 12, 1968, the law applied to all employers of 25 or more people and included, under the Fair Labor Standards Act, labor unions and employment agencies.[5]

Just weeks before the measure took effect, *U.S. News & World Report* reminded its business readers the law was coming; that it barred discrimination against the 40-to-65 age group in hiring, compensation and terms of employment; that it covered all firms with 25 or more employees, if the company was in an industry affecting interstate commerce. Overall, the law was estimated to cover 37 million employees in 350,000 firms. Also noted was that if the employer could show that older people could not handle the work, an employer could refuse to hire people in the 40-to-65 age group.[6]

That same magazine conducted a survey of employers about two weeks after the law took effect and declared; "Employers generally say they have not been discriminating against older applicants and so will not have to change their employment practices." Within the approximately two dozen states which had measures in force similar to the federal law, officials reported they had received relatively few complaints of violations. One of them explained, "Employers usually know the law; they don't say they won't hire someone because of his age, but find some other excuse." In Chicago a personnel man said, "I don't expect to see any changes in personnel policies of companies. Age may be the reason a person is not hired, but the fact won't be broadcast." Michigan's law had been in operation for 16 months but had generated only 67 complaints filed; Ohio received five complaints over three years. Since the New York State measure had taken effect a decade earlier, 885 complaints of age discrimination had been received, yet that represented only 13 percent of all the complaints alleging discrimination in employment.[7]

When the law took effect, Labor Department representatives did not expect the new measure to change the situation overnight. As one of them explained, "To the extent it's publicized and law-abiding employers obey voluntarily, it could be helpful. But the Volstead Act didn't end drinking, and this act isn't going to end age discrimination." The National Employment Association, which represented 7,000 private employment agencies in the United States, expected the new law to have its most immediate and visible impact in newspaper help-wanted ads. Association executive John Holmes instructed the group's members to avoid using in their ads phrases such as "age 25 to 35," "recent college grad," "young," "boy," and "girl." However, as was often pointed out in business publications, there was an out—older people could be rejected because of their age when there was a bona fide occupational qualification reasonably necessary to the normal operation of the particular business. For example, it was all right to advertise for a young girl to model teenage fashions. If, in the course of investigating a complaint, the Labor Department found that a worker had been denied a job or promotion solely because of his age, then the Labor Department had the legal powers to force reimbursement of lost wages, among other remedies.[8]

During the fiscal year ending June 30, 1971, the Labor Department found that 2,522 employers and employment agencies discriminated against workers aged 40 to 65 because of their age. They reported that their investigations during that year had resulted in the hiring, rehiring, or retention of 615 workers.[9]

For the year ending June 30, 1973, the Labor Department was involved in 25,000 age-discrimination cases. Of those, more than 6,000 reached the stage of formal investigation, and 36 percent of them turned up violations. The total number of unduplicated establishments not in compliance with ADEA that year was 2,185; breaking it down, there were 2,489 employers not in compliance, 516 agencies, and one labor organization. By employers: 818 were not in compliance for refusal to hire; 1,003 for illegal advertising; 186 for illegal discharge; 339 for promotional barriers; and 143 for other reasons. By employment agencies: 186 were not in compliance for failure to refer; 295 for illegal advertising; 35 for other reasons. The one labor organization was not in compliance for having a bar to referral. Age bias turned up most frequently in ads for job openings. Said Labor Department spokesman F.W. McGowan, "We consider it discrimination if an advertisement calls for recent college graduates. There are damned few 40-year-olds who just got out of college." Much of the Department's activity had dealt with professional and white-collar workers. "They know their rights," explained McGowan. Richard McMullan of the Labor Department's Division of Equal Pay and Age Discrimination observed that a lot of people who became unemployed at the age of 58 or so just gave up. They were no longer counted as unemployed. The cost squeeze of the last few years led to many being out of work and, "in practice the forced exits of recent times have centered on the 37 million workers in the over-40 bracket."[10]

A great deal of publicity was generated for the ADEA in the spring of 1974 when the Standard Oil Company of California agreed to pay $2 million in back wages to 160 employees it had discharged and to rehire 120 of them. By far it was the largest settlement under the ADEA. As in all negotiated settlements, the company did not, as a matter of legal technicality, admit that it had broken the law. According to a Labor Department official, about 200 cases had been brought since funds first became available for enforcement of the act, in mid–1969. The largest previous award of back pay was $250,000 to 29 employees of Pan American World Airways. Those discharged from Standard Oil (all were age 40 to 65) held a variety of jobs, from engineers to area sales managers to retail gas station employees. Annual salaries for the positions ranged from $8,000 to $40,000. All were discharged between December 1, 1970, and December 31, 1973, because of what the company called "declining manpower requirements." Besides dealing with direct complaints from workers, the Labor Department also made inspections of employers where there had been no complaints and found that 43 percent of them were not in compliance with the act, according to Assistant Secretary Bernard DeLury. Other Department officials remarked that pervasive violations had been found in employer advertising. While relatively few cases had been litigated—with a resultant lack of court clarification—the Labor Department believed all advertising was illegal that contained phrases such as "recent college graduate," "boy," "girl," "draft deferred," or "maximum two years experience."[11]

As expected, the Standard Oil case was covered extensively in the business press. When it was covered by *U.S. News & World Report*, it was portrayed as part of a government campaign then picking up speed to "get tough" on age discrimination against workers. Said one Labor Department spokesman, "From now on, the age-bias law is likely to become better known in the corporate boardroom and the plant locker room." Reportedly, a special task force of lawyers had been set up in the Department's legal division just to handle age-bias cases. Labor Department solicitor William Kilberg observed that "some companies tend to discharge older workers in order to bring in younger persons at lower wage scales." Sometimes, he added, it appeared that workers were terminated a year or so before they were due to get vesting rights in a pension plan. "People in the 40-to-65 age group ... tend to earn higher wages, they tend to be vested in their pension rights or to be close to vesting, which boosts pension costs, and so it is often more profitable to discharge the older, rather than the younger worker," elaborated Kilberg.[12]

In its coverage, *Business Week* commented that it was notoriously hard to prove age discrimination, and mainly for that reason, antidiscrimination officials had played down age bias and concentrated on cases involving blacks or women. Back-pay settlements for cases involving sex or color bias in employment had topped $30 million in each category.[13]

Early in 1975 a U.S. District Court in Newark, New Jersey, awarded $750,000 to the widow of an Exxon Research and Engineering company employee who was forced to retire at 60 "as part of a campaign to prune older, higher-salaried employees from the payroll." Age-bias cases by fiscal year were as follows: year ending June 30, 1972, 1,862 complaints, 964 employees awarded damages, amounts paid were $1,655,000; 1973, 2,208, 1,031, $1,866,226; 1974, 3,040, 1,648, $6,315,484 (including Standard Oil's $2 million).[14]

Not every case resulted in a government victory. The Greyhound bus company had set a policy that 35 was the maximum age for hiring bus drivers. The Department of Labor was alerted and a complaint was begun, finally reaching the court stage. Department lawyers called upon Greyhound to prove in court that older workers were a risk to the safety of its passengers, while the government marshaled an impressive array of experts and studies to show that older workers were capable and competent. The court was persuaded, and Greyhound's "no hires over 35" policy was declared illegal. The bus company appealed with the thrust of its defense being that the human body began to degenerate around 35, with a detrimental effect on driving ability, so that the age limit was a BFOQ (bona fide occupational qualification). The Labor Department argued the company itself knew better, because Greyhound had many drivers in their 60s who were driving every day and doing a good job. However, the company's defense was successful with the three-man Court of Appeals decision unanimously reversing the lower court. Thus, the age bar was allowed to stand. Shortly thereafter the United States Supreme Court declined to hear the government's appeal of that decision.[15]

Other jurisdictions were also active. In New York City, Major John Lindsay signed executive orders in August 1970 formally barring discrimination on the basis of age and sex in city employment and in the execution of contract work for the city. Those orders did not apply in those cases where sex and age were genuine occupational qualifications or where a retirement plan or statutory requirement had established an age limitation. The effect of the new order on New York City employment was that the Commission on Human Rights was then instructed to initiate an investigation of all qualifications as to age and sex that were then required for those people applying for jobs and promotions. Where such qualifications appeared to be unjustified, the Commission was to make recommendation for changes. Until Lindsay signed the new orders, the law against job discrimination covered only race, creed, color, and national origin.[16]

When *Newsweek* surveyed the current situation in April 1974, it cited Howard Eglit of the Chicago chapter of the American Civil Liberties Union, who observed that both subtly and blatantly society had exalted youth and shrunk from what were euphemistically called the golden years. And that pervasive attitude, declared *Newsweek*, translated itself into "widespread job discrimination against older workers." Mentioned were the then still mostly in force police and fire department age limitations along with the then-recent Greyhound bus decision in favor of the company's 35-year cutoff age. Alice Brophy, director of New York City's Office for the Aging, agreed with that conclusion. According to one management consultant it was not a conscious bias but represented "an underlying corporate value." Ironically, many federally funded job-training programs limited entrance to people under 28. An increasingly worrisome aspect of ageism to the magazine was forced early retirement. Once an optimal benefit that allowed workers to retire in their mid-50s with reduced pension payments, said *Newsweek*, "it has now become a widely used management tool to cut costs and trim the payroll."[17]

Within the field of engineering a report published in 1966 summarized the experience of some 1,200 engineers laid off during the 1963–1965 period. Findings indicated that age was the only significant difference between working and laid-off engineers (that is, the older ones were terminated). According to the report, the length of unemployment was directly related to age, as 56 percent of those age 56 or older were unemployed for 18 weeks or longer; only 26 percent of those under 35 suffered the same fate. A November 1969 study of engineers laid off from four West Coast aerospace firms indicated that 50 percent of those were over 40. Of the remainder, 30 percent were over 30. That is, 65 percent were over age 30. When a New York agency that specialized in manpower advertising conducted a 1971 survey it found that most firms then advertising for engineers wanted people who had no more than five years experience and were willing to work for $14,000 yearly. As well, several personnel managers and representatives of employment agencies admitted candidly to journalist Francis Lavoie that the over-40 engineer probably did have more trouble getting a job than did the younger man. The term most often heard in interviews by older engineers was "overqualified"—a code word for "too old." One study looked at engineers who kept up with the changes in their profession, devoting two to five hours per week to this self-education. According to that 1966 report, such continuing education had no noticeable effect on who was or was not laid off.[18]

Business reporter Richard Williams posed the question in 1972 as to whether or not there was life after 40 to various advertising agency people. Hank Seiden, senior vice president at Hicks & Griest, replied, "If you should lose your job after 40, you're dead" (assuming the person was not an established "star"). Replied Marion Kabat, personnel executive at the Judd-Falk Agency, "There are fewer and fewer jobs as you get older. And if you're competing for a job with a kid, the kid will win. For one thing, he'll come in at a lot less money." George Allen Jr., vice president at Grey Advertising, said, "Life after 40 in advertising? I'd say it's closer to 35. If you haven't made it by then, what life is left is quickly beaten to death." Jerry Della Femina, president of Della Femina, Travisano & Partners commented, "What I think is that it's a terrible way to judge a person. Awful. But if a 42-year-old writer says he's 37, it might make all the difference. Tragically, not only is there life after 40, there's death. Especially in creative areas. So I'm for lying." Agreeing that lying about one's age was sometimes necessary was Ronald Plummer, creative director at Buchen Advertising, who added, "In fact, I'm for anything else that will keep a talented guy marketable. Including wigs and face lifts." Those comments caused Williams to conclude you had to be a lot more at 40 than you were at 25—a superstar, supervisor, a vice president, or an agency owner. "But what you can't be is just another writer or art director. No matter how professional, talented, dedicated, hardworking."[19]

In 1975 the Connecticut Commission on Human Rights and Opportunities ordered the Shelton Police Department to offer its next available patrolman's post to 44-year-old Robert Silverman, who contended he had been denied a job because of his age. The Police Department denied the charge, claiming Silverman was not physically fit. However, a state hearing examiner found that applicants with lower test grades had been hired, including a 260-pound 5' 10" applicant.[20]

Nevertheless, such victories were rare, especially in the 1970s. At the end of that decade a survey of 4,500 people of all ages revealed that 80 percent of them believed that employers discriminated unfairly against older people and made employment more difficult for them. That view

was supported by 97 percent of those surveyed who had personal responsibility for hiring and firing. Gruman Aerospace corporation personnel
director Daniel P. Knowles remarked that "of all the different types of discrimination, age bias is the most insidious. The very people who display
age bias are themselves middle-aged." The Forty Plus Club advised its
members to submit resumes giving eight or ten important achievements
rather than a straight chronological account of their education and
employment that revealed their age. "But sooner or later, employers insist
on resumes with dates," said John Silverthorn, director of the New York
branch of Forty Plus. Club members got only a three percent response
rate to their applications. Of the replies, only one percent invited the
applicant to a job interview.[21]

At the Chicago chapter of Forty Plus in 1983, the standard was said
to be that you must have earned a salary of at least $25,000 in a prior job
in order to qualify as a potential member. The chapter was then open to
both men and women. There were no women at the club the day reporter
Bob Greene dropped in but he observed there was a difference. "Some-
how there is no shame for a woman to be unemployed; if a woman, especially a married woman, finds that she is going to be staying home full
time, she can be safe in knowing that no one will be whispering about
her or avoiding her gaze on the sidewalk."[22]

Phyllis Worne had a private employment agency for people over 50
in Marlton, New Jersey, a suburb near Philadelphia. Regarding the 1984
employment picture for people over 50 she said, "It's an outrage. Discrimination is rampant. Employers think an older worker won't fit the
company's 'youthful' image, whatever that means." Many of her clients
were men in their 50s who were victims of corporate mergers or payroll
cuts. This account said that Forty Plus Clubs sometimes made exceptions
for women to join who had held managerial positions without reaching
the salary level. Each member paid $300 to join the organization, $5 a
week as a "housekeeping fee" and a $200 exit fee when they got a job.
Also, each member was still required to devote 2½ days a week to club
work.[23]

Researcher Robert Hutchens looked at the evidence on the link
between age and job opportunities, computed from the January 1983 Current Population Survey. If older workers faced more restricted job opportunities, he supposed, then recently hired young workers should be more
evenly (or equally) distributed across industries and occupations than
recently hired older workers. Additionally, if older workers tended to be
employed in but not hired for some jobs, then one would expect recently

hired older employees to be less equally distributed across industries and occupations than all older workers. The age groups compared here were workers older than 55, and those 55 and younger. When Hutchens examined the data he concluded that, consistent with expectations, recently hired older workers were less equally distributed across industries and occupations than both recently hired young workers and all older workers. Although the results did not constitute unambiguous proof that job opportunities declined with age, said the researcher, they reinforced other evidence supportive of that hypothesis. Other studies indicated that older workers making job changes reaped smaller wage gains than younger workers, and they often suffered wage losses. Also, once unemployed, older workers were less likely to move from unemployment to employment than younger workers. The evidence presented here, declared Hutchens, "adds to the weight of the evidence indicating that job opportunities decline with age."[24]

Writing in *Modern Maturity* in 1989, Roy Hoopes stated ominously, "All across the country, an insidious and sometimes illegal discrimination is being practiced against older job seekers." Christopher Mackaronis, manager of the Advocacy Programs section of the American Association of Retired Persons (AARP) worker equity department, declared that age discrimination was "rampant." However, he added that it was virtually impossible to prove. Inevitably, he thought, there was information on a resume that would generally reflect someone's age and could well cause their rejection, "but you have no way to prove it." One new problem mentioned by Hoopes was that, under the Immigration Reform and Control Act of 1986, employers and employment agencies required people to show that they could be legally hired, which usually meant providing some sort of official identification such as a birth certificate or a driver's license. One person wrote to Representative Claude Pepper to complain, "Isn't the Immigration and Naturalization Service now making it possible for prospective employers to covertly discriminate?" Hoopes characterized the enforcement record of the ADEA as "dismal"—especially in cases where job applicants had been denied work because of age.[25]

In a March 5, 1991, *Washington Post* story, NBC News president Robert Wright was paraphrased as saying that television stations could cut costs by replacing highly paid, experienced people with "hungry twenty-three-year-olds." The next day an NBC spokesperson said the comment had been taken out of context, that Wright was referring to a hypothetical situation, not network policy. On that same day Wright issued a memo to all NBC employees restating the network's policy against discrimination of all kinds, including age bias. That same month several NBC workers were offered buyouts. Twenty-two of those were moved from regular jobs into a "pool." Half of them were over 50; all but one were over 40. In that pool most had little to do; instead they sat around waiting for something to do.[26]

When Mortimer Zuckerman bought the New York *News*, all 544 members of the editorial arm of that newspaper were fired. He rehired all but 182 of them in very public fashion. Zuckerman maintained that the firing decisions were based on evaluations from the employees' immediate bosses. "[We] were not given any information on gender, race, age, or sex," he declared. The entire process was said to be based on merit, taking into account reporting and writing ability, story ideas, accuracy, cooperation and teamwork, and the ability to meet deadlines. All were supposedly professional standards. Of those 182 who were fired, 24 percent were under 40, 27 percent were between 40 and 50, and 49 percent were over 50. Commenting on that situation and others, a spokesman for a Wall Street securities firm said, "It doesn't matter what company or what industry you work in these days. If you're over 40, you're old. Does it worry me? You bet." Thomas Moloney, public-policy expert at the Institute for the Future, observed that until 1980 there was a deal—a tacit social agreement—that there was a lifetime earnings curve. A person was underpaid in the beginning of his career, that person came out all right in the middle, around age 35 to 45, and then was overpaid a little at the end. What business was saying then, in 1993, thought Moloney, was, "Okay, the deal's off. We're going to lop off that premium, even though we know you worked your tail off and were underpaid in the beginning."[27]

In New York that recession of the early 1990s brought a doubling in unemployment rates for workers under 55, but nearly a tripling for those over 55. According to reporter Marilyn Webb, economists were saying the increase in the firing of those in their 40s and 50s was prompted not only by the desire to stop paying high salaries "but by underfunded pension plans, prejudice about age (and sex), lack of respect for experience, and the cult of the young." Fifty years of age seemed to be the great divide, though in fields like cosmetics, televisions, investment banking, and advertising, 40 was the cutoff. Remarked Anne Vladeck, a lawyer who had represented dismissed employees in age discrimination lawsuits, "The thinking is that people who are not chiefs—people who are still at mid-level when they're in their fifties—must not be so good." Ads for help wanted each Sunday in the *New York Times* classifieds regularly contained phrases such as "graduates of the classes of 1986 to 1990 wanted." The Equal

Employment Opportunity Commission (EEOC—which was then in charge of enforcing the ADEA) acknowledged that such ads were illegal but was overwhelmed by complaints and had no resources to police advertisements. Kidder Peabody's investment banking division was sued for age discrimination by the EEOC in 1992 on behalf of a class of former employees. Louis Graziano, of the EEOC, explained that his agency felt that young people had been hired to replace the ones let go. It seemed that older workers were being discharged while younger ones were being hired. Asked if that was astounding Graziano said; "No, I've seen it over and over again ... You don't always get the discrimination verbalized ... They say these people weren't performing that well, but on the evidence we have, we can dispute that." As in all previous periods, age discrimination hit women harder than men. Males experienced big employment drops in their mid 50s; it came 10 years earlier for women.[28]

Nationally, in America, from 1989 to 1992, the number of people 50 and over who were unemployed jumped 68.1 percent, compared with a 40.6 percent increase for people under 50. Through October 1993, the average number of unemployed people who were 50 and over dropped 4.5 percent from one year earlier, compared with a 5.1 percent decline for workers who were under 50.[29]

A 1994 article by Esther Fein was pessimistic about the fact that little headway had been made against age discrimination in employment despite decades of educational work, numerous studies that showed older workers to be as good as younger ones, and so on. Karen Davis, executive vice president of the Commonwealth Fund, explained that in the beginning she was more optimistic that if the stereotype was corrected, if older workers' productivity was documented, it would help change attitudes. "I really thought the reports would have had more of a positive impact. But we are running against economic trends and some deep-rooted bias. I still think it may turn around, but it's clearly going to be an uphill struggle to make it happen." Vice president for ICF, Michael Barth, said he wished he could say that because of all the case studies, companies were running out in droves to hire older workers. "But if anything, they are finding more ways to get rid of them and the reason is because there is a lot of pure bias, of behaving toward older workers totally in the context of their age, not their ability." In a study issued in 1993, the AARP and the Society for Human Resource Management surveyed about 1,000 managers in a variety of businesses. Martin Sicker, director of Work Force Programs for the AARP, commented that everybody saw older workers as reliable, like Saint Bernards. "They love them, but they won't hire them and we really couldn't get at why." He concluded that, "It does just come down to ageism and we haven't found a way to crack it."[30]

According to a 1994 study by the AARP, older people were discriminated against more than 25 percent of the time when applying for jobs. That study was conducted for the AARP by the Fair Employment Council (FEC) of Greater Washington, who mailed comparable resumes for two job applicants, one aged 57, the other 32, to a random sample of 775 companies. For the 79 firms who had job openings, 43 percent favored the younger applicant and 17 percent favored the older one. One set of test resumes was sent to a Fortune 500 firm for the same position of management information systems specialist. Both applicants were listed as having 10 years experience while, in addition, the older one was listed as having had 25 years experience as a mathematics teacher. FEC director Claudia Withers remarked, "The amount of hiring discrimination uncovered by this study is extremely significant. Our findings indicate that all too often older job seekers face barriers that are totally unrelated to their ability to do the job."[31]

Later that same year business journalist Genevieve Capowski observed that on the surface, the corporate rationale for instituting early retirement programs, rather than adhering to the last hired, first fired philosophy for reducing the payroll, appeared to be pure economics. Many saw the rationale for that option running deeper: "They point to an underlying, insidious element that's becoming more and more apparent in our business practice—ageism." Helen Dennis, lecturer at the Andrus Gerontology Center at the University of Southern California, said there was enough research that showed older workers were dependable, could learn, could change, and so forth. But what society had not come to grips with was that research and management practice were not always related. With regard to firms downsizing by age and the lawsuits that sometimes resulted, Cathy Ventrell-Monsees, manager of worker equity at the AARP, noted that the disturbing trend was that employers had become more callous. They were more willing to risk age-discrimination lawsuits because the courts had become more conservative over the past dozen years. In fact, employers won only about 60 percent of the cases, and those were from the cases that actually made it to trial. A recent survey by Jury Verdict Research showed that successful age-bias claims resulted in average awards of $302,914, compared with $255,734 for sex discrimination, $176,578 for race bias, and $151,421 for disability discrimination. The reason for the difference was reportedly that victims of age bias tended to be more highly paid employees because they had been with the company longer, and damages were based on the amount of lost income.[32]

When Pacific Telesis carried out a downsizing in December 1995, the firm fired 1,469 people. Like many other companies engaged in reducing staff, PacTel targeted what it believed to be its most expensive people: older, more experienced employees entitled to generous benefits. Most of those 1,469 people fired were just a few years short of full benefit entitlement. On pensions alone the company was said to have saved an average of $326,632 per firing. For example, one of those fired was John Kelley, a 23-year employee, who was fired 2½ years before he became eligible for his full pension. PacTel saved some $337,000 in pension payments and avoided the cost of lifetime health insurance guaranteed to the company's retirees. Age discrimination, said reporter Ann Monroe, was the dark underbelly of downsizing with older workers failing to appear in downsizing statistics because firms described their exit as "early retirement." With new jobs hard to get, most quickly dropped out of the labor pool. In her view, job discrimination lawsuits dramatized the problem but understated it, since many corporate employers demanded a promise not to sue before they handed out severance payments. Managers laid off older workers not only for economic reasons, but also because managers saw them as less flexible and innovative. Ken Olsen, founder and former president of Digital Equipment Corporation, campaigned for younger workers. Lowell Hoffman, downsized at age 49 from IBM said, "We had a bunch of younger people coming in and learning the job as we were being pressured to leave."[33]

Writing in *The Nation* in 1998, Margaret Gullette declared that full-time work might soon become a privilege denied to middle-aged people, since 50 was the end of the line, even for those who were well educated. She added that ageism was useful to employers in both business and government because "it imputes losses of ability, slower reflexes and techno-retardation to justify downgrading of midlife employees."[34]

In a lengthy article in a 1999 issue of *Fortune* magazine, Nina Munk studied the current scene and declared that once a person reached 55 it was almost impossible to find a job in business. "But a new trend is emerging: In corporate America, 40 is starting to look and feel old. Since the early 1980s large companies had been getting rid of people. For a long time seniority mattered, with the result that if people had to be fired, younger, junior people were usually the first to go." But firms today, said Munk, had less and less tolerance for people they believed were earning more than their output warranted. At Westech Career Expos, the country's largest technology-related job fairs, the registration form asked those attending to indicate their "professional minority status." One option was "Over 40." David Opton, executive director of Exec-U-Net (a network of 5,000 executives looking for leads on new positions) commented that, "The age bar is lowering on what is considered old. I often tell people who are between 40 and 45 and thinking of getting a new job to hurry, because the door closes at 45."[35]

Nor was it just high-tech firms who were engaging in these practices, wrote Munk. In 1998, when management consulting firm Watson Wyatt Worldwide asked 773 chief executive officers at what age they felt people's productivity peaked, the average response was: 43. A recent study done for the AARP noted that the message was consistent; managers generally saw older workers as less suitable for the future work environment than other segments of the workforce. When Gerber Products got rid of 389 salespeople in January 1998, it was revealed that nearly 70 percent of them were over the age of 40. In a study of all the age-bias suits filed in federal courts in 1996, it was found that 26 percent were brought by plaintiffs in their 40s. That was an increase of 18 percent from that found in an earlier study that looked at age discrimination suits filed between 1968 and 1986. Most firms looking to dump older workers left no traces. Richard Posner, chief judge of the United States Court of Appeals for the Seventh Circuit, explained that within companies the ADEA had forced a vocabulary purge. Companies knew they could no longer say "We need new blood," but they could not be prevented from thinking it. Posner added, "If you believe you have too many old people, you can simply offer them early retirement. And it's said that if you want to fire an older person, you just fire a disposable younger person along with him in order to avoid a lawsuit." Munk concluded that, "Suing for age bias is expensive, emotionally exhausting, and rarely successful." By 2003, predicted Munk, half of the nation's workers would be 40 and over. That would be the first time ever.[36]

One opinion maker who weighed in on the topic in this period was columnist William Safire who said, in 1977, "Old people get older and usually less productive, and they ought to retire so that business can be better managed and more economically served." He thought the elderly should be treated with respect, but if politicians started to invent "rights" for them that cut productivity, "they infringe on the consumer's right to a product at the lowest cost."[37]

Mostly, though, there was an increase in the presentation of management's point of view, mainly hostile. William Martin, Director of the

Management Centre of the University of Michigan and Wayne State University, told an audience of 800 members of the Personnel Association of Toronto, in 1970, that half the employees over 55 in any company should be fired within the next three to five years. The reason for this was to open up the lines of promotion for the "young chargers," the development men. According to Martin at least five American corporations were then engaged in firing half of their workforce over the age of 55, especially at the executive level. He added that studies showed that 40 percent of the discharged older employees found other jobs and were "happy doing bookkeeping three days a week." Reportedly, Martin's presentation ended to loud applause.[38]

A major source of criticism against middle-aged workers came from the pages of *Fortune* magazine in a column titled "Keeping Up." That column contained news items from other media sources, was unsigned, and looked like an editorial. In the February 17, 1986, issue the column observed that a point infrequently made about ageism was that it tended to make a lot of economic sense. "The principal point of our existing laws against age discrimination is to override economics." Arguing that the ADEA was bad enough at the outset, it had since been "disimproved substantially." In numerous circumstances, "it is now not necessary for the plaintiff to prove that the managers are biased; as in other corners of anti-discrimination law, it is now sufficient to establish that some company policy has a 'disparate impact' on the oldies." Since older workers were more likely to have vested pension rights and to receive higher pay the argument presented here was that older employees and younger workers were two different types of workers. Thus, an employer trying to make purely economic decisions about different kinds of employees "can easily commit ageism. If he has to cut back the workforce, he is an ageist if he decides to lop off those who will be cushioned by pensions." In earlier periods employers tried to pass themselves off as humane for not hiring older people because they did not want to eventually retire them without a pension. This column tried to paint employers who got rid of older workers as humane since those people did have some pension benefits.[39]

Two weeks later that same column criticized the 15 or so states that had by then enacted bans on age-based retirement (a federal ban was on the way). Exceptions were generally included for specific occupations, such as police officer. The New York State statute also allowed an exemption for any job for which age was a bona fide occupational qualification (BFOQ). The columnist complained that he could think of almost no occupation in which age would be a BFOQ.[40]

A few months later this column declared that it was time again to restate the case in favor of age discrimination. This time the column was signed by Daniel Seligman. Congress was then trying to remove all age limitations on retirement. But, he said, "employers have to live with the fact of reduced mental ability—especially ability to learn—among the elderly." Seligman then observed that the problem was that the declines in workers' brainpower were hard to track and measure, making it often wildly impractical to identify the point at which each individual had slipped to some unacceptable level. Because of these difficulties Seligman rejected the idea being put forward in Congress that chronological age was meaning less and employers should make individual evaluations of their employees' physical and mental condition.[41]

Four years later Seligman was back in the "Keeping Up" column with another rant. "Age discrimination is rational because in the typical case, critical mental functions decline with age—and because it is ordinarily not practical to test the brainpower of employees claiming to be untypical." As you age, he stated, your skull thickens and your brain shrinks. This time Seligman had some precise numbers; by age 65 the brain has typically lost about six percent of its weight at age 20, and IQ scores were perhaps 15 percent lower. He added that people held up well in "crystallized intelligence"—the ability to perform familiar tasks. Where people supposedly crashed with age was in "fluid intelligence"—the ability to learn new tasks, see things in different ways, and respond creatively. Seligman presented no evidence to support his argument.[42]

Another columnist who made similar arguments to those of Seligman and who was just as critical toward older workers was Gary Becker, writing in *Business Week*. In a 1986 column he remarked that government regulation of labor markets had been growing rapidly in the United States and Europe in recent years, at the same time that air travel, banking and other industries had been deregulated. Most important of that government intervention, he thought, was the increasing regulation of the market for older workers. As background, Becker said that about 60 percent of men over 65 were privately employed in the United States at the beginning of the century. A similar percentage then existed in the United Kingdom. There was a gradual decline in the rate from the time of the Civil War to the 1930s. After 1930 the rate at which men over 65 participated in the labor market declined rapidly and was well under 20 percent by 1986. The participation rate of males 55 to 64 dropped from 87 percent in 1960 to less than 70 percent in 1986. Becker declared, "The reason for these rapid changes is not any growing discrimination against the elderly in modern industrial economies; the culprit is public policies that discourage employment of the elderly." Pension plans and Social Security had enabled many to retire, he said, while recent laws required companies to maintain the health insurance of former employees for up to 18 months. Because of this, and other regulations, "official figures must overstate, possibly by a lot, the actual decline in the number of elderly who are working." Also, many large companies were said to prefer having a fixed retirement age (by then mostly legally banished). It all made sense to Becker because those company policies "are a recognition both of the decline in the health and productivity of a significant fraction of elderly workers and of the inability of most large companies to pick and choose among their older workers in order to retain only the productive ones."[43]

Four years later Becker was back to announce that the problem wasn't simply a case of discrimination. That Social Security rules, government interference in labor markets, and "confusion in the courts" limited the number of jobs available for older people. Noting that the federal government was extensively involved in regulating the labor market for older workers and that federal and state courts were filled with cases brought by older workers for age discrimination, Becker, nevertheless, went on to declare, "Yet no evidence exists of widespread discrimination against these workers." Then he threw in a non sequitur by observing that men aged 60 to 64 who worked year round earned almost as much as those who were 45 to 54, and much more than men aged 24 to 44. The plain fact, he said, was that older workers formed "an elite" who were generally valued by employers for their experience, knowledge, reliability, and loyalty. Courts had an impossible task imposed on them because, it was said, they lacked clear-cut guidelines as to what constituted bias. Fearful of court decisions, companies then settled out of court even when they had done nothing wrong. And those firms guarded against such lawsuits from older employees "by simply not hiring them"—although that action left them vulnerable to lawsuits from those who weren't hired. So, in the end, the columnist said, "the very policies supposed to protect the rights of elderly workers sometimes end up hurting them." Becker here used faulty logic by confusing cause and effect. The right to sue for age discrimination, which was then less than 20 years old at the federal level, did not explain the existing age bias for the decades before its existence. In fact, that right was granted only after much protest from older people, trade unions, and so forth. That right was implemented only after exhortation, moral suasion, and other methods short of legislation were all unsuccessful in getting companies to stop discriminating in employment on the basis of age.

In conclusion Becker said, "The labor market for older workers will function much better if pay and employment are left to private negotiations among workers, unions, and companies."[44]

More formal surveys and studies of the problem in this period, as in past times, continued to document the widespread incidence of age bias. A report by the United States Senate Special Committee on Aging delivered in 1971, after a two-year study, emphasized that unemployment of workers over 45 had jumped from 596,000 to 1,017,000 in those two years. That committee found that Americans over 45 represented nearly one-third of those out of work for more than 15 weeks, and nearly 43 percent of those idle for longer than six months. Those over 45 who were no longer actively seeking work rose from 4.1 million in 1950 to 8.3 million by December 1970.[45]

A New York organization called Women Office Workers contacted 100 employment agencies in 1976, either directly or by phone. One test was performed by a man who phoned all 100 agencies. He told them his company (a nonexistent one) was looking for a young, pretty, receptionist/secretary type who was between 23 and 25 years old. His order was taken. As well, the group sent two women with equal skills, training and background—Dorothy, 50, and Marge, 25, to ten employment agencies. The only difference between them in their fictional background was experience, 20 years versus six years. At two agencies Dorothy was told there were no jobs yet at the same two agencies Marge was sent out to job interviews.[46]

A sample of 398 black, 373 Mexican Americans, and 373 white residents of Los Angeles County, aged 45 to 74, was asked about their experiences with race and age discrimination in finding or staying on a job in 1977. Until that time, according to researcher Patricia Kasschau, there had been only one study of self-reported data on age bias. It found that more than half of a sample of 273 aerospace engineers still active in the labor force claimed to have personally experienced age discrimination in their work career since reaching middle age, and an additional 25 percent of the sample claimed knowledge of a friend's similar experience with bias. Kasschau, in her study, found that 23.4 percent of the blacks said they had experienced job discrimination because of age; 15.8 percent of the Mexicans and 13.1 percent of the whites made the same assertion. When asked if any of their friends had experienced age discrimination in finding or staying on a job because of age, 38.2 percent of blacks said they had, 27.1 percent of Mexicans, and 25.7 percent of whites. When respondents were asked if they thought job discrimination based on age was common in America then, the figures for those replying yes were: blacks, 87.4 percent; Mexicans, 78.6 percent, whites, 87.7 percent.[47]

A brief news account late in 1982 indicated that the unemployment rate among Americans over the age of 55 had risen 24 percent since the start of that year, versus a 16 percent increase in the overall jobless rate. Those older workers were also out of work for a longer period of time than were their younger counterparts.[48]

When the Wyatt company conducted a 1989 study, it was found that 30 of the 50 largest corporations in America had recently offered retirement incentive programs; government surveys indicated that five million workers were displaced between 1981 and 1986. It was also estimated that about one million managers would have lost their jobs between 1980 and 1990. Those myths surrounding older workers as inferior persisted still and that meant, said reporter Roy Hoopes, that "the oldest workers are targeted for downsizing. The tragedy of the 1980s is that it is primarily the older worker who has borne the brunt of the corpocracy fitness programs and the raids, buy-outs and takeovers on Wall Street." David Gamse, director of the AARP's Worker Equity Department, added that although the law prohibited employer retaliation, filing an age discrimination complaint against your employer could make your situation "difficult."[49]

About 80 percent of the Fortune 100 companies offered an early-retirement program between 1979 and 1988; 30 percent of those required workers to sign waivers. According to a report from the General Accounting Office (GAO), such waivers were becoming increasingly common. For the period 1987–1988, 35 percent of firms offering such programs required their employees to sign them. Those waivers declared that the election to take early retirement was voluntary. Companies then contended those signed waivers barred workers from suing for age bias.[50]

Journalist Susan Dentzer noted that the percentage of United States males aged 55 to 64 in the labor force in 1948 was 91 percent, 62 percent in 1989. The numbers for females were, respectively, 22 percent, 42 percent. Dentzer said, "It is questionable whether market forces will prompt private employers to make way for many older workers anytime soon." That was because a much publicized labor shortage had not yet arrived, and might never come.[51]

One study conducted by the AARP involved mailing out virtually identical resumes to large companies. The only substantial difference on the resumes was in the ages of applicants, younger versus older in the matched pairs sent out. Results found were that companies discriminated

26.5 percent of the time against the older fictional applicant. Successful firms displayed less bias than did less successful firms, which caused the AARP to observe that discrimination did not pay.[52]

Of the 3,551 cases filed in one year in the mid–1990s with the Massachusetts Commission Against Discrimination (MCAD), 16 percent were complaints of age discrimination. It led MCAD to set up its own sting operation. MCAD would send out testers in pairs. A search was then made for pairs of women, older and younger, who were similar in every respect—looks, mannerisms, education—except for their ages. For example, one pair had a 45-year-old and a 22-year-old who were trained for a job search in the Boston area, assigned to target retail stores. Their resumes were modified to make them similar. From the twelve businesses to which Tish (older) and Rebecca (younger) simultaneously applied, Rebecca received nine offers, six for full-time permanent employment, three for seasonal. Tish was offered four jobs, all of them seasonal. Similar results were obtained by three different decoy teams. As a result of its investigation MCAD charged seven of the 42 businesses it had tested with violations of the state's antidiscrimination law. MCAD found probable cause that discrimination had occurred in four of those cases; two were cleared of charges, and one faced further investigation. Also noted in connection with the decoy operation was the rude treatment of the older women, in some cases, when they entered stores to apply for positions.[53]

Researchers Karen Leppel and Suzanne Clain observed that official measures of unemployment understated joblessness in the economy, and that in investigating the "discouraged worker" effect its presence and magnitude had been found to vary with gender and age. However, most researchers had reported that discouragement was greater among older workers than among prime-aged workers. Leppel and Clain's work explored the influence of unemployment on labor force participation for men and women aged 56 to 60, with comparisons made to 31- to 35-year-old men and women and with 16- to 19-year-olds. When the unemployment rate increased, concluded the study, displaced prime-aged women workers remained in the workforce as unemployed workers, while displaced older women workers exited the labor force. Displaced younger women workers did both. Similar results were found for the male group. Results confirmed earlier studies which found that older workers who became unemployed were less likely to be counted among the officially unemployed than were the other age groups.[54]

The National Longitudinal Survey of Older Men collected data in 1966 on a national sample of 5,020 males aged 45 to 59, then made periodic follow-ups until 1990, when the men were 69 to 83. In the 1971, 1976, and 1980 follow-ups, those men were asked if they had experienced any age discrimination in their work in the previous five years. Overall, about seven percent of the respondents reported they had experienced such bias; however, only three percent reported such discrimination from their current employer. Incidence of reports of bias were similar for workers under 60 and for those aged 60 and over. Men who reported they had experienced age bias were 50 to 100 percent more likely to separate from their jobs as were workers who reported no age discrimination.[55]

For the older worker living outside the United States the situation was just as bad as it was for the ones living in America. The International Labour Organization (ILO) reported in 1974 that the practice then in Western Europe appeared to be to refuse to employ manual workers over 50 and white-collar workers over 40, especially in small enterprises. In France, Belgium, West Germany, Greece, Italy, and Sweden, the average time between jobs for workers over 45 was four times longer than for workers under 20. Long-term joblessness in Canada accounted for 37.4 percent of all unemployment among workers over 45, as compared to 25 percent in the 25–45 age group. The chance of finding a job diminished gradually up to the age of 50, said the study, but after that the difficulty accelerated sharply. Another conclusion drawn was that "the unemployment rate for ageing women has long been somewhat higher than for men. This gap has been widening recently, in good times as well as bad."[56]

That same ILO survey found that people over 50 made up two-thirds of those who had been unemployed for more than six months. One British survey determined that every second managerial or administrative job advertised in a major daily paper was closed to people 40 and older. Commenting on the fact that the United States had outlawed age discrimination in 1967, and that Costa Rica did the same in 1970, the study added that to be effective such legislation had to be supported by a change in attitude, with an end to the existing stereotypes about older workers. The ILO report reinforced that little had changed for the older workers since the time of Milton Barron, who wrote in the 1950s. Barron believed older workers were at a disadvantage in all the world's labor markets, East, West, free enterprise or socialist. He had written, "There is no evidence available that indicates that anywhere in the world employers generally are free from prejudice against the hiring of older workers. On the other hand clear and unmistakable evidence exists that even in areas of labour shortages, employers are reluctant to hire older workers."[57]

At the end of the 1970s job ads in Western European newspapers still openly listed age limits. The United Kingdom's Department of Employment, which campaigned vigorously against racial discrimination and for equal opportunity for women and the disabled, regularly published job advertisements with strict age limits. Help for the Aged, a UK charitable organization devoted to helping older people, had recently advertised for a housing manager "aged 35 to 45." France did have a law by then which made it illegal to set strict age limits in job ads, and in that country, as in America, companies advertised for "recent college graduates" or "people of youthful appearance." Job applicants in France were also regularly asked to submit photos of themselves with their resumes.[58]

Despite widespread evidence to the existence of the problem abroad, the business publication *International Management* took, not unexpectedly, a different position. In its April 1982 issue it said that, while age discrimination was a major issue in the United States, it was debatable whether or not it was a major issue with European companies. European attitudes towards age bias were said to contrast strongly with those in America; "certainly the lack of legislation banning age discrimination in Europe indicates that it is not a pressing problem." After this periodical conducted its own survey of the issue, it went on to declare that the results confirmed the view that age discrimination was less of a problem in Europe than "even moderate corporate critics think it is." That survey explored, among other issues, hiring practices, and was sent to a random sample of 3,000 executives in 10 Western European nations. Questionnaires were received back from 878 executives, a return rate of 29.3 percent.[59]

Two questions were posed on the issue of hiring practices. One asked if the respondent thought it should be against the law to specify age limits in job ads. Overall, 70.4 percent said no, 27.4 percent yes, 2.2 percent gave no answer. Highest yes response came from French executives, 49.2 percent, followed by Spain, 32.9 percent. Highest no responses came from German executives, 77.7 percent; next were Italians, at 75.6 percent. The other question asked the respondent if his company specified age limits in any job advertisement. Overall, 36.5 percent of executives replied yes, 63.5 percent said no. Yes percentages were as follows: the Netherlands, 64.5 percent; Italy, 48.8 percent; Spain, 47.1 percent; UK, 41.8 percent; Belgium, 37.1 percent; Denmark, 36.2 percent; Switzerland, 32.4 percent; Germany, 31.9 percent; France, 18.5 percent; Sweden 8.6 percent. Since all respondents answered the question, the yes and no responses for each country summed to 100. Despite its own data the magazine concluded, "The widely held belief that companies actually have policies or practices that encourage, either overtly or covertly, age discrimination is not borne out by the results of the survey."[60]

Even more oddly, the magazine went on to present some specific examples. Sweden was said to have long had a tradition not to state ages in job ads, but it was pointed out that companies got around that by listing such things as the number of years of experience, and so on. All of the requirements gave a good indication of an applicant's age. France remained the only country of the 10 surveyed that had any legislation aimed specifically at age discrimination. Under that law, described as "vague," it was illegal to state strict age limits in job ads. However, in practice it meant that French job ads were allowed to carry broad age bands. They could not, for example, advertise for someone not over 35, but they could request applicants who were "about 35 years of age." When age limits were specified in job listings, top management was responsible for setting them in about 75 percent of the cases, according to the survey respondents. From that, *International Management* concluded that "age discrimination is often a simple matter of older managers discriminating against their own contemporaries." It was a strange idea which had never been aired before, outside or inside the United States, and would not surface again.[61]

Looking at the European situation from a different perspective was Guy Standing, who presented his study in 1986 in the ILO's *International Labour Review*. He argued that in Western Europe much attention was devoted to teens and young workers as victims of high unemployment, while far less attention was paid to workers in their 50s and 60s who had been those most affected by the job shedding that had gone on there since the mid–1950s. Statistics typically used as indicators of labor market performance were not the best indicators of older workers' labor market position, he believed, since their plight was concealed. Many older workers withdrew from the labor market if unemployed, either in discouragement or into "early retirement." Since the rise of mass unemployment in Western Europe, official policies towards older workers had radically changed, and in many countries concerted efforts had been made to reduce the labor supply of those over about the age of 55. In Germany men aged 60 to 65 were encouraged to retire early, so that by 1980 only a third of that group was employed. Until 1983 the French government operated a scheme whereby workers over 55 were paid a lump sum if they retired early. In Italy the steel industry instituted a scheme in 1984 to encourage workers to retire at 50. Policies such as these meant older workers were increasingly marginalized, without that necessarily showing in a worsening of their relative unemployment rate. According to a European Economic Community (EEC) survey, the active (people seeking and available in the reference week) unemployment rate was highest for teens, declining to a low point for the 45 to 49 age group, then it rose slightly for those aged 50 to 54. In all ten EEC nations of the time, the groups 50 to 54, 55 to 59, and 60 to 64 had unemployment rates well below the overall average. In most of those countries the unemployment rates for older women were higher than for their male cohorts. Although older workers appeared to have relatively low unemployment rates, Standing felt that largely reflected statistical practices and the tendency for older workers to withdraw in discouragement from the labor force into passive unemployment. The incidence of long-term unemployment in the majority of EEC nations was highest among older workers. By age group the percentage of job seekers having sought work for 12 or more months in 1983, in nine EEC countries (Germany, Belgium, Denmark, France, Greece, Ireland, Italy, the Netherlands, and the UK), were as follows: 14 to 19 age group, 35.3 percent; 20 to 24, 46.9 percent; 25 to 54, 49.4 percent; 55 and over, 59 percent.[62]

While the populations of industrialized countries had been steadily aging, the labor force participation rates had declined. Between 1975 and 1982 the activity rates of men aged 60 to 64 fell from about 85 percent to less than 70 percent in the UK. Similar figures were recorded in other European nations. By 1983, in most of those countries, said Standing, the majority of older workers in employment had only part-time jobs. Among men, particularly high proportions of the employed 60 and over were working part-time in France, the Netherlands, and the UK, and apparently most male part-time workers were older workers, a fact consistent with their relatively low average incomes. In those same nations the great majority of women aged 50 and over who had any job at all were in part-time work, with the highest proportions being in Denmark, the Netherlands, and the UK.[63]

A problem, in Standing's view, was that with the aging population the dependency burden was growing. In Western Europe the ratio of the workforce to the total population was expected to continue to decline until about 2015. He argued that as a response to long-term unemployment, a guaranteed basic income paid regardless of age and work status was preferable to a lowering of the retirement age, because all such measures to reduce the labor supply were implicitly discriminatory. Regarding early retirement schemes in general, an earlier ILO report, from 1962, had warned that great care needed to be taken when implementing such programs to ensure they were not used to force older workers out of the employment market, or used as an excuse for not actively seeking appropriate employment for them. "Such arrangements affect the behavior and expectations of employers, unions and workers themselves, so encouraging discrimination. Indeed, all early retirement schemes that involve selective criteria are essentially arbitrary and thus unfair."[64]

Diana Cornish was the managing director of an employment agency based in London, England. With respect to English employers she said, in 1991, that their age prejudice was widespread and socially acceptable. They believed a person's age determined whether they could do a particular job. "Many personnel officers, whatever their own ages, seem to share the same bias against employing older people. Even older officers make statements like: 'You can't learn after 50,'" she explained. Cornish added that, for whatever reason, ageism did not come into play when hiring temporary workers.[65]

Britain's largest chain of do-it-yourself stores was called B&Q. As an experiment the company staffed a suburban Manchester outlet entirely with workers aged 50 and older. Against four comparison stores with similar market areas and sales levels that Manchester outlet had profits that were 18 percent higher, turnover that was 16 percent less, 40 percent fewer days missed by employees, and almost 60 percent less inventory loss through theft, damage, and so on. Business writer James Krohe, Jr., remarked that the ambivalent way our society treated the aging worker mirrored the way we treated aging parents. Americans, he added, had become accustomed to throwing away usable resources, including people. That tendency was reinforced by one of America's most enduring national myths, "that the United States is still a young nation where energy is worth more than wisdom."[66]

Back in 1981 in the Netherlands, 75 percent of those unemployed for more than a year were older than 50; in 1990 it was 73 percent. While there had been a recovery in job opportunities in the second half of the 1980s, older people benefited the least from that recovery. Researcher Kene Henkens felt the reentry of older people into the work force occurred to some degree in the United States, but it happened hardly at all in France, the UK, Germany, or the Netherlands. Thus, many resigned and discouraged older workers did not apply for jobs at all any more. Henkens looked at a group of 242 men in the Netherlands aged 40 to 55 who were followed for about seven years after they became involuntarily unemployed. Two-thirds of the men finally obtained another job within the seven years. But half of them did so within one year of separation. The probability of reemployment steadily decreased after that first year, reaching a minimum after 2½ years following separation. Probability of never finding another job increased from 33 percent to around 80 percent in the period from one to 2½ years after separation. Those results caused Henkens to question the value of official retraining programs which did not commence until the subject had been unemployed for some minimum period of time, such as six months, or two years.[67]

Age Concern was an antiageist UK charity. Despite pressure from Age Concern, and its own pre-election promise notwithstanding, the British government, in 1998, shelved its own planned legislation and would not be supporting a private member's bill to outlaw ageist job ads. According to employment minister Andrew Smith, any such legislation would involve "a minefield of complexity and whole rafts of people going to industrial tribunals." Exactly the same was said of gender and race bias, before they were outlawed. In the UK then, as in the United States in the late 1990s, companies engaged in downsizing were dumping older and more expensive employees.[68]

A 1996 survey of Hong Kong establishments showed that, as in America, many firms employed older workers but did not hire them. No laws in Hong Kong prohibited age discrimination or required uniform fringe benefit provision. Newly hired older workers remained concentrated in a narrow set of industries and occupations. Researcher John Heywood mailed a survey to a random sample of establishments in Hong Kong, receiving 770 responses, a return rate of 31 percent. Using 55 as the age cutoff, the study found that 52 firms had not hired even one older worker; 50.4 percent of the managers indicated a preference for new hires who were 35 or younger; 16.8 percent preferred new hires above the age of 35; 32.8 percent said they had no preference between the two age categories. Heywood concluded that his examination of managerial attitudes corroborated the evidence of reduced hiring opportunities for older workers. In establishments where hiring opportunities for older people were reduced, managers were more likely to express a preference for hiring younger workers. "This type of corroborative evidence is hard to replicate in economies in which the government prohibits age discrimination. It seems unlikely that over 50% of managers in such countries would admit to a preference that, if followed, would violate the law."[69]

During this period that old, unfounded idea that pension cost kept firms from hiring older workers was used less frequently than in the past. Nonetheless, the supposed higher costs for older employees were still mentioned. Late in 1990 President George Bush signed the Older Workers' Benefit Protection Plan which required employers to provide older

workers with benefits at least equal to those provided for younger workers, under complex rules. It meant employees over 40 had to receive either
equal benefits or have an equal expenditure made for them, even if the
benefit was less. Writing in *Management Review* Thomas Wiencek argued
that companies employing younger staffs generally ended up paying less
in benefit costs. As a result those firms with an older workforce often
attempted to curtail costs by offering different benefit packages to older
and younger employees. It was, of course, precisely such activity that
prompted the law which Bush signed.[70]

According to Dan Lacey, editor of the newsletter *Workplace Trends*,
health care costs "are an increasingly important reason they are pushing
out older employees—which for many companies means people as young
as 40, when costs start to rise notably." No evidence was cited to support
that claim. If Washington continued to lay more obligations for health
care on employers, Lacey told the Joint Economic Committee in 1992,
"we will succeed only in accelerating the staff cutting, causing even more
pain." He claimed a growing proportion of job cuts could be traced to the
rising health care burden, but cited no evidence. "As health care raised
the cost per worker, companies responded in a panic by cutting back on
the most expensive ones," he concluded.[71]

One new slant on the problem in this time period revolved around
a so-called solution to the unemployment of older workers: using them
as temporary workers. Richard Ross, president of Mature Temps, Inc.,
was touting that solution back in 1977 when he pointed out that using
older people as temporary workers was a handy solution to a workforce
problem since hiring those temps could mean reducing expenses between
$1 and $1.25 per hour, compared to a regular company employee. Because
of that, many business managers were said to be no longer limiting their
use of temporary help to such traditional areas as filling in for a vaca-
tioning secretary, but were scheduling operations to include older temporary workers on a regular basis. Ross argued that older people were
more reliable in their work habits, were less frequently absent and, contrary to the stereotype, were more adaptable, since they had learned over
the years to adjust to change. Unlike students, transients, or temporarily
unemployed workers, many older people were available for repeat assign-
ments. Some firms, declared Ross, were "staffing an entire operation with
mature temporary help."[72]

A decade later, journalist Jim Peters announced that older workers
and the disabled represented tremendous sources of talent, in part-time
service jobs, but warned that "both groups have special needs and

considerations." John Cauley, president of the Massachusetts-based Friendly Restaurant corporation, stated that the most difficult situation then facing the hospitality industry was the shortage of labor. Young employees, the mainstay of the service industry, were said to be a declining proportion of the workforce. Besides the increasing availability of older workers, Peters reported they were more reliable, flexible, and more skilled at public relations and accommodating guests. That growing percentage of older workers could also result in higher productivity growth, since those workers generally had substantial work experience and, said Peters, tended "to be the most productive."[73]

It was an idea that seemed to catch on, because a year later Frederick Demicco reported that McDonald's, Kentucky Fried Chicken (KFC), Marriott, and Pizza Hut had led the service industry in tapping the labor pool of mature workers. McDonald's McMasters program had brought the percentage of older workers in the chain's labor force to above 13 percent. In 1987 KFC sponsored a conference (co-presented by the National Restaurant Association and the AARP) linking individuals and agencies serving older people and offering information on where to find older workers, "how to hire them, and how to develop a working environment conducive to retaining them." At KFC, a program called the Colonel's Tradition established a new part-time managerial position for older people. Still, Demicco admitted that none of that had yet triggered a service industry-wide movement to incorporate older workers into long-range staffing plans. Questionnaires distributed to 480 firms, all National Restaurant Association members, revealed the mean percentage of hourly workers over the age of 50 to be 9.75 percent, while the figure for managers over 50 was 13.3 percent. Highest percentage of both older workers and managers was found in the institutional segment; lowest percentage was located in the fast-food segment. Another finding was a negative correlation between the number of older workers and managers under 25, no correlation when managers were 25 to 50, and a positive correlation when managers were over 50. In other words, young managers hired young workers, while older managers hired mature workers. Perhaps one of the biggest benefits was that the government often paid some of the cost. In the McMasters program, experienced McDonald's employees, trained as job coaches, provided intensive personal training for new McMasters recruits. Job coaches devoted 15 to 20 hours per week to each recruit during a four-week period. In order to help create jobs for older workers the contracting government agency and McDonald's shared the training and administrative costs.[74]

In 1986 Days Inns of America, the nation's third largest hotel chain, staffed its 24-hour-a-day reservation center in Atlanta almost exclusively with young people. The problem was that the turnover rate was 100 percent. One of the reasons was that entry wage rates for reservation agents were less than those paid at local fast food outlets. Days Inns decided that a wage increase might decrease turnover rates but declined to implement one on the ground that it would drive them out of business. Instead it turned to hiring older (over 49) people. Within a few years older people comprised 25 percent of the telephone reservation agents. Originally Days Inns segregated its agent trainees by age but soon stopped the practice when the energies brought to the workplace by the mature people were wanted as role models for young workers. Initially, the campaign to attract older workers was not successful. Traditional recruiting methods such as newspaper ads touting openings for persons of all ages received few responses. One possible explanation was that older people may have assumed such ads were intended more to satisfy equal opportunity requirements than to seriously recruit. After shifting its focus to direct recruitment through senior citizen centers and the like, Days Inns was able to hire a significant number of workers aged 50 and over. Then word of mouth began to help, and after that there was no shortage of applicants.[75]

When the New York-based Commonwealth Fund heard of this project it commissioned the consulting firm ICF to conduct a study at Days Inns to compare the performance of those workers 50 and over with those under 50. Records of the hotel chain for the years 1987 to 1990 were studied. On the surface the job of reservation agent required many talents that conventional wisdom did not expect of older workers, such as handling sophisticated technologies, working quickly, and executing multiple tasks simultaneously. In the younger group were 138 people: 48 male, 90 female; in the older group were 187: 67 men, 120 women. For older workers the average career was three years; for younger ones it was one year. After one year, 87.3 percent of the older group were still on the job, 73.3 percent after two years, 54.7 percent after three years, 32.8 percent after four years. For the younger group those figures were, respectively, 29.9, 20.1, 10.7, and 6.1 percent. Although the cost of recruiting and training was the same, when annualized per worker, that cost was lower for the older group because they stayed longer. The much higher turnover rate in the younger group meant more people had to be hired and trained. Wages were slightly higher for the older group, for the same reason—they stayed longer and thus moved up the wage scale a little. Days Inns matched all employee contributions to the pension plan, up to five percent of pay;

28 percent of the older group participated, eight percent of the younger group. The older group was also slightly more productive than the younger ones, with 40.5 percent of their calls leading to a reservation, compared to 40.1 percent. The study found the typical older worker cost $11,173 per year, versus $12,253 for the typical younger employee, a nine percent saving, although virtually all of that difference came from differing turnover rates and the resulting recruitment and retraining costs. Those annual costs were broken down as follows: training, $1,646 younger, $584 older; recruitment, $96, $34; wages, $9,441, $9,572; incentive pay $323, $188; health insurance, $674, $663; pensions, $28, $84; life insurance, $45, $48. When the researchers developed two hypothetical models of a Days Inns reservation center, one staffed entirely by workers aged 50 and over, and one staffed by people under 50, they concluded "the costs are essentially the same."[76]

In the fall of 1995 a training program which was jointly sponsored by New York City's Department for the Aging and the Riese organization, a Manhattan-based firm that owned 200 chain-restaurant franchises, was instituted. Training took place in a full-scale mock-up of a fast-food restaurant. That first class had 19 trainees, all aged 55 or older. Riese donated $100,000 to create the center. Company chief executive officer Dennis Riese said, "This ought to be a win-win-win situation. We're helping the seniors get jobs, helping employers expand their labor pool and helping the city in the process."[77]

One month after the end of the first 10-week program, 10 of the 19 participants were employed, four in Riese restaurants. Despite seeing many help-wanted signs in fast-food restaurants, the other nine failed to find jobs. One remarked, "The main problem is age discrimination." Another one said, "They're looking for young people." Reportedly McDonald's was one company that was still actively recruiting older workers.[78]

The few studies done in this period continued to show older workers to be at least the equal of their younger counterparts. When the Bureau of Labor Statistics reviewed three major studies it had conducted to compare age and productivity, the general finding, in each case, was that there was no decline in productivity until after the age of 65. In those instances where there was a substantial physical effort, there was a slight decrease. Each of those studies was conducted in a different industry: (a) men's footwear and household goods-furniture; (b) office workers, primarily insurance; (c) post office mail sorters.[79]

In an exhaustive study the Department of Labor collected data from more than one million workers' compensation records from agencies in 30 states, for the year 1977. Work injury ratios by age were as follows: 16–17 age group, 3.2 percent of total workers, 1.9 percent of total injuries, work/injury ratio of .59; 18–19 years, 5.3 percent, 6.8 percent, 1.28; 20–24 years, 15.2 percent, 21 percent, 1.38; (16–24 years, 23.7 percent, 29.7 percent, 1.25); 25–34 years, 26.4 percent, 30.3 percent, 1.15; 35–44 years, 18.7 percent, 16.7 percent, .89; 45–54 years, 17.6 percent, 13.6 percent, .77; 55–64 years, 11.4 percent, 8.8 percent, .77; 65 and older, 2.2 percent of all workers, 0.9 percent of all injuries, work/injury ratio of .41. As can be seen from the data, older workers had considerably fewer injuries on the job.[80]

During this period a variety of attitude studies were conducted. All had in common the result that older workers were viewed in more negative ways than were younger workers. Benson Rosen and Thomas Jerdee looked at the nature of job-related age stereotypes in a study in which 56 realtors and 50 undergraduate business students rated the average 60-year-old and average 30-year-old on 65 personal characteristics scored on four worker-qualification dimensions. Results were that the 60-year-old was rated lower on performance capacity and lower on potential for development; the 30-year-old was rated lower on stability. No difference was found on ratings of interpersonal skills. On the measure of performance capacity the younger man was seen as more productive, efficient, motivated, and capable of working under pressure. As well, the younger man was perceived to be more innovative, creative, and logical. The older man was seen to be more accident-prone. On the potential for development measure, the younger man was perceived as more ambitious, eager, future-oriented, receptive to new ideas, more capable of learning, more adaptable and more versatile. The older man was viewed as being more rigid and more dogmatic. With regard to stability, the older worker was perceived as more reliable, dependent, honest, trustworthy, and less likely to quit or miss work for personal reasons. Female respondents evaluated the older man more favorably than did male respondents. Regarding the age of respondents, there was only one significant difference: older respondents perceived a smaller difference than did younger respondents between the capacity of older and younger men to meet the job demands. With that exception it appeared, said the researchers, that the respondent's age did not affect age stereotypes. Noting that the accuracy of the age stereotypes was largely unsupported or even contradicted by research, Rosen and Jerdee concluded that "a serious inconsistency exists between the age stereotypes identified in this study and research evidence on aging."[81]

Eight years later James Crew replicated the study by Rosen and

Jerdee. In this case the same 65 questions were given to a group of white and black undergraduate students. Crew obtained the same results as in the first study, with the older man perceived as significantly worse than the younger man on the performance capacity and potential for development scales, while being rated slightly better on the stability measure. Results were in the same direction for both white and black students. However, the black students rated the older man significantly more negatively than did the white respondents.[82]

Rosen and Jerdee conducted a second study which was an in-basket exercise used to investigate the influence of age stereotypes on the simulated managerial decisions of 142 undergraduate business students, aged 21 to 29. A younger and older employee version was created for each of six in-basket items covering a variety of managerial problems. For example, one item on trainability depicted a computer programmer whose technical skills had become obsolete due to changes in computer operations. That programmer was described as either 30 or 60 and of average ability. Far fewer respondents elected to retrain the older person. Rosen and Jerdee said, "Results confirmed the hypothesis that stereotypes regarding older employees' physical, cognitive, and emotional characteristics lead to discrimination against older workers."[83]

A year later Rosen and Jerdee repeated their in-basket study. This time they surveyed subscribers to the *Harvard Business Review,* sending out 6,000 questionnaires to a national sample of the publication's subscribers. Returned surveys numbered 1,570, 26 percent. Findings were that managers perceived older employees to be relatively inflexible and resistant to change. Accordingly, managers made much less effort to give an older person feedback about needed changes in performance. Few managers provided organizational support for the career development and retraining of older employees. Promotion opportunities for older people were found to be somewhat restricted. Almost 20 percent of the respondents were aged 50 and over. They were slightly easier on the older worker, leading the researchers to observe that for older people the best prospects for fair treatment appeared to be in working for an older boss. Rosen and Jerdee speculated in conclusion that the differential treatment of older and younger employees in the in-basket decisions was the result of respondents' unconscious age stereotypes rather than conscious discrimination.[84]

James Haefner interviewed 286 employees from Illinois to determine their assessments of hypothetical job candidates with various characteristics for a semiskilled position. Results indicated that the race of a potential employee was not important in hiring decisions. However, the age, sex, and competence of the potential employee were found to affect decisions. The 25-year-old worker was preferred over the 55-year-old, males over females, and highly competent over barely competent. Average age of respondents was 44. Haefner concluded that age discrimination "against highly competent older workers clearly exists in the employment setting for semiskilled jobs." An earlier study found similar results for American personnel directors who indicated that they preferred not to hire 55-year-old people at lower levels in the organization.[85]

Haefner did a second study in which he surveyed 588 employees from Illinois to determine the types of discriminatory feelings that existed in the work environment. It was found that race, sex, age, and competence were significant forms of discrimination. Employees would prefer not to work with blacks, women, older individuals, or barely competent persons. When the sample of respondents was split on the basis of the demographic characteristics of sex, age, and race, it was found that blacks preferred working with other blacks, whereas females preferred working with other females. Older employees indicated that age made no difference in their preference for fellow employees.[86]

A study of 120 college students by James Perry assessed their attitudes toward a worker described in scenarios using the dimensions of competence and age. Seven questions were rated by the respondents. Students viewed the older worker as making fewer future valuable contributions and as catching on to new ideas less quickly.[87]

A study done in 1985 was a replication of one done 30 years earlier. Both studied the attitudes of mostly male workers, hourly paid, and supervisors in a Midwest nonunion manufacturing plant, to older workers. Results were similar in both studies. Hourly workers held more positive attitudes toward older employees than did supervisors, and attitude score correlated strongly with the age of hourly workers but not with the age of supervisors. Also found was a "modest but reliable" negative correlation between amount of education and attitude score, indicating a tendency for more highly educated employees to hold more negative attitudes toward older workers. Researchers in this latest study concluded that whatever negative bias supervisors held was not a function of their own age and that "our results are consistent with the Rosen and Jerdee research, which found that biases against older workers are quite pervasive."[88]

When 168 Canadian senior executives were surveyed in 1998 they indicated that they believed an employee's performance peaked at the age of 44 and declined after the age of 57.[89]

Returning to the Age Discrimination in Employment Act (ADEA), the Labor Department reported that from mid–1968 to the end of 1976 some 9,000 employees—including some from the biggest, most famous firms—were awarded nearly $30 million in age-bias cases. Since then, through early 1979, the department said the age discrimination caseload had "accelerated sharply." From mid–1968 through 1976 the number of court cases totaled more than 300, yet over the next two years there were another 150. Author Peter Chew declared, "Age discrimination in employment after age 40 in this country is pervasive, it is brutal, it is stupid and it is costly in both human and monetary terms." Tom Jackson, who specialized in outplacement, agreed that age discrimination problems were on the rise.[90]

The ADEA was amended in 1978 to extend protection beyond the age of 65, with no upper age limit in the Federal sector (effective September 30, 1978) and until the age of 70 for most other workers in the United States (effective January 1, 1979). In 1979 the Equal Employment Opportunity Commission (EEOC) assumed administrative responsibility for enforcing the ADEA, taking over from the Civil Service Commission (which covered federal departments) and the Labor Department (all others). The EEOC also enforced antidiscrimination protection under Title VII of the 1964 Civil Rights Act, which prohibited bias in employment on the grounds of race, color, religion, sex, and national origin.[91]

When *Business Week* ran a 1980 story about the increasing number of lawsuits filed against companies under ADEA, mostly by executives, it went on to declare: "For some companies, firing or forcing early retirement on highly paid older executives has two perceived advantages: It cuts salary costs and pension liabilities and, at the same time, makes room at the top for young achievers."[92]

Under the pressure of a lawsuit brought by the EEOC, the city of Virginia Beach entered into a consent decree in June 1980 to employ an applicant for a position of police officer without previous experience and who was about to turn age 51. Over the objections of the police chief the city also agreed that it would not adopt, maintain, or utilize any form of maximum hiring age for the employment of police officers in the future. Prior to this agreement the city had applied a 35-year age limit. Contributing to the city's decision to compromise was the fact that the city attorney regarded it as unlikely that age could be established as a BFOQ for police work. Burden was on the employer to prove that any age restriction was an essential BFOQ for the job involved. A presumption of discrimination was made unless the employer could prove that an age limitation was a BFOQ. It was all too much for William Nelson, writing in the *Journal of Police Science and Administration*, who declared, "Under the federal law on age discrimination, as applied by zealous bureaucrats, the logical can become the absurd. The ADEA makes no provision for the use of a 'reasonable' age restriction on employment..."[93]

Age bias charges filed with the EEOC rose to nearly 9,500 during 1981, an increase of 75 percent over the 1979 total. Said Representative Claude Pepper (D-Fla.); "Age discrimination has oozed into every pore of the workplace." A survey of those cases showed that age bias affected all types of employment and workers of all ages, although it was most common among those in their 50s. About half of those cases were in manufacturing, 20 percent were in service industries and 12 percent were in wholesale and retail trades. The House Select Committee on Aging commented that the dramatic increase in complaints could be the result of "intensified discriminatory activity by employers" or new attention devoted by the EEOC after it was given jurisdiction over age discrimination. As well, since the law was enacted, the population over age 40 increased 21 percent, from 57 million to 69 million. According to the Labor Department those who were 45 and over, and unemployed, took an average of 17.4 weeks to find work, 26 percent longer than did the rest of the working population.[94]

Complaints of age bias continued to grow faster than complaints of sex and race discrimination, according to the EEOC. More than 11,000 age-bias charges were filed with that agency in 1982, more than twice as many as in 1975 and about 10 times as many as in 1969. Over 28 million civilian workers were then covered by the law. Daniel Knowles, vice president at Grumman Aerospace in New York, observed that whatever money companies were spending to defend themselves in court should be spent on preventive medicine: "Most companies aren't doing anything to protect themselves." With a recession then underway, the number of cases was expected to continue to climb since firms were looking for ways to reduce payrolls and bring in new blood, "which sometimes means younger and less expensive blood." Age discrimination complainants tended to be better educated than persons who complained of other types of job bias. Cathie Shattuck, vice chair of the EEOC, surveyed age plaintiffs in 1982 and found that 84 percent were male, and 80 percent were in white-collar positions. Average annual pay for the male complainants was $30,024. Noted John Tysse, director of labor law at the United States Chamber of Commerce, "It's the equal employment statute for white males." Also revealed in the survey was that the statute was rarely used in hiring cases.

Ninety percent of the complaints challenged firing decisions. The number of cases of age discrimination filed with the federal government were as follows: 1975, 5,424; 1976, 5,826; 1977, 5,535; 1978, 4,612; 1979, 5,347; 1980, 8,779; 1981, 9,479; 1982, 11,063.[95]

While America's over-55 population grew from 41 million to 48 million between 1975 and 1985, the over-55 workforce declined from 15.7 million to 14.2 million in that same period. United States Bureau of Labor Statistics senior economist Deborah Klein remarked that there was a school of thought that once the mandatory retirement age was raised from 65 to 70 in 1978, there would be a lot more older people in the labor force. "Employers wouldn't know how to get rid of them. But it hasn't happened." In 1983 age-bias claims filed under ADEA jumped to 21,000.[96]

In 1986 Congress eliminated mandatory retirement at age 70 or any other age. There were some minor exceptions in occupations such as law enforcement and fire fighting where mandatory retirement would continue in force for at least a number of years. That new legislation marked the first major change in age-bias laws since 1978. About one-third of major corporations were then making use of golden handshakes to induce older workers to retire early. IBM had recently announced that some 10,000 of its U.S. employees had elected to take early retirement under an inducement plan. When IBM first made the plan public, its stated goal was 5,000. Age-bias complaints to the EEOC moved to 24,830 in 1985. Critics charged that the agency's investigations moved at a very slow pace. In 1986 the agency filed 118 lawsuits in the area of job discrimination, the highest total in the EEOC's history. Still, the ratio of complaints to lawsuits was greater than 200 to one.[97]

Deidre Fanning, writing in *Forbes*, reported that in 1986 the number of age-bias cases filed with the EEOC was 17,500. She explained that the number of cases had been rising rapidly because the ADEA "makes it easy—and potentially very lucrative—to go to court, whether a plaintiff has a bona fide discrimination case or not." Fanning noted that in substance the act was similar to the race- and sex-discrimination laws that were part of Title VII of the Civil Rights Act of 1964, with one key difference: The ADEA "is much more favorable to the plaintiff." Title VII cases were decided exclusively by judges—a reflection of the 1960s-era belief that it was difficult in many states to provide unbiased juries for victims of race bias, she explained. No such prejudice was thought to exist in age discrimination, so plaintiffs were granted the right of a trial by jury, if they so opted. As well, the ADEA gave plaintiffs a right to double damages if the complainant was successful in showing willfulness at the trial.

Average age of juries was said to be increasing—along with that of the general population—while many people on juries were retired and some may themselves have felt age bias. "The effect of these provisions in the suit-happy 1980s," said Fanning, "has been to stack the cards against employers from the moment a firm lets go almost anyone over 40." However, she did admit that "few of the cases filed by 40-year-olds so far have actually been won by the plaintiffs." She felt that was because the prospect of doubled damages typically frightened companies into "paying a juicy out-of-court settlement to avoid the risk of actually going to court." Agreeing that no one wanted to see an employee fired just because he turned 40 and that some law was "obviously" needed to make sure such actions didn't happen, Fanning went on to say that a lot had changed since the ADEA was passed, "and maybe it's time to think anew about this social engineering relic." She felt it had become little more than another of the legal profession's endlessly multiplying opportunities to litigate.[98] Christopher Mackaronis was a lawyer who specialized in EEOC age-bias cases. In 1987 he said that only one in three cases was won in court by the plaintiffs.[99]

U.S. News & World Report said more than 20,000 cases came to the EEOC in 1987 but the overworked agency could only file 80 court cases, mostly involving large groups of workers. Individuals could proceed in court on their own, but it could be a costly exercise.[100]

There were five EEOC commissioners, appointed by the President and confirmed by the Senate for staggered five-year terms. As a rule, one commissioner came up for reappointment every year. The law said that no more than three commissioners could be from the same party as the President. During most of the Ronald Reagan era the EEOC, said reporter Roy Hoopes, had been dominated by pro-management conservatives, which had an impact in all its areas of concern. Late in 1988 a report by the United States Government General Accounting Office criticized the agency for not fully investigating many of its cases. Richard Seymour, with the Lawyers' Committee for Civil Rights Under Law, called the EEOC performance "pitiful." A worker who felt he was a victim of age discrimination had 180 days to file a claim with the EEOC (300 days in states that had their own age-bias laws) and two years to file a lawsuit. Because the agency failed to warn so many complainants that the statute of limitations for a lawsuit would run out after two years, in 1988 Congress passed the Age Discrimination Claims Assistance Act. That forced the EEOC to notify certain complainants that although the statute had run out, they would still be permitted to file lawsuits. When the Senate Committee on Aging compelled the EEOC to acknowledge how many people it had to notify, the agency admitted to more than 7,500. Conceding that it had made some mistakes, the EEOC claimed it was underfunded. While the number of age complaints filed with the agency rose from 8,000 in 1981 to 20,000 in 1987, the number of court cases initiated by the EEOC fell from 96 to 81 over the same period. Illustrating the problems at the EEOC was a class action case involving Xerox. Some 1,300 employees alleged they were fired because of their age. At the same time Xerox was hiring 22,000 new people, most of them were under 40. The television program *20/20* investigated and "found evidence that some of the commissioners were not only sympathetic to Xerox, but looking for ways to help the company." Pages of evidence from a Senate hearing showed that the EEOC lawyers felt they had the evidence to bring a case against Xerox, "but the commissioners overruled them." That General Accounting Office report found that in six EEOC field offices and in five state agencies, 40 to 87 percent of the cases closed "were not fully investigated."[101]

When confirmation hearings were held on Clarence Thomas' nomination to the United States Court of Appeals, reporter Viveca Novak remarked that most senators made few inquiries about the EEOC's handling of age-bias cases during Thomas's eight years as its chairman. About 25 percent of the agency's caseload were age-discrimination cases. Novak reported that the EEOC had allowed the statute of limitations to expire in over 13,000 age-bias claims. As well, in the two years after April 1988, another 1,500 claims had been allowed to lapse.[102]

When researcher Barbara Bessey reviewed some studies done on ADEA court cases, she found that one study of 153 cases revealed that more than 80 percent of complainants were male and more than 50 percent of the cases were brought by professional or managerial employees. A second study of 280 federal court cases found that 84 percent of the plaintiffs were white males and 59 percent were managerial or professional employees. Bessey concluded: "What these results suggest is that the ADEA may have become a viable mechanism for higher paid White males who believe that they have received an adverse employment action— the beneficiaries are not the lower paid blue-collar workers whom Congress in 1967 [when the ADEA was passed] thought might suffer adverse actions due to increased use of technology in the workplace."[103]

On the 25th anniversary of the passage of ADEA Robert Maxwell, president of the AARP, commented in an editorial in *Modern Maturity* that there were still people who refused to recognize that age discrimination was harmful not only to its individual victims but also to the nation's economy. "So age discrimination is still practiced—albeit more subtly—in both offices and factories."[104]

Age-bias cases began to decline somewhat. For 1993 17,491 complaints of age discrimination were filed with the EEOC, about 20 percent of all charges of discrimination filed with the agency. Of all those age-bias cases filed in 1993, fewer than four percent resulted in a finding that a violation had occurred. EEOC spokesperson Dorcas Vancil commented, "Age cases are very difficult [for the victim] to prove."[105]

Reporter Marianne Lavelle said that more than 86 percent of age-bias complaints in the mid–1980s were filed by men, 79 percent by white-collar workers and 57 percent by managers. Thirty years after the passage of ADEA Lavelle noted that, in 1997, older people were still discriminated against and that the amount of bias they faced was about the same as that directed against African-Americans and Hispanics of all ages. EEOC complaints were reported here as moving from 24,813 in fiscal year 1990 to 32,145 in 1996 (that is, complaints filed with the EEOC or state and local agencies; some accounts gave just the number lodged with the EEOC while others used the second, and higher, figure). According to Lavelle the EEOC calculated that in fiscal year 1996 employers paid more than ever in per-worker precourt resolution of age cases: $40.9 million to settle 1,931 cases. Researchers found that when looking for work older applicants could boost their chances only by hiding their age or emphasizing their youthful qualities. The worst strategy for an older applicant to follow was to emphasize experience, stability, loyalty and maturity—stereotypical qualities associated with age, even though they were positive traits. More than one in every three such resumes was rejected outright.[106]

During 1997 the EEOC handled 18,279 complaints filed under the ADEA. However, said Nina Munk, writing in *Fortune* in 1999, 61 percent of them were found to have "no reasonable cause." Besides, to receive severance pay and benefits, most workers who were fired or took "early retirement" were required to sign away their right to sue. Munk declared; "Even if an employee manages to take his case to court, it's unlikely he will win." Partly that was because of a 1993 United States Supreme Court decision. In that case (Hazen Paper Co. vs. Biggins) the court suggested that just because a firm took an action that happened to be more harmful to older workers than to younger employees, it did not necessarily constitute age discrimination. That is, laying off mostly older, more highly paid, workers, if done as a cost measure, might not constitute bias. As the

1990s ended, an estimated 90 percent of all age-bias claims were settled long before any complaints were filed with the EEOC, said Munk. One study of 325 cases filed federally under the ADEA found that only 19 went before a jury; 17 of those were decided in favor of the plaintiff. Under the federal statute, recovery was limited to back pay, possibly front pay (if it was clear that an employee would have a hard time finding another job) and attorney fees. If a jury decided the discrimination was willful, back pay damages were doubled. Larger financial settlements were possible under state laws, some of which allowed punitive damages as well as damages for emotional distress.[107]

Age discrimination in employment seems to have started in the latter part of the 1800s. It was a period in American history when the nature of employment itself changed drastically. Prior to that time most people earned their living through a connection to the land. Working the land was a family affair with all members contributing to the task, from the youngest to the oldest, according to their abilities. Older people tended to be cared for by their extended families, as their ability to labor waned. During this time, and earlier, people who worked away from the land were artisans and craftspeople: tinsmiths, carpenters, cobblers, and the like. Mainly they were self-employed and thus worked whatever schedule they liked. With tools of that era being less precise than today's equivalents and with materials being more inconsistent and harder to work with, age and experience probably were marks of expertise. For example, the goldsmith with 30 years experience was probably a more skilled artisan than he was when he had 20 years experience. Age discrimination in employment did not happen very much to people because employment in today's sense of working for a large, impersonal corporation was something most people did not experience.

From, roughly, the Civil War through the early 1900s all that changed as huge factories, offices, and retail outlets sprang up everywhere and the percentage of people employed in agriculture fell away to a tiny minority. As workers moved from rural to urban settings seeking jobs, the role of the extended family began to wither. Its place would be taken by the nuclear family. More mobile in chasing after jobs, it also left is members more vulnerable to any age-related lack of work, potentially disastrous in a pre-pension era. The coming of big enterprises was accompanied by a drastic de-skilling of a great many jobs. A worker on the Ford assembly line was skilled at his limited task within a few days of starting his employment, perhaps even before that. From that point forward there was no change. At the same time, theories of so-called scientific management came to dominate boardrooms, sometimes known as Taylorism, after its popularizer, Frederick Taylor. Emphasis there was on speed, time and motion studies, and still more speed. Prior to World War II, age bias was a fact of industrial and commercial life. However, it was rarely mentioned; perhaps it was just considered part of the natural order of things. Factory work was long and hard. Pollution and toxins were a greater part of the workplace than they are today. If a 50-year-old slowed from some factory norm he was summarily dismissed. He would not likely get another job easily. The fact that he may have slowed down because he had spent 30 years in a plant exposed to its toxins would not save him from dismissal. But it would, just as certainly, work against him in his search for new work.

Prior to 1927 the only real media stir raised about age bias came around 1905—and continued off and on for some time—when famed physician William Osler essentially wrote off everybody who had passed the age of 40. Critics of Osler refuted the doctor by pointing out the great number of works of art created by individual men of merit past that age, such as Dante. However, this had little or no relevance for the average man of 50 or more who was looking for a job.

Age bias only hit the media in a big way starting in 1927. From that time forward it has never been absent for any length of time. Why it shot so suddenly into the public eye is not clear. Perhaps the problem was affecting a greater percentage of people. As well, during the 1920s the problem began to hit more office workers and lower-level managers, as fallout from the business merger mania that was a part of that decade. It meant that age bias was hitting people who were more highly educated and more articulate. Perhaps that group of people had an easier time in attracting media attention than did factory hands. Also surfacing then was the initially mysterious Mr. Action who tried to form a self-help and lobby group for older, unemployed people. His short quotes and refusal to give his name or background—for a time—must have appealed to the press.

Age bias was dully noted in the 1930s but no specific action was taken. Of course, the Depression itself brought hard times for all. During World War II any and all out-groups, including older workers, had a much easier time in finding work. Studies showed they performed as well as young workers, often in jobs they had not usually been allowed to hold prior to the war. That led some to hope that age bias would not resurface at all at war's end.

Such was not the case. Survey after survey and study after study verified the existence and scope of the problem. Individual states began to enact laws barring the practice. Yet little changed. Initially, the federal government was loathe to step in; in 1964 when the landmark Civil Rights Act was passed, bias in employment was prohibited on several grounds—notable by its absence was age discrimination. Finally, a few years later, age bias in employment was banned by the federal government, under its own statute. What has happened in the last few decades has been the removal of all the obvious trappings of age bias. One no longer sees help-wanted ads specifying an age range; one is not asked one's age on application forms. What has not happened is the disappearance of the practice itself. While the ADEA was designed in theory to aid older people who had been fired or had been refused to be hired solely because of age, in practice the law has helped within a very narrow range, mainly white males in managerial positions who have been fired. Someone who has not been hired for a job solely because of age would have a next-to-impossible task in trying to prove it.

For a hundred years companies, when asked why they would not hire people over a certain age, have tended to give the same answers, to evoke the same stereotypes about the older worker being unable to learn, slow to adapt, and so forth. For at least half that long, an increasing number of studies have debunked all those stereotypes. In fact, if anything, the older worker sometimes comes out slightly ahead of his younger counterparts. One irony over time has been that firms which won't hire older workers almost always have some on staff whom they usually value and rate highly. Yet still they won't hire new ones. One other constant for a century has been that age bias hits women harder than men.

Age bias in employment has the potential to strike all of us. Unlike racial or gender discrimination which attacks people for what they are, age discrimination attacks us for what we become.

Notes

CHAPTER 1

1. "Woes of the middle-aged." *New York Times*, July 17, 1907, p. 8.
2. "The anti-age limit league." *New York Times*, October 20, 1905, p. 8.
3. H. L. Douse. "Discrimination against older workers." *International Labour Review* 83 (April, 1961): 350.
4. Waldemar Kaempffert. "The man over 40: a machine-age dilemma." *New York Times Magazine*, March 6, 1938, pp. 1–2, 22.
5. William Graebner. "Help wanted: age discrimination in Buffalo, New York, 1895–1935." *New York History* 65 (October, 1984): 351–353.
6. *Ibid.*, pp. 353–354.
7. *Ibid.*, pp. 355–356.
8. *Ibid.*, pp. 364–365.
9. Roger L. Ransom and Richard Sutch. "The labor of older Americans." *Journal of Economic History* 46 (March, 1986): 17.
10. "Davis says worker is at peak at 60." *New York Times*, January 29, 1928, p. 20.
11. Michael Cope. "What role for the old and displaced worker." *Executive* 6 (January, 1964): 23.
12. Judith C. Hushbeck. *Old and Obsolete: Age Discrimination and the American Worker, 1860–1920*. New York: Garland, 1989, p. 190.
13. *Ibid.*, pp. 191–194.
14. "The Osler dead line." *New York Times*, October 4, 1908, pt. 5, p. 11.
15. "Graybeards must walk with the boys—Osler." *New York Times*, December 20, 1905, p. 11.
16. "Osler only half right says Dr. Felix Adler." *New York Times*, January 8, 1906, p. 6.
17. "Dr. Osler's theory refuted." *New York Times*, June 9, 1908, p. 5.
18. "Expresses a forlorn hope." *New York Times*, November 11, 1910, p. 8.
19. "No place for the old men?" *New York Times*, November 12, 1910, p. 8.
20. "Gives men of 40 no hope." *New York Times*, November 6, 1911, p. 6.

21. "Hunting a job when a man is over forty-five." *New York Times*, July 10, 1910, pt. 5, p. 15.

22. *Ibid.*

23. "The handicap of age." *New York Times*, April 24, 1915, p. 10.

24. "The drawbacks to age." *New York Times*, April 29, 1915, p. 12.

25. "Looking for work in old age." *New York Times*, May 1, 1915, p. 12.

26. "Aged office boys go to aid of business." *New York Times*, November 29, 1916, p. 4.

27. "The office boy passes." *Literary Digest* 54 (April 14, 1917): 1128.

28. "Elderly men hired as office boys." *New York Times*, November 30, 1916, p. 12.

29. B. C. Bean. "Is your job keeping up with your age?" *American Magazine* 83 (June, 1917): 44.

30. "Jobs for the men over 45." *New York Times*, August 2, 1917, p. 8.

31. "The middle-aged woman." *New York Times*, October 14, 1922, p. 12.

32. "Would protect the idle." *New York Times*, October 2, 1921, p. 2.

33. "Old and out of a job." *New York Times*, July 15, 1925, p. 16.

CHAPTER 2

1. "The unwanted middle-aged men." *New York Times*, July 17, 1927, sec. 7, p. 9; "Disadvantages of age." *New York Times*, July 29, 1927, p. 18.

2. "Finding jobs for the middle-aged." *New York Times*, August 15, 1927, p. 16.

3. "Workers, jobless at 40, organize for fight." *New York Times*, August 20, 1927, p. 17.

4. "Mr. Action musters his jobless hosts." *New York Times*, August 24, 1927, p. 14.

5. "Revolt of the jobless middle-aged." *Literary Digest* 94 (September 10, 1927): 9.

6. *Ibid.*

7. "Jobless body asks public for a name." *New York Times*, August 25, 1927, p. 7; "Jobless middle-aged form organization." *New York Times*, August 31, 1927, p. 3.

8. "Mr. Action drops veil of incognito." *New York Times*, September 3, 1927, p. 32.

9. "Declare pretty girls keep them from jobs." *New York Times*, September 4, 1927, p. 13.

10. "Work for the middle-aged." *New York Times*, September 27, 1927, p. 26.

11. "Mr. Action asks for jobs." *New York Times*, September 30, 1927, p. 23.

12. "Few come to Mr. Action." *New York Times*, November 19, 1927, p. 19.

13. "Finds apathy bars aid to middle-aged." *New York Times*, May 12, 1928, p. 19.

14. "Jobs for the middle-aged." *New York Times*, May 30, 1928, p. 18; "Not jobs for middle-aged." *New York Times*, June 4, 1928, p. 20.

15. "Problem of the middle-aged is still far from solution." *New York Times*, October 20, 1929, sec. 3, p. 5.

16. "For the middle-aged unemployed." *New York Times*, July 13, 1929, p. 14.

17. "Unemployment studied." *New York Times*, August 23, 1929, p. 11.

18. Walter S. Hiatt. "Weighing the worth of the man past forty." *New York Times*, October 2, 1927, sec. 9, p. 4.

19. Fred H. Colvin. "Shall we chloroform 'em at 40?" *Magazine of Business* 56 (July, 1929): 59.

20. Stuart Chase. "Laid off at forty." *Harper's Magazine* 159 (August, 1929): 340–342.

21. *Ibid.*, p. 343.

22. "Years prove handicap to women in business." *New York Times*, September 25, 1927, sec. 8, p. 15.

23. *Ibid.*

24. "St. Barnabas House aided 1,584 in year." *New York Times*, July 1, 1928, sec. 3, p. 7.

25. Daisy A. Kugel. "The status of the older woman in home economics." *Journal of Home Economics* 21 (December, 1929): 911–912.

26. Ernest McCullough. "The case of the middle-aged." *New York Times*, August 4, 1929, sec. 3, p. 5.

27. "Shall we starve men over 40?" *Literary Digest* 100 (March 9, 1929): 10.

28. "Green says labor enters on new era." *New York Times*, September 3, 1929, p. 4.

29. "Raises spectre of unemployment." *New York Times*, October 2, 1929, p. 33.

30. "Labor council asks union drive in South." *New York Times*, October 7, 1929, p. 27.

31. "Pledges premier support of labor." *New York Times*, October 8, 1929, p. 3.

32. "Says workers dye hair in fear of losing jobs." *New York Times*, November 15, 1929, p. 32.

33. James J. Davis. "'Old age' at fifty." *Monthly Labor Review* 26 (June, 1928): 1096–1100.

34. "Shall we starve men over 40?" *Literary Digest* 100 (March 9, 1929): 10.

35. "Employment and adjustment of the older worker." *Monthly Labor Review* 29 (December, 1929): 1258.

36. "Calls age a tragedy." *New York Times*, September 3, 1928, p. 24.

37. "Thomas advocates city job bureau." *New York Times*, October 11, 1929, p. 4.

38. "Urges job analysis for older workers." *New York Times*, November 10, 1929, sec. 2, p. 6.

39. "Henry Ford's viewpoint on the elderly worker." *Monthly Labor Review* 29 (August, 1929): 337–338; "Ford says he prefers employes, 35 to 60." *New York Times*, June 29, 1929, p. 3.

40. "Age distribution of workers in a small group of establishments." *Monthly Labor Review* 29 (November, 1929): 1060–1062.

41. "Age limits on employment by American manufacturers." *Monthly Labor Review* 28 (May, 1929): 1024–1025; "Employment age limit survey is undertaken." *New York Times*, May 26, 1929, sec. 10, p. 11.

42. Stuart Chase. Op. cit., p. 343.

43. "Employment and adjustment of the older worker." *Monthly Labor Review* 29 (December, 1929): 1255–1256.

44. *Ibid.*, pp. 1256–1258.

45. "Workers discarded too young, he says." *New York Times*, April 11, 1928, p. 8.

46. Stuart Chase. Op. cit., p. 345.

47. "The jobless man of 45." *New York Times*, October 6, 1929, sec. 3, p. 5.

48. "Revolt of the jobless middle-aged." *Literary Digest* 94 (September 10, 1927): 9.

49. "Accidents to older workers: relation of age to extent of disability." *Monthly Labor Review* 29 (October, 1929): 841–843.

50. "Revolt of the jobless middle-aged." *Literary Digest* 94 (September 10, 1927): 9; Stuart Chase. Op. cit., p. 344.

51. "Shall we starve men over 40?" Op. cit., p. 10.

52. "The middle-age deadline." *New York Times*, July 28, 1929, sec. 3, p. 5.

53. "Group insurance." *New York Times*, November 19, 1929, p. 28.

54. Stuart Chase. Op. cit., p. 344.

55. "The middle-age deadline." Op. cit., p. 5.

56. "Caring for the aged." *New York Times*, November 8, 1927, p. 26.

57. "A job for insurance activities." *New York Times*, November 13, 1929, p. 26.

58. "Uruguayan bill would force employment of men over 45." *New York Times*, November 12, 1929, p. 10.

CHAPTER 3

1. Frank Ernest Hill. "At what age should a man quit work?" *New York Times Magazine*, August 12, 1934, pp. 6–7.

2. "Better management saves older workers." *Business Week*, February 12, 1930, p. 15.

3. "Over forty." Literary Digest 122 (December 12, 1936): 13–14.

4. Benjamin Colby. "Jobless over 45 handicapped." *New York Times*, December 6, 1936, sec. 4, p. 12.

5. *Ibid.*

6. Waldemar Kaempffert. "The man over 40: a machine-age dilemma." *New York Times Magazine*, March 6, 1938, pp. 1–2.

7. "Young and old at the employment office." *Monthly Labor Review* 46 (January, 1938): 12.

8. "Find women of 40 capable in business." *New York Times*, December 8, 1930, p. 6.

9. "Women in industry." *Monthly Labor Review* 39 (August, 1934): 340–342.

10. Anne Petersen. "Challenge issued to remedy plight." *New York Times*, February 20, 1938, sec. 6, p. 5.

11. "Engineer condemns forty-year deadline." *New York Times*, January 12, 1930, p. 16.

12. "We cast off men in prime of life." *New York Times*, March 15, 1931, sec. 3, p. 2.

13. Agnes Camilla Hansen. "Age limit to placement." *Library Journal* 65 (November 15, 1940): 960.

14. "Navy Yard workers oppose age limit." *New York Times*, March 5, 1930, p. 14.

15. "Secretary Hull." *The Nation* 137 (November 15, 1933): 552.

16. "Asks if age bars jobs." *New York Times*, October 31, 1933, p. 17.

17. Ray Giles. "Men over forty preferred." *Reader's Digest* 32 (March, 1938): 97.

18. "The age factor in employment." *Monthly Labor Review* 30 (April, 1930): 782.

19. "Age limit for city service." *New York Times*, February 5, 1937, p. 20; "Civil service limit on age is disputed." *New York Times*, March 17, 1937, p. 6.

20. "Earning while learning." *New York Times*, April 20, 1937, p. 24.

21. "Civil suit heard." *New York Times*, June 15, 1937, p. 48.

22. "Court overrules city age limit." *New York Times*, July 9, 1937, p. 23.

23. "Civil service board asks stay of writ." *New York Times*, July 17, 1937, p. 13.

24. "Civil service board loses appeal on test." *New York Times*, July 18, 1937, p. 22.

25. "Civil service aides held in contempt." *New York Times*, July 21, 1937, p. 6.

26. "Plans to aid middle-aged." *New York Times*, March 13, 1930, p. 46.

27. "Job drive planned by older workers." *New York Times*, March 31, 1930, p. 2; "250 elderly seek jobs daily." *New York Times*, May 18, 1930, sec. 2, p. 18.

28. "Drive to get jobs for aging opens." *New York Times*, February 28, 1937, p. 33.

29. "Middle-aged jobless band to seek work." *New York Times*, June 5, 1937, p. 3.

30. Ray Giles. "Men over 40 preferred." Op. cit., p. 97.

31. "Urge jobs for men over 40." *Business Week*, July 16, 1938, p. 24.

32. Ray Giles. "Hired after forty—Boston style." *Reader's Digest* 33 (December, 1938): 1–3.

33. "Forty Plus club grows." *New York Times*, March 17, 1939, p. 17; "Pittsburgh club finds jobs for many over 40." *New York Times*, July 27, 1939, p. 36.

34. "Job club rejoices at low membership." *New York Times*, January 26, 1941, p. 40.

35. "Job plight of women over 35 is stressed." *New York Times*, May 21, 1940, p. 23.

36. Helen Welshimer. "When employers says 'too old.'" *Independent Woman* 16 (October, 1937): 308; "Over 40 project to advertise." *New York Times*, November 27, 1937, p. 22.

37. "Forty Plus resumes." New York Times, April 6, 1946, p. 19; "Employment and the older worker." *Monthly Labor Review* 62 (March, 1946): 386–390.

38. "Gray hairs in business." *New York Times*, January 13, 1931, p. 26.

39. "The truth about men over 40." *New York Times*, September 29, 1931, p. 20.

40. "Plan job survey for middle-aged." *New York Times*, September 4, 1930, p. 11.

41. "Middle-aged workers." *New York Times*, November 22, 1932, p. 20.

42. "Ford looks to men of 40." *New York Times*, June 25, 1933, p. 20.

43. "Says employers bar many older than 35." *New York Times*, February 8, 1937, p. 6.

44. "Jobs few for older men." *New York Times*, September 18, 1933, p. 2.

45. "Too old for a job at 35." *New York Times*, December 12, 1936, p. 18.

46. Channing Pollock. "Death begins at forty." *The Forum* 98 (November, 1937): 211–216.

47. "After 40." *Literary Digest* 123 (March 27, 1937): 26–27.

48. Frances Maule. "Beat that deadline." *Independent Woman* 19 (March, 1940): 77, 88.

49. Helen Sloan Stetson. "You, too, can find a career." *Independent Woman* 20 (September, 1941): 271.

50. Antoinette Gilman. "Forty leads the field." *The Forum* 90 (November, 1933): 314–316.

51. Clara Belle Thompson and Margaret Lukes Wise. "P.S. she didn't get the job." *Independent Woman* 18 (January, 1939): 9.

52. Otto Pollak. "Discrimination against older workers in industry." *American Journal of Sociology* 50 (September, 1944): 99, 104–105.

53. *Ibid.*, pp. 105–106.

54. "Employment of the older worker." *Monthly Labor Review* 30 (March, 1930): 542.

55. C. R. Dooley. "The large corporation and the older worker." *The Annals of the American Academy of Political & Social Science* 154 (March, 1931): 45, 47.

56. *Ibid.*, pp. 46–47.

57. "Denies men over 40 are barred from jobs." *New York Times*, February 22, 1930, p. 15.

58. "Employment of the older worker." *Monthly Labor Review* 30 (March, 1930): 541–546.

59. *Ibid.*, pp. 544–545.

60. "Age limits in industry in Maryland and California." *Monthly Labor Review* 32 (February, 1931): 284–285.

61. *Ibid.*, pp. 287–290.

62. *Ibid.*, pp. 290–293.

63. "Older men barred from 59% of jobs." *New York Times*, November 19, 1932, p. 17.

64. "Urges provision for older worker." *New York Times*, February 20, 1933, p. 4.

65. "Age limit for jobs found little used." *New York Times*, April 10, 1937, p. 21.

66. Channing Pollock. Op. cit., pp. 212–215.

67. Lucile Eaves. "Discrimination in the employment of older workers in Massachusetts." *Monthly Labor Review* 44 (June, 1937): 1359–1376.

68. *Ibid.*, pp. 1380–1386.

69. Helen Welshimer. Op. cit., pp. 308, 332.

70. "Age of 35 is peak in average hiring." *New York Times*, March 6, 1938, p. 16.

71. Hal Borland. "Does life end at forty?" *New York Times Magazine*, January 21, 1940, p. 2.

72. *Ibid.*, p. 17.

73. Helen Welshimer. Op. cit., pp. 332–333.

74. "Maximum hiring ages in Canadian industry." *Monthly Labor Review* 46 (March, 1938): 662

75. "Problem of the older worker in the United States and Europe." *Monthly Labor Review* 48 (February, 1939): 258–259, 268.

76. *Ibid.*, pp. 260–261, 266.

77. "New York employers shift their accent." *The Commonweal* 31 (April 5, 1940): 503

78. "The age factor in employment." *Monthly Labor Review* 30 (April, 1930): 783; Dwight L. Palmer and John A. Brownell. "Influence of age on employment opportunities." *Monthly Labor Review* 48 (April, 1939): 780.

79. Abraham Epstein. "The older workers." *The Annals of the American Academy of Political & Social Science* 154 (March, 1931): 28–29.

80. Joseph Ernest McAfee. "Middle-aged white collar workers on the economic rack." *The Annals of the American Academy of Political & Social Science* 154 (March, 1931): 32–36.

81. "Causes of discrimination against older workers." *Monthly Labor Review* 46 (May, 1938): 1138–1143.

82. *Ibid.*, p. 1139.

83. Anton J. Carlson. "The older worker." *Hygeia* 21 (May, 1943): 376.

84. Howard A. Meyerhoff. "The older worker." *Scientific Monthly* 59 (November, 1944): 404.

85. "Age factor in industrial accidents." *Monthly Labor Review* 35 (October, 1932): 844–845.

86. "Unemployment of older workers in New York." *Monthly Labor Review* 49 (August, 1939): 365.

87. "Persons in fifties sell more goods, study finds." *New York Times*, September 2, 1937, p. 30.

88. "Employment at 40 kept at '23 rate." *New York Times*, January 8, 1939, p. 2.

89. Amy Hewes. "Employment of older persons in Springfield, Mass., department stores." *Monthly Labor Review* 35 (October, 1932): 773–781.

90. "Perkins asks work for those over 45." *New York Times*, September 7, 1937, p. 2.

91. "Best workers of WPA average 47 in age." *New York Times*, November 8, 1937, p. 1; "Topics of the Times." *New York Times*, November 9, 1937, p. 22.

92. "Workers past 40." *New York Times*, February 26, 1938, p. 14.

93. Frances Perkins. "Too old at 40." *New York Times Magazine*, March 13, 1938, pp. 3, 19, 22.

94. *Ibid.*

95. James M. Mead. "Our older people." *Vital Speeches of the Day* 4 (March 1, 1938): 319–320.

96. Felix Belair, Jr. "Roosevelt scores ban on middle age." *New York Times*, April 28, 1939, p. 1.

97. "Roosevelt asks jobs for citizens over 40." *New York Times*, April 20, 1940, p. 9.

98. "President's appeal for hiring of older workers." *Monthly Labor Review* 52 (May, 1941): 1151–1152.

99. "Employment conditions and unemployment relief." *Monthly Labor Review* 37 (July, 1933): 25.

100. *Ibid.*, p. 26.

101. *Ibid.*, pp. 27–28.

102. "Law held no cure for job loss at 40." *New York Times*, January 20, 1938, p. 11.

103. "Civil service curb on ageing scored." *New York Times*, January 21, 1938, p. 21.

104. "Age curbs upheld by Mayor." *New York Times*, January 22, 1938, p. 16.

105. "Conclusions of New York legislative committee on older workers." *Monthly Labor Review* 51 (July, 1940): 74–79; "Less bias found on middle-aged." *New York Times*, March 21, 1940, p. 12.

106. "Findings on the older employee problem." *The Commonweal* 29 (March 31, 1939): 619.

107. "Employment problems of older workers." *Monthly Labor Review* 48 (May, 1939): 1077–9.

108. "Jobs after forty." *The Nation* 149 (September 23, 1939): 308.

109. "Age discrimination barred in public employment in New Jersey." *Monthly Labor Review* 30 (June, 1930): 1304.

110. "Protection of older workers against discrimination in Louisiana." *Monthly Labor Review* 39 (December, 1934): 1386.

111. "After 40." *Literary Digest* 123 (March 27, 1937): 26–27.

112. Dwight L. Palmer. Op. cit., pp. 767, 780; "Law held no cure for job loss at 40." *New York Times*, January 20, 1938, p. 11.

113. "Unemployment of older workers in New York." *Monthly Labor Review* 49 (August, 1939): 364; "Assembly passes job age waiver." *New York Times*, February 22, 1938,

p. 20; Warren Moscow. "Moratorium bills signed by Lehman." *New York Times*, April 8, 1938, p. 5; "Sees a rush for city jobs." *New York Times*, April 8, 1938, p. 19.

114. "Hiring of older workers by War and Navy Departments." *Monthly Labor Review* 51 (September, 1940): 622.

115. "'40 Plus' at work." *Newsweek* 17 (May 19, 1941): 51–52.

116. Dorothy C. Reid. "Pull yourself together." *Independent Woman* 21 (November, 1942): 333–334.

117. Edsel Ford. "Why we employ aged and handicapped workers." *Saturday Evening Post* 215 (February 6, 1943): 16–17.

118. Ross L. Holman. "Old age and industrial efficiency." *American Mercury* 61 (September, 1945): 311–313.

CHAPTER 4

1. "Employers asked to hire older men." *New York Times*, October 18, 1948, p. 39.

2. "Life begins at Forty Plus." *Business Week*, May 1, 1948, p. 26.

3. "Experience, loyalty, skill—come with age." *Occupations* 27 (February, 1949): 302–304.

4. "Support rallied for handicapped." *New York Times*, November 2, 1948, p. 43.

5. "New move to aid workers over 40." *New York Times*, March 13, 1949, sec. 3, pp. 1, 5.

6. Thomas C. Desmond. "America must age successfully." *Christian Century* 65 (August 18, 1948): 829; "More middle-aged found losing jobs." *New York Times*, April 6, 1949, p. 34.

7. "Avalanche of applications from oldsters answers ad for $34-a-week position." *Occupations* 29 (March, 1951): 469.

8. Alfred R. Zipser, Jr. "Industry revamps personnel policy." *New York Times*, January 28, 1951, sec. 3, p. 7.

9. Louis A. Ferman and Michael Aiken. "Mobility and situational factors in the adjustment of older workers to displacement." *Human Organization* 26 (Winter, 1967): 236.

10. Sumner Marcus and Jon Christoffersen. "Discrimination and the older worker." *Business Horizons* 12 (October, 1969): 88.

11. "After 45 it's hard to get a job." *U.S. News & World Report* 38 (April 1, 1955): 88–89.

12. "Is 45 too old to work? Many doors are shut." *U.S. News & World Report* 39 (September 1955): 107, 109.

13. William Vassallo. "The phony age barrier." *American Mercury* 88 (May, 1959): 76–77.

14. "Old men of 30, crones of 35 now feel first hiring bars because of age." *Business Week*, July 20, 1957, p. 38.

15. Margaret S. Gordon. "The older worker and hiring practices." *Monthly Labor Review* 82 (November, 1959): 1198–1203.

16. "Age limit explained." *New York Times*, August 23, 1958, p. 5.

17. "Business now holds women 'old' at 35." *New York Times*, April 11, 1950, p. 34.

18. Mary K. Pirie. "No one over thirty-five need apply." *Independent Woman* 29 (February, 1950): 42.

19. "U.S. to seek jobs for older women." *New York Times*, October 3, 1956, p. 35.

20. "More jobs taken by older women." *New York Times*, February 25, 1954, p. 27.

21. "The employment of older women." *International Labour Review* 72 (July, 1955): 61–73.

22. "House panel hears complaint of stewardesses." *New York Times*, September 3, 1965, p. 12.

23. Aute L. Carr. "Are ministers obsolete at 50?" *Christian Century* 75 (April 16, 1958): 463.

24. "Life begins at Forty Plus." *Business Week*, May 1, 1948, p. 26.

25. Laurie Johnston. "It's one for all and all for one in job-hunt club for men over 40." *New York Times*, February 20, 1950, p. 27.

26. Raymond Schuessler. "Success begins at Forty Plus." *American Mercury* 82 (April, 1956): 54–56.

27. "City's jobless now are put at 400,000." *New York Times*, February 23, 1950, p. 19.

28. "Unemployment among older workers, 1945–1949." *Labour Gazette* 49 (November, 1949): 1392.

29. "Jobs after forty." *Business Week*, December 17, 1949, pp. 90–91.

30. Thomas C. Desmond. "The plight of the elderly." *Today's Health* 30 (August, 1952): 19–20.

31. "Baruch opposes age hiring law." *New York Times*, December 10, 1956, p. 33.

32. "Business leaders chided on 'over-45 scrap pile.'" *New York Times*, April 30, 1950, p. 9.

33. H. L. Douse. "Discrimination against older workers." *International Labour Review* 83 (April, 1961): 349–351, 366.

34. "The 'aged'—management's dilemma." *Office Management* 21 (January, 1960): 36.

35. "Does business discriminate against employees above 45?" *Business Management* 31 (November, 1966): 22–24.

36. "Age closes jobs to many in state." *New York Times*, March 17, 1948, p. 26.

37. Howard A. Rusk. "Retiring of workers at 65 producing vital problems." *New York Times*, April 23, 1950, p. 51.

38. Charles E. Odell. "Employment of older workers." *Occupations* 30 (October, 1951): 15–18.

39. "Over-40 hiring bias tied to relief load." *New York Times*, May 28, 1951, p. 23.

40. Albert J. Abrams. "Barriers to the employment of older workers." *Annals of the American Academy of Political & Social Science* 279 (January, 1952): 62.

41. *Ibid.*, pp. 62–63.

42. *Ibid.*, pp. 63, 65.

43. *Ibid.*, pp. 64, 66.

44. "Hirers approve older workers." *U.S. News & World Report* 35 (November 13, 1953): 99.

45. "Jobs for older workers." *New York Times*, September 13, 1954, p. 22.

46. Thomas C. Desmond. "Wanted: jobs for the forty-plus." *Today's Health* 34 (October, 1956): 32.

47. "Workers past 45 face lack of jobs." *New York Times*, March 10, 1957, p. 111.

48. "Age alone no criterion of job performance." *Personnel & Guidance Journal* 35 (December, 1956): 205.

49. John I. Saks. "Status in the labor market." *Monthly Labor Review* 80 (January, 1957): 16–19.

50. Abraham Stahler. "Job problems and their solution." *Monthly Labor Review* 80 (January, 1957): 22–23.

51. *Ibid.*, pp. 23–24.

52. *Ibid.*, pp. 24–26.

53. "Older workers face hiring problems." *Office Management* 19 (June, 1958): 8, 12.

54. C. E. Grinder. "Research roundup." *Office Executive* 33 (July, 1958): 39.

55. *Ibid.*, pp. 39–40.

56. C. E. Grinder. "Research roundup." *Office Executive* 34 (September, 1959): 62–63.

57. "Hiring policies, prejudices, and the older worker." *Monthly Labor Review* 88 (August, 1965): 968.

58. *Ibid.*, pp. 968–969.

59. "Over forty." *The Economist* 176 (August 20, 1955): 608.

60. "Employment of older men and women." *Labour Gazette* 57 (September, 1957): 1054–1058.

61. "Older men at work." *The Economist* 117 (December 31, 1955): 1196–1197.

62. "Progress in dealing with problem of older worker." *Labour Gazette* 48 (January/February, 1948): 7.

63. Harold C. Hudson. "The older worker." *Canadian Welfare* 23 (January 15, 1948): 20, 23.

64. "The problem of the older worker." *Canadian Unionist* 27 (April, 1953): 117–118.

65. Sidney Katz. "Sheltered employment for older people." *Canadian Welfare* 31 (May 1, 1955): 38–39.

66. Raymond Varela. "Over 40 ... are you really too old?" *Financial Post* 51 (November 30, 1957): 44.

67. Winston O. Cameron. "Men over 40 need not apply." *Western Business & Industry* 38 (April, 1964): 62.

68. George Harry. "The problem of job-hunters over forty." *Industrial Canada* 55 (May, 1954): 59, 62, 64.

69. "Employment of the older worker." *Canadian Welfare* 31 (May 1, 1955): 36–37.

70. Robert Majoribanks. "Pension plans block over-35 job hunters." *Financial Post* 53 (February 21, 1959): 38.

71. "Ont. bans age discrimination." *Canadian Labour* 11 (May, 1966): 116.

72. "The problem of the employment of older workers." *International Labour Review* 69 (June, 1954): 594–597.

73. *Ibid.*, pp. 598–600.

74. *Ibid.*, p. 600

75. *Ibid.*, p. 601.

76. *Ibid.*, p. 602.

77. *Ibid.*, pp. 602–604.

78. *Ibid.*, p. 605.

79. *Ibid.*, pp. 610–611.

80. *Ibid.*, pp. 617–618.

81. Anna-Stina Ericson. "The employment of older workers." *Monthly Labor Review* 83 (March, 1960): 270–274.

82. J. W. Willard. "Employment problems of older workers." *Public Affairs* 11 (July, 1948): 135–139.

83. "Workers over 45 backed as able." *New York Times*, May 26, 1957, p. 76.

84. Leonard M. Leonard. "Why don't they hire older workers?" *Science Digest* 40 (September, 1956): 53–57.

85. "At 45, a pension liability?" *Business Week*, November 5, 1949, pp. 72, 74.

86. Peter F. Drucker. "The mirage of pensions." *Harper's Magazine* 200 (February, 1950): 31–32.

87. "Pensions vs. jobs for older workers." *U.S. News & World Report* 28 (May 5, 1950): 18–19.

88. A. R. Mosher. "The problem of employment for older workers." *Canadian Unionist* 26 (May, 1952): 139.

89. "It costs too much." *Business Week*, May 9, 1953, p. 178.

90. J. Gordon Coburn. "Pensions as a stumbling block to employment." *Industrial Canada* 55 (September, 1954): 57–59.

91. "Eisenhower cites pensions problem." *New York Times*, January 21, 1955, p. 9.

92. "Is 45 too old to work? Many doors are shut." *U.S. News & World Report* 39 (September 10, 1955): 109.

93. J. E. McMahon. "Older persons held eligible for hiring." *New York Times*, October 21, 1956, sec. 3, pp. 1, 11.

94. "After 45 it's hard to get a job." *U.S. News & World Report* 38 (April 1, 1955): 90–91.

95. Burt K. Scanlan. "Effects of pension plans on labor mobility and hiring older workers." *Personnel Journal* 44 (January, 1965): 29–33.

96. *Ibid.*, pp. 33–34.

97. Alfred R. Zipser Jr. "Insurance no bar to older workers." *New York Times*, April 3, 1949, sec. 3, p. 9.

98. Joseph Arkin. "Are older workers too expensive?" *Business Management* 22 (May, 1962): 55–57.

99. "Plight of the over-45." *America* 93 (September 24, 1955): 606.

100. Ronald Schiller. "Help wanted: for the 40-plus." *Reader's Digest* 71 (July 1957): 157–8.

101. "New views on older worker." *Science Digest* 23 (March, 1948): 29–30.

102. William H. Bowers. "An appraisal of worker characteristics as related to age." *Journal of Applied Psychology* 36 (October, 1952): 296, 300.

103. "Labor Dept. comes to aid of oldsters with data on work efficiency." *Business Week*, December 29, 1956, p. 70.

104. Charles E. Odell. "Productivity of the older worker." *Personnel & Guidance Journal* 37 (December, 1958): 289.

105. Lucien R. Sellett. "Age and absenteeism." *Personnel Journal* 43 (June, 1964): 309–313.

106. Jacob Tuckman and Irving Lorge. "Attitudes toward older workers." *Journal of Applied Psychology* 36 (June, 1952): 149–153.

107. Jacob Tuckman. "Experts' biases about the older worker." *Science* 115 (June 20, 1952): 685–686.

108. *Ibid.*, pp. 686–687.

109. Wayne Kirchner, Theodore Lindblom and Donald G. Paterson. "Attitudes toward the employment of older people." *Journal of Applied Psychology* 36 (June, 1952): 154–155.

110. "The older worker." *Time* 62 (October 19, 1953): 100.

111. "Tobin attacks age ban." *New York Times*, January 24, 1952, p. 29.

112. "Mitchell attacks over-45 work ban." *New York Times*, December 22, 1954, p. 25.

113. James P. Mitchell. "After 45—are you too old to work?" *Collier's* 135 (January 7, 1955): 38–40.

114. James P. Mitchell. "Life doesn't end at 45." *Catholic World* 180 (January, 1955): 246–249.

115. "65,000,000 jobs set U.S. record." *New York Times*, September 5, 1955, pp. 1, 6.

116. "Job plea for mid-age." *New York Times*, February 21, 1957, p. 23.

117. Warren Weaver Jr. "Harriman policy on aging scored." *New York Times*, October 3, 1957, p. 31.

118. "Desmond asks steps to aid older worker." *New York Times*, September 24, 1948, p. 27.

119. "Keeping older men from jobs scored." *New York Times*, December 10, 1948, p. 29.

120. "Age job bias law urged for state." *New York Times*, December 15, 1950, p. 50.

121. Thomas C. Desmond. "Let's give the older worker a chance." *Hygeia* 27 (February, 1949): 92.

122. Damon Stetson. "Prejudice noted in jobs for aging." *New York Times*, December 11, 1959, p. 30.

123. "Hiring gain is found for older workers." *New York Times*, August 25, 1961, p. 49.

124. Alfred R. Zipser Jr. "State law to aid older workers is off until 1951 session in Albany." *New York Times*, March 5, 1950, sec. 3, p. 1.

125. "State ban on barring jobs to aged put off." *New York Times*, December 9, 1951, sec. 5, p. 8.

126. Warren Weaver Jr. "State urged to bar age bias in hiring." *New York Times*, January 27, 1957, pp. 1, 60.

127. "Governor opposes ban on age bias." *New York Times*, December 11, 1957, p. 35.

128. Warren Weaver Jr. "Harriman signs a ban on age bias." *New York Times*, April 16, 1958, p. 35.

129. "The age discrimination law." *New York Times*, June 16, 1958, p. 22.

130. "New age-bias law draws objections." *New York Times*, June 19, 1958, p. 31.

131. "Law on age assailed." *New York Times*, June 20, 1958, p. 46.

132. "Job forms soften questions on age." *New York Times*, June 30, 1958, p. 21.

133. "S.C.A.D. finds gains in fight on age bar." *New York Times*, November 8, 1959, p. 13.

134. Charles Grutzner. "Age limit on jobs yielding slowly." *New York Times*, January 17, 1960, pp. 1, 78.

135. *Ibid.*

136. Warren Weaver Jr. "State puts curbs on authorities." *New York Times*, April 20, 1961, p. 21.

137. "Unions act to save older men's jobs." *New York Times*, November 27, 1949, p. 83.

138. Thomas C. Desmond. "Wanted: jobs for the forty-plus." Op. cit., p. 34.

139. Margaret S. Gordon. Op. cit., p. 1198.

140. Charles E. Odell. "Productivity of the older worker." Op. cit., p. 289.

141. Thomas C. Desmond. "Older-worker laws: good or bad." *Today's Health* 40 (October, 1962): 27, 68, 70.

142. Robert J. Fjerstad. "Is it economical to hire the over forty-five worker?" *Personnel Administration* 28 (March/April, 1965): 22, 26.

143. "Old before their time." *America* 113 (August 14, 1965): 147–148.

144. "Johnson issues job order banning age discrimination." *New York Times*, February 14, 1964, p. 35.

145. John Herbers. "House told laws are needed on age discrimination in jobs." *New York Times* July 1, 1965, p. 14.

CHAPTER 5

1. Sumner Marcus and Jon Christoffersen. "Discrimination and the older worker." *Business Horizons* 12 (October, 1969): 84.

2. *Ibid.*, pp. 84, 88.

3. *Ibid.*, pp. 84, 86.

4. *Ibid.*, p. 86.

5. "Job law signed." *New York Times*, December 17, 1967, p. 62.

6. "No more 'too old for job.'" *U.S. News & World Report* 64 (May 27, 1968): 87.

7. "Helping older job seekers—how federal law will work." *U.S. News & World Report* 65 (July 1, 1968): 63.

8. Richard J. Levine. "Age bias comes under fire." *Supervisory Management* 13 (August, 1968): 34–36.

9. "Agency lists cases of bias against workers over age." *New York Times*, December 18, 1971, p. 60.

10. George J. McManus. "You are only as old as the company feels you should be." *Iron Age* 211 (March 1, 1973): 40–41.

11. Eileen Shanahan. "Oil concern to pay age-bias settlement." *New York Times*, May 17, 1974, pp. 1, 8.

12. "Fired for being 'too old'? Government is on your side." *U.S. News & World Report* 76 (June 3, 1974): 76; "Age discrimination moves into the limelight." *Business Week*, June 15, 1974, p. 104.

13. "Age discrimination moves into the limelight." *Business Week*, June 15, 1974, p. 104.

14. "The courts reinterpret old-age discrimination." *Business Week*, February 24, 1975, p. 91.

15. Lawrence Stessin. "The ax and older workers." *New York Times*, June 23, 1974, sec. 3, p. 3; "The courts reinterpret old-age discrimination." *Business Week*, February 24, 1975, p. 91.

16. "Mayor's order bans sex discrimination on jobs." *New York Times*, August 25, 1970, p. 15.

17. "Thinking young." *Newsweek* 83 (April 29, 1974): 80.

18. Francis J. Lavoie. "The plight of the over-40 engineer." *Management Review* 60 (February, 1971): 27–29.

19. C. Richard Williams. "Is there a life after forty?" *Advertising Age* 43 (March 6, 1972): 40, 42.

20. "Job applicant, 44, wins bias case." *New York Times*, August 9, 1975, p. 21.

21. Gerard Tavernier. "The age of discrimination." *International Management* 34 (September, 1979): 19.

22. Bob Greene. "The high price of joblessness." *Esquire* 99 (June, 1983): 427–428.

23. Dawn Raffel. "The search for jobs." *50 Plus* 24 (November, 1984): 72, 74.

24. Robert M. Hutchens. "Do job opportunities decline with age?" *Industrial and Labor Relations Review* 42 (October, 1988): 89, 92, 98.

25. Roy Hoopes. "On the outside looking in." *Modern Maturity* 32 (June/July, 1989): 32, 35, 39.

26. Rod Benson. "Drowning pool?" *Columbia Journalism Review* 30 (May/June, 1991): 13–14.

27. Marilyn Webb. "How old is too old?" *New York* 26 (March 29, 1993): 67.

28. *Ibid.*, pp. 67–70.

29. Lori Bongiorno. "Jobless at 50? It's not hopeless." *Business Week*, December 20, 1993, p. 82.

30. Esther B. Fein. "Frustrating fight for acceptance." *New York Times*, January 4, 1994, pp. B1, B6.

31. "Older and wiser may not help in job hunt." *Management Review* 83 (June, 1994): 6.

32. Genevieve Capowski. "Ageism: the new diversity issue." *Management Review* 83 (October, 1994): 11–15.

33. Ann Monroe. "Getting rid of the gray." *Mother Jones* 21 (July/August, 1996): 29.

34. Margaret Morganroth Gullette. "The end of the workday—II." *The Nation* 266 (January 5, 1998): 21–22.

35. Nina Munk. "Finished at forty." *Fortune* 139 (February 1, 1999): 50.

36. *Ibid.*, pp. 52–54+.

37. William McNaught and Michael C. Barth. "Are older workers 'good buys'? A case study of Days Inns of America." *Sloan Management Review* 33 (Spring, 1992): 53.

38. Peggy Butler. "Problems of the older worker." *Labour Gazette* 70 (November, 1970): 780–1.

39. "And now a kind word for age discrimination." *Fortune* 113 (February 17, 1986): 120.

40. "Ageism again." *Fortune* 113 (March 3, 1986): 92.

41. Daniel Seligman. "The case against old age." *Fortune* 114 (November 10, 1986): 163, 166.

42. Daniel Seligman. "Slipping." *Fortune* 122 (December 17, 1990): 183–184.

43. Gary S. Becker. "What really hurts the job market for older workers." *Business Week*, October 6, 1986, p. 15.

44. Gary S. Becker. "What keeps older workers off the job rolls?" *Business Week*, March 19, 1990, p. 18.

45. "Senate panel on aging, after a 2-year-study, says retirement problem has reached crisis stage." *New York Times*, January 18, 1971, p. 11.

46. Nadine Brozan. "Job discrimination charged by women workers." *New York Times*, March 5, 1976, p. 22.

47. Patricia L. Kasschau. "Age and race discrimination reported by middle-aged and older persons." *Social Forces* 55 (March, 1977): 727–736.

48. "Rate for older workers soar." *New York Times*. October 8, 1982, p. B7.

49. Roy Hoopes. "Working late: the railroad to retirement." *Modern Maturity* 32 (February/March, 1989): 42–44.

50. Gillian Sandford. "Lawmakers seeking to fortify older workers' protection." *Congressional Quarterly Weekly Report* 47 (April 22, 1989): 891.

51. Susan Dentzer. "Do the elderly want to work?" *U.S. News & World Report* 108 (May 14, 1990): 49.

52. "Job applicants face age bias, study finds." *New York Times*, February 23, 1994, p. A15.

53. Carolyn Magnuson. "You're too old!" *Good Housekeeping* 219 (October, 1994): 242, 244.

54. Karen Leppel and Suzanne Heller Clain. "The effect of increases in the level of unemployment on older workers." *Applied Economics* 27 (October, 1995): 901–904.

55. Richard W. Johnson and David Neumark. "Age discrimination, job separations, and employment status of older workers." *The Journal of Human Resources* 32 (Fall, 1997): 779–793.

56. "Middle-aged misfits." *Labour Gazette* 75 (March, 1975): 156–157.

57. Gerard Tavernier. "The age of discrimination." Op. cit., pp. 19–20.

59. "The age factor—does it really lead to job discrimination." *International Management* 37 (April, 1982): 14–16.

60. *Ibid.*

61. *Ibid.*

62. Guy Standing. "Labour flexibility and older worker marginalisation." *International Labour Review* 125 (May-June, 1986): 329–331.

63. *Ibid.*, pp. 332–333.

64. *Ibid.*, pp. 343–346.

65. Diana Cornish. "Bias against older workers is absurd." *Financial Post* 85 (July 8, 1991): 12.

66. James Krohe, Jr. "An old story." *Across the Board* 28 (November, 1991): 35, 37.

67. Kene Henkens, Maarten Sprengers and Frits Tazelaar. "Unemployment and the older worker in the Netherlands." *Aging and Society* 16 (September, 1996): 562–568.

68. Mary Riddell. "Mary Riddell." *New Statesman* 127 (February 6, 1998): 13.

69. John S. Heywood, Lok-Sang Ho and Xiangdong Wei. "The determinants of hiring older workers: evidence from Hong Kong." *Industrial and Labor Relations Review* 52 (April, 1999): 444–458.

70. Thomas J. Wiencek. "Washington targets benefits in fight against age discrimination. *Management Review* 80 (August, 1991): 31.

71. Lenore Schiff. "Is health care a job killer?" *Fortune* 125 (April 6, 1992): 30.

72. Richard Ross. "One way to get good workers." *Nation's Business* 65 (September, 1977): 39–40.

73. Jim Peters. "Alternative labor pool." *Restaurant Business* 86 (September 1, 1987): 183–184.

74. Frederick J. Demicco and Robert D. Reid. "Older workers." *The Cornell Hotel and Restaurant Administration Quarterly* 29 (May, 1988): 56–59.

75. James Krohe Jr. "Days Inns: older workers need apply." *Across the Board* 28 (November, 1991): 38–39; William McNaught and Michael C. Barth. Op. cit., pp. 53–63.

76. *Ibid.*

77. Jeffery C. Rubin. "McSeniors." *Time* 146 (December 4, 1995): 25.

78. Marjorie Coeyman. "Two takes on seniors." *Restaurant Business* 95 (March 1, 1996): 58.

79. D. N. Williams. "You can trust anybody over 50." *Iron Age* 204 (July 10, 1969): 64.

80. Norman Root. "Injuries at work are fewer among older employees." *Monthly Labor Review* 104 (March, 1981): 30–31.

81. Benson Rosen and Thomas H. Jerdee. "The nature of job-related age stereotypes." *Journal of Applied Psychology* 61 (April, 1976): 180–183.

82. James C. Crew. "Age stereotypes as a function of race." *Academy of Management Journal* 27 (June, 1984): 431–435.

83. Benson Rosen and Thomas H. Jerdee. "The influence of age stereotypes on managerial decisions." *Journal of Applied Psychology* 61 (August, 1976): 428–429.

84. Benson Rosen and Thomas H. Jerdee. "Too old or not too old." *Harvard Business Review* 55 (November, 1977): 98, 105.

85. James F. Haefner. "Race, age, sex, and competence as factors in employer selection of the disadvantaged." *Journal of Applied Psychology* 62 (April, 1977): 199–202.

86. James E. Haefner. "Sources of discrimination among employees: a survey investigation." *Journal of Applied Psychology* 62 (June, 1977): 265, 268.

87. James S. Perry. "College students' attitudes toward workers' competence and age." *Psychological Reports* 42 (June, 1978): 1319, pt. 2.

88. "Thirty years later: attitudes toward the employment of older workers." *Journal of Applied Psychology* 71 (August, 1986): 515–517.

89. Katherine Gay. "The other side of the hill." *CGA Magazine* 32 (July/August, 1998): 24.

90. Elizabeth M. Fowler. "Protection for older workers." *New York Times*, April 18, 1979, p. D19.

91. Julia Stone. "Age discrimination in employment act: a review of recent changes." *Monthly Labor Review* 103 (March, 1980): 33–35.

92. "Wounded executives fight back on age bias." *Business Week*, July 21, 1980, p. 109–110.

93. William R. Nelson. "Age discrimination in police employment." *Journal of Police Science and Administration* 9 (December, 1981): 428–429, 439.

94. Warren Weaver Jr. "Age discrimination charges found in sharp rise in U.S." *New York Times*, February 22, 1982, p. A12.

95. Tony Mauro. "Age bias charges: increasing problem." *Nation's Business* 71 (April, 1983): 44–46.

96. Mark Reiter. "Age discrimination in the workplace." *50 Plus* 25 (May, 1985): 18.

97. Jack Mitchell. "Age bias: the uphill battle." *50 Plus* 27 (March, 1987): 32, 95.

98. Deidre Fanning. "Employer beware." *Forbes* 139 (May 18, 1987): 82, 86.

99. Frank Greve. "Age bias: the uphill battle." *50 Plus* 27 (March, 1987): 35.

100. Ted Gest. "When you get pushed out early." *U.S. News & World Report* 104 (March 7, 1988): 71.

101. Roy Hoopes. "The case of the myopic watchdog." *Modern Maturity* 32 (April/May, 1989): 36–39+.

102. Viveca Novak. "Doubting Thomas." *The Nation* 250 (March 26, 1990): 405.

103. Barbara L. Bessey and Srijati M. Ananda. "Age discrimination in employment." *Research on Aging* 13 (December, 1991): 415, 422.

104. Robert B. Maxwell. "A silver jubilee for the ADEA." *Modern Maturity* 35 (April/May, 1992): 8–9.

105. Carolyn Magnuson. "You're too old!" Op. cit., pp. 137, 242.

106. Marianne Lavelle. "On the edge of age discrimination." *New York Times Magazine*, March 9, 1997, pp. 67–69.

107. Nina Munk. "Suspect age bias? Try proving it." *Fortune* 139 (February 1, 1999): 58.

Bibliography

Abrams, Albert J. "Barriers to the employment of older workers." *Annals of the American Academy of Political and Social Science* 297 (January, 1952): 62–71.

"Accidents to older workers: relation of age to extent of disability." *Monthly Labor Review* 29 (October, 1929): 841–843.

"After 40." *Literary Digest* 123 (March 27, 1937): 26–27.

"After 45 it's hard to get a job." *U.S. News & World Report* 38 (April 1, 1955): 88–91.

"Age alone no criterion of job performance." *Personnel & Guidance Journal* 35 (December, 1956): 204–205.

"Age closes jobs to many in state." *New York Times*, March 17, 1948, p. 26.

"Age curbs upheld by Mayor." *New York Times*, January 22, 1938, p. 16.

"Age discrimination barred in public employment in New Jersey." *Monthly Labor Review* 30 (June, 1930): 1304.

"The age discrimination law." *New York Times*, June 16, 1958, p. 22.

"Age discrimination moves into the limelight." *Business Week*, June 15, 1974, p. 104.

"Age distribution of workers in a small group of establishments." *Monthly Labor Review* 29 (November, 1929): 1060–1062.

"The age factor—does it really lead to job discrimination." *Industrial Management* 37 (April, 1982): 14–16.

"The age factor in employment." *Monthly Labor Review* 30 (April, 1930): 781–785.

"Age factor in industrial accidents." *Monthly Labor Review* 35 (October, 1932): 844–845.

"Age job bias law urged for state." *New York Times*, December 15, 1950, p. 50.

"Age limit explained." *New York Times*, August 23, 1958, p. 5.

"Age limit for city service." *New York Times*, February 5, 1937, p. 20.

"Age limit for jobs found little used." *New York Times*, April 10, 1937, p. 21.

"Age limits in industry in Maryland and California." *Monthly Labor Review* 32 (February, 1931): 284–293.

"Age limits on employment by American manufacturers." *Monthly Labor Review* 28 (May, 1929): 1024–1025.

"Age of 35 is peak in average hiring." *New York Times*, March 6, 1938, p. 16.

197

"The 'aged'—management's dilemma." *Office Management* 21 (January, 1960): 35–37.
"Aged office boys go to aid of business." *New York Times*, November 29, 1916, p. 4.
"Ageism again." *Fortune* 113 (March 3, 1986): 92.
"Agency lists cases of bias against workers over age." *New York Times*, December 18, 1971, p. 60.
"And now, a kind word for age discrimination." *Fortune* 113 (February 17, 1986): 120.
"The anti-age limit league." *New York Times*, October 20, 1905, p. 8.
Arkin, Joseph. "Are older workers too expensive?" *Business Management* 22 (May, 1962): 55–57.
"Asks if age bars jobs." *New York Times*, October 31, 1933, p. 17.
"Assembly passes job age waiver." *New York Times*, February 22, 1938, p. 20.
"At 45, a pension liability?" *Business Week*, November 5, 1949, pp. 72, 74.
"Avalanche of applications from oldsters answers ad for $34-a-week position." *Occupations* 29 (March, 1951): 469.
"Baruch opposes age hiring law." *New York Times*, December 10, 1956, p. 33.
Bean, B. C. "Is your job keeping up with your age?" *American Magazine* 83 (June, 1917): 44–45.
Becker, Gary S. "What keeps older workers off the job rolls?" *Business Week*, March 19, 1990, p. 18.
Becker, Gary S. "What really hurts the job market for older workers." *Business Week*, October 6, 1986, p. 15.
Belair, Felix Jr. "Roosevelt scores ban on middle age." *New York Times*, April 28, 1939, pp. 1, 13.
Benson, Rod. "Drowning pool?" *Columbia Journalism Review* 30 (May/June, 1991): 13–14.
Bessey, Barbara L. and Srijati M. Ananda. "Age discrimination in employment." *Research on Aging* 13 (December, 1991): 413–457.
"Best workers of WPA average 47 in age." *New York Times*, November 8, 1937, p. 1.
"Better management saves older workers." *Business Week*, February 12, 1930, p. 15.
Bongiorno, Lori. "Jobless at 50? It's not hopeless." *Business Week*, December 20, 1993, pp. 82–83.
Borland, Hal. "Does life end at forty?" *New York Times*, January 21, 1940, pp. 1–2, 17.
Bowers, William H. "An appraisal of worker characteristics as related to age." *Journal of Applied Psychology* 36 (October, 1952): 296–300.
Brozan, Nadine. "Job discrimination charged by women workers." *New York Times*, March 5, 1976, p. 22.
"Business leaders chided on 'over-45 scrap pile.'" *New York Times*, April 30, 1950, p. 9.
"Business now holds women 'old' at 35." *New York Times*, April 11, 1950, p. 34.
Butler, Peggy. "Problems of the older worker." *Labour Gazette* 70 (November, 1970): 775–782.
"Calls age a tragedy." *New York Times*, September 3, 1928, p. 24.
Cameron, Winston O. "Men over 40 need not apply." *Western Business & Industry* 38 (April, 1964): 62–63.
Capowski, Genevieve. "Ageism: the new diversity issue." *Management Review* 83 (October, 1994): 10–15.
"Caring for the aged." *New York Times*, November 8, 1927, p. 26.
Carlson, Anton J. "The older worker." *Hygeia* 21 (May, 1943): 338–339+.
Carr, Aute L. "Are ministers obsolete at 50?" *Christian Century* 75 (April 16, 1958): 463–464.
"Causes of discrimination against older workers." *Monthly Labor Review* 46 (May, 1938): 1138–1143.
Chase, Stuart. "Laid off at forty." *Harper's Magazine* 159 (August, 1929): 340–347.
"City's jobless now are put at 400,000." *New York Times*, February 23, 1950, p. 19.
"Civil service aides held in contempt." *New York Times*, July 21, 1937, p. 6.
"Civil service board asks stay of writ." *New York Times*, July 17, 1937, p. 13.
"Civil service board loses appeal on test." *New York Times*, July 18, 1937, p. 22.

"Civil service curb on ageing scored." *New York Times*, January 21, 1938, p. 21.

"Civil service limit on age is disputed." *New York Times*, March 17, 1937, p. 6.

"Civil suit heard." *New York Times*, June 15, 1937, p. 48.

Coburn, J. Gordon. "Pensions as a stumbling block to employment." *Industrial Canada* 55 (September, 1954): 57–59.

Coeyman, Marjorie. "Two takes on seniors." *Restaurant Business* 95 (March 1, 1996): 56–58.

Colby, Benjamin. "Jobless over 45 handicapped." *New York Times*, December 6, 1936, sec. 4, p. 12.

Colvin, Fred H. "Shall we chloroform 'em at 40?" *Magazine of Business* 56 (July, 1929): 59–60.

"Conclusions of New York legislative committee on older workers." *Monthly Labor Review* 51 (July, 1940): 74–79.

Cope, Michael. "What role for the older and displaced worker." *Executive* 6 (January, 1964): 22–25.

Cornish, Diana. "Bias against older workers is absurd." *Financial Post* 85 (July 8, 1991): 12.

"Court overrules city age limit." *New York Times*, July 9, 1937, p. 23.

"The courts reinterpret old-age discrimination." *Business Week*, February 24, 1975, p. 91.

Crew, James C. "Age stereotypes as a function of race." *Academy of Management Journal* 27 (June, 1984): 431–435.

Davis, James J. "'Old age' at fifty." *Monthly Labor Review* 26 (June, 1928): 1095–1100.

"Davis says worker is at peak at 60." *New York Times*, January 29, 1928, p. 20.

"Declare pretty girls keep them from jobs." *New York Times*, September 4, 1927, p. 13.

Demicco, Frederick J. and Robert D. Reid. "Older workers." *The Cornell Hotel and Restaurant Administration Quarterly* 29 (May, 1988): 56–61.

"Denies men over 40 are barred from jobs." *New York Times*, February 22, 1930, p. 15.

Dentzer, Susan. "Do the elderly want to work?" *U.S. News & World Report* 108 (May 14, 1990): 48–50.

"Desmond asks steps to aid older worker." *New York Times*, September 24, 1948, p. 27.

Desmond, Thomas C. "America must age successfully." *Christian Century* 65 (August 18, 1948): 828–830.

Desmond, Thomas C. "Let's give the older worker a chance." *Hygeia* 27 (February, 1949): 92–93+.

Desmond, Thomas C. "Older-worker laws: good or bad." *Today's Health* 40 (October, 1962): 27+.

Desmond, Thomas C. "The plight of the elderly." *Today's Health* 30 (August, 1952): 18–22.

Desmond, Thomas C. "Wanted: jobs for the forty-plus." *Today's Health* 34 (October, 1956): 32–35+.

"Disadvantages of age." *New York Times*, July 29, 1927, p. 18.

"Does business discriminate against employees above 45?" *Business Management* 31 (November, 1966): 22–24.

Dooley, C. R. "The large corporation and the older worker." *The Annals of the American Academy of Political & Social Science* 154 (March, 1931): 45–48.

Douse, H. L. "Discrimination against older workers." *International Labour Review* 83 (April, 1961): 349–368.

"Dr. Osler's theory refuted." *New York Times*, June 9, 1908, p. 5.

"The drawbacks to age." *New York Times*, April 29, 1915, p. 12.

"Drive to get jobs for aging opens." *New York Times*, February 28, 1937, p. 33.

Drucker, Peter F. "The mirage of pensions." *Harper's Magazine* 200 (February, 1950): 31–38.

"Earning while learning." *New York Times*, April 20, 1937, p. 24.

Eaves, Lucile. "Discrimination in the employment of older workers in Massachusetts." *Monthly Labor Review* 44 (June, 1937): 1359–1386.

"Eisenhower cites pensions problem." *New York Times*, January 21, 1955, p. 9.

"Elderly men hired as office boys." *New York Times*, November 30, 1916, p. 12.

"Employers asked to hire older men." *New York Times*, October 18, 1948, p. 39.

"Employment age limit survey is undertaken." *New York Times*, May 26, 1929, sec. 10, p. 11.

"Employment and adjustment of the older worker." *Monthly Labor Review* 29 (December, 1929): 1255–1258.

"Employment and the older worker." *Monthly Labor Review* 62 (March, 1946): 386–396.

"Employment at 40 kept at '23 rate." *New York Times*, January 8, 1939, p. 2.

"Employment conditions and unemployment relief." *Monthly Labor Review* 37 (July, 1933): 25–29.

"Employment of older men and women." *Labour Gazette* 57 (September, 1957): 1054–1058.

"The employment of older women." *International Labour Review* 72 (July, 1955): 61–77.

"Employment of the older worker." *Monthly Labor Review* 30 (March, 1930): 541–546.

"Employment of the older worker." *Canadian Welfare* 31 (May 1, 1955): 35–37.

"Employment problems of older workers." *Monthly Labor Review* 48 (May, 1939): 1077–1081.

"Engineer condemns forty-year deadline." *New York Times*, January 12, 1930, p. 16.

Epstein, Abraham. "The older workers." *The Annals of the American Academy of Political & Social Science* 154 (March, 1931): 28–31.

Ericson, Anna-Stina. "The employment of older workers." *Monthly Labor Review* 83 (March, 1960): 270–274.

"Experience, loyalty, skill—come with age." *Occupations* 27 (February, 1949): 301–306.

"Expresses a forlorn hope." *New York Times*, November 11, 1910, p. 8.

Fanning, Deidre. "Employer beware." *Forbes* 139 (May 18, 1987): 82, 86.

Fein, Esther B. "Frustrating fight for acceptance." *New York Times*, January 4, 1994, pp. B1, B6.

Ferman, Louis A. and Michael Aiken. "Mobility and situational factors in the adjustment of older workers to displacement." *Human Organization* 26 (Winter, 1967): 235–241.

"Few come to Mr. Action." *New York Times*, November 19, 1927, p. 19.

"Find women of 40 capable in business." *New York Times*, December 8, 1930, p. 6.

"Finding jobs for the middle-aged." *New York Times*, August 15, 1927, p. 16.

"Findings on the older employee problem." *The Commonweal* 29 (March 31, 1939): 618–619.

"Finds apathy bars aid to middle-aged." *New York Times*, May 12, 1928, p. 19.

"Fired for being 'too old'? Government is on your side." *U.S. News & World Report* 76 (June 3, 1974): 75–76.

Fjerstad, Robert J. "Is it economical to hire the over forty-five worker?" *Personnel Administration* 28 (March/April, 1965): 22–28.

"For the middle-aged unemployed." *New York Times*, July 13, 1929, p. 14.

Ford, Edsel. "Why we employ aged and handicapped workers." *Saturday Evening Post* 215 (February 6, 1943): 16–17.

"Ford looks to men of 40." *New York Times*, June 25, 1933, p. 20.

"Ford says he prefers employes, 35 to 60." *New York Times*, June 29, 1929, p. 3.

"'40 plus' at work." *Newsweek* 17 (May 19, 1941): 51–52.

"Forty Plus club grows." *New York Times*, March 17, 1939, p. 17.

"Forty Plus resumes." *New York Times*, April 6, 1946, p. 19.

Fowler, Elizabeth M. "Protection for older workers." *New York Times*, April 18, 1979, p. D19.

Gay, Katherine. "The other side of the hill." *CGA Magazine* 32 (July/August, 1998): 23–29.

Gest, Ted. "When you get pushed out too early." *U.S. News & World Report* 104 (March 7, 1988): 71.

Giles, Ray. "Hired after forty—Boston style." *Reader's Digest* 33 (December, 1938): 1–5.

Giles, Ray. "Men over forty preferred." *Reader's Digest* 32 (March, 1938): 97–100.

Gilman, Antoinette. "Forty leads the field." *The Forum* 90 (November, 1933): 314–316.

"Gives men of 40 no hope." *New York Times*, November 6, 1911, p. 6.

Gordon, Margaret S. "The older worker and hiring practices." *Monthly Labor Review* 82 (November, 1959): 1198–1205.

"Governor opposes ban on age bias." *New York Times*, December 11, 1957, p. 35.

Graebner, William. "Help wanted: age discrimination in Buffalo, New York, 1895–1935." *New York History* 65 (October, 1984): 349–365.

"Gray hairs in business." *New York Times*, January 13, 1931, p. 26.

"Graybeards must walk with the boys—Osler." *New York Times*, December 20, 1905, p. 11.

"Green says labor enters on new era." *New York Times*, September 3, 1929, p. 4.

Greene, Bob. "The high price of joblessness." *Esquire* 99 (June, 1983): 427–428+.

Greve, Frank. "Age bias: the uphill battle." *50 Plus* 27 (March, 1987): 33–36.

Grinder, C. E. "Research roundup." *Office Executive* 33 (July, 1958): 38–40.

Grinder, C. E. "Research roundup." *Office Executive* 33 (October, 1958): 43.

Grinder, C. E. "Research roundup." *Office Executive* 34 (September, 1959): 62–63.

"Group insurance." *New York Times,* November 19, 1929, p. 28.

Grutzner, Charles. "Age limit on jobs yielding slowly." *New York Times*, January 17, 1960, pp. 1, 78.

Gullette, Margaret Morganroth. "The end of the workday—II." *The Nation* 266 (January 5, 1998): 21–22.

Haefner, James. F. "Race, age, sex, and competence as factors in employer selection of the disadvantaged." *Journal of Applied Psychology* 62 (April, 1977): 199–202.

Haefner, James E. "Sources of discrimination among employees: a survey investigation." *Journal of Applied Psychology* 62 (June, 1977): 265–270.

"The handicap of age." *New York Times*, April 24, 1915, p. 10.

Hansen, Agnes Camilla. "Age limit to placement." *Library Journal* 65 (November 15, 1940): 960–961.

Harry, George. "The problem of job-hunters over forty." *Industrial Canada* 55 (May, 1954): 59, 62, 64.

"Helping older job seekers—how federal law will work." *U.S. News & World Report* 65 (July 1, 1968): 63.

Henkens, Kene, Maarten Sprengers and Frits Tazelaar. "Unemployment and the older worker in the Netherlands." *Aging and Society* 16 (September, 1996): 561–578.

"Henry Ford's viewpoint on the elderly worker." *Monthly Labor Review* 29 (August, 1929): 337–338.

Herbers, John. "House told laws are needed on age discrimination in jobs." *New York Times*, July 1, 1965, p. 14.

Hewes, Amy. "Employment of older persons in Springfield, Mass., department stores." *Monthly Labor Review* 35 (October, 1932): 773–781.

Heywood, John S., Lok-Sang Ho and Xiangdong Wei. "The determinants of hiring older workers: evidence from Hong Kong." *Industrial and Labor Relations Review* 52 (April, 1999): 444–460.

Hiatt, Walter S. "Weighing the worth of the man past forty." *New York Times*, October 2, 1927, sec. 9, p. 4.

Hill, Frank Ernest. "At what age should a man quit work?" *New York Times Magazine*, August 12, 1934, pp. 6–7, 19.

"Hirers approve older workers." *U.S. News & World Report* 35 (November 13, 1953): 99.

"Hiring gain is found for older workers." *New York Times*, August 25, 1961, p. 49.

"Hiring of older workers by War and Navy departments." *Monthly Labor Review* 51 (September, 1940): 622–623.

"Hiring policies, prejudices, and the older worker." *Monthly Labor Review* 88 (August, 1965): 968–970.

Holman, Ross L. "Old age and industrial efficiency." *American Mercury* 61 (September, 1945): 311–315.

Hoopes, Roy. "The case of the myopic watchdog." *Modern Maturity* 32 (April/May, 1989): 36–39+.

Hoopes, Roy. "On the outside looking in." *Modern Maturity* 32 (June/July, 1989): 32–35+.

Hoopes, Roy. "Working late: the railroad to retirement." *Modern Maturity* 32 (February/March, 1989): 34–37+.

"House panel hears complaint of stewardesses." *New York Times*, September 3, 1965, p. 12.

Hudson, Harold C. "The older worker." *Canadian Welfare* 23 (January 15, 1948): 20–23.

"Hunting a job when a man is over forty-five." *New York Times*, July 10, 1910, pt. 5, p. 15.

Hushbeck, Judith. *Old and Obsolete: Age Discrimination and the American Worker, 1860–1920.* New York: Garland, 1989.

Hutchens, Robert M. "Do job opportunities decline with age?" *Industrial and Labor Relations Review* 42 (October, 1988): 89–99.

"Is 45 too old to work? Many doors are shut." *U.S. News & World Report* 39 (September 10, 1955): 107–110.

"It costs too much." *Business Week*, May 9, 1953, p. 178.

"Job applicant, 44, wins bias case." *New York Times*, August 9, 1975, p. 21.

"Job applicants face age bias, study finds." *New York Times*, February 23, 1994, p. A15.

"Job club rejoices at low membership." *New York Times*, January 26, 1941, p. 40.

"Job drive planned by older workers." *New York Times*, March 31, 1930, p. 2.

"A job for insurance activities." *New York Times*, November 13, 1929, p. 26.

"Job forms soften questions on age." *New York Times*, June 30, 1958, p. 21.

"Job law signed." *New York Times*, December 17, 1967, p. 62.

"Job plea for mid-age." *New York Times*, February 21, 1957, p. 23.

"Job plight of women over 35 is stressed." *New York Times*, May 21, 1940, p. 23.

"Jobless body asks public for a name." *New York Times*, August 25, 1927, p. 7.

"The jobless man of 45." *New York Times*, October 6, 1929, sec. 3, p. 5.

"Jobless middle-aged form organization." *New York Times*, August 31, 1927, p. 3.

"Jobs after 40." *The Nation* 149 (September 23, 1939): 308–309.

"Jobs after forty." *Business Week*, December 17, 1949, pp. 90–91.

"Jobs few for older men." *New York Times*, September 18, 1933, p. 2.

"Jobs for men over 45." *New York Times*, August 2, 1917, p. 8.

"Jobs for older workers." *New York Times*, September 13, 1954, p. 22.

"Jobs for the middle-aged." *New York Times*, May 30, 1928, p. 18.

"Johnson issues job order banning age discrimination." *New York Times*, February 14, 1964, p. 35.

Johnson, Richard W. and David Neumark. "Age discrimination, job separations, and employment status of older workers." *The Journal of Human Resources* 32 (Fall, 1997): 779–793.

Johnston, Laurie. "It's one for all and all for one in job-hunt club for men over 40." *New York Times*, February 20, 1950, p. 27.

Kaempffert, Waldemar. "The man over 40: a machine-age dilemma." *New York Times Magazine*, March 6, 1938, pp. 1–2, 22.

Kasschau, Patricia L. "Age and race discrimination reported by middle-aged and older persons." *Social Forces* 55 (March, 1977): 728–742.

Katz, Sidney. "Sheltered employment for older people." *Canadian Welfare* 31 (May 1, 1955): 38–41.

"Keeping older men from jobs scored." *New York Times*, December 10, 1948, p. 29.

Kirchner, Wayne, Theodore Lindblom and Donald G. Paterson. "Attitudes toward the employment of older people." *Journal of Applied Psychology* 36 (June, 1952): 154–156.

Krohe, James Jr. "An old story." *Across the Board* 28 (November, 1991): 35–37+.

Krohe, James Jr. "Days Inns: older workers need apply." *Across the Board* 28 (November, 1991): 38–39.

Kugel, Daisy A. "The status of the older woman in home economics." *Journal of Home Economics* 21 (December, 1929): 911–913.

"Labor council asks union drive in south." *New York Times*, October 7, 1929, p. 27.

"Labor Dept. comes to aid of oldsters with data on work efficiency." *Business Week*, December 29, 1956, p. 70.

Lavelle, Marianne. "On the edge of age discrimination." *New York Times Magazine*, March 9, 1997, pp. 66–69.

Lavoie, Francis J. "The plight of the over-40 engineer." *Management Review* 60 (February, 1971): 27–30.
"Law held no cure for job loss at 40." *New York Times*, January 20, 1938, p. 11.
"Law on aged assailed." *New York Times*, June 20, 1958, p. 46.
Leonard, Leonard M. "Why don't they hire older workers?" *Science Digest* 40 (September, 1956): 53–57.
Leppel, Karen and Suzanne Heller Clain. "The effect of increases in the level of unemployment on older workers." *Applied Economics* 27 (October, 1995): 901–906.
"Less bias found on middle-aged." *New York Times*, March 21, 1940, p. 12.
Levine, Richard J. "Age bias comes under fire." *Supervisory Management* 13 (August, 1968): 34–36.
"Life begins at Forty Plus." *Business Week*, May 1, 1948, p. 26.
"Looking for work in old age." *New York Times*, May 1, 1915, p. 12.
Magnuson, Carolyn. "You're too old!" *Good Housekeeping* 219 (October, 1994): 137+.
Majoribanks, Robert. "Pension plans block over-35 job hunters." *Financial Post* 53 (February 21, 1959): 38.
Marcus, Sumner and Jon Christoffersen. "Discrimination and the older worker." *Business Horizons* 12 (October, 1969): 83–89.
Maule, Frances. "Beat that deadline." *Independent Woman* 19 (March, 1940): 77+.
Mauro, Tony. "Age bias charges: increasing problem." *Nation's Business* 71 (April, 1983): 44–46.
"Maximum hiring ages in Canadian industry." *Monthly Labor Review* 46 (March, 1938): 662–663.
Maxwell, Robert B. "A silver jubilee for the ADEA." *Modern Maturity* 35 (April/May, 1992): 8–9.
"Mayor's order bans sex discrimination on jobs." *New York Times*, August 25, 1970, p. 15.
McAfee, Joseph Ernest. "Middle-aged white collar workers on the economic rack." *The Annals of the American Academy of Political & Social Science* 154 (March, 1931): 32–37.
McCullough, Ernest. "The case of the middle-aged." *New York Times*, August 4, 1929, sec. 3, p. 5.
McMahon, J. E. "Older persons held eligible for hiring." *New York Times*, October 21, 1956, sec. 3, pp. 1, 11.
McManus, George J. "You are only as old as the company feels you should be." *Iron Age* 211 (March 1, 1973): 40–41.
McNaught, William and Michael C. Barth. "Are older workers 'good buys?' A case study of Days Inn of America." *Sloan Management Review* 33 (Spring, 1992): 53–63.
Mead, James M. "Our older people." *Vital Speeches of the Day* 4 (March 1, 1938): 319–320.
Meyerhoff, Howard A. "The older worker." *Scientific Monthly* 59 (November, 1944): 404.
"The middle-age deadline." *New York Times*, July 28, 1929, sec. 3, p. 5.
"Middle-aged jobless band to seek work." *New York Times*, June 5, 1937, p. 3.
"Middle-aged misfits." *Labour Gazette* 75 (March, 1975): 156–157.
"The middle-aged woman." *New York Times*, October 14, 1922, p. 12.
"Middle-aged workers." *New York Times*, November 25, 1932, p. 20.
"Mitchell attacks over-45 work ban." *New York Times*, December 22, 1954, p. 25.
Mitchell, Jack. "Age bias: the uphill battle." *50 Plus* 27 (March, 1987): 32, 95.
Mitchell, James P. "After 45—are you too old to work?" *Collier's* 135 (January 7, 1955): 38–41.
Mitchell, James P. "Life doesn't end at 45." *Catholic World* 180 (January, 1955): 246–251.
Monroe, Ann. "Getting rid of the gray." *Mother Jones* 21 (July/August 1996): 29.
"More jobs taken by older women." *New York Times*, February 25, 1954, p. 27.
"More middle-aged found losing jobs." *New York Times*, April 6, 1949, p. 34.
Moscow, Warren. "Moratorium bills signed by Lehman." *New York Times*, April 8, 1938, p. 5.
Mosher, A. R. "The problem of employment for older workers." *Canadian Unionist* 26 (May, 1952): 139–140.

"Mr. Action asks for jobs." *New York Times*, September 30, 1927, p. 23.

"Mr. Action drops veil of incognito." *New York Times*, September 3, 1927, p. 32.

"Mr. Action musters his jobless hosts." *New York Times*, August 24, 1927, p. 14.

Munk, Nina. "Finished at forty." *Fortune* 139 (February 1, 1999): 50–54+.

Munk, Nina. "Suspect age bias? Try proving it." *Fortune* 139 (February 1, 1999): 58.

"Navy Yard workers oppose age limit." *New York Times*, March 5, 1930, p. 14.

Nelson, William R. "Age discrimination in police employment." *Journal of Police Science and Administration* 9 (December, 1981): 428–440.

"New age-bias law draws objections." *New York Times*, June 19, 1958, p. 31.

"New move to aid workers over 40." *New York Times*, March 13, 1949, sec. 3, pp. 1, 5.

"New views on older worker." *Science Digest* 23 (March, 1948): 29–30.

"New York employers shift their accent." *The Commonweal* 31 (April 5, 1940): 503.

"No more 'too old for job.'" *U.S. News & World Report* 64 (May 27, 1968): 87.

"No place for the old men?" *New York Times*, November 12, 1910, p. 8.

"Not jobs for middle-aged." *New York Times*, June 4, 1928, p. 20.

Novak, Viveca. "Doubting Thomas." *The Nation* 250 (March 26, 1990): 405.

Odell, Charles E. "Employment of older workers." *Occupations* 30 (October, 1951): 15–20.

Odell, Charles E. "Productivity of the older worker." *Personnel & Guidance Journal* 37 (December, 1958): 288–291.

"The office boy passes." *Literary Digest* 54 (April 14, 1917): 1128.

"Old and out of a job." *New York Times*, July 15, 1925, p. 16.

"Old before their time." *America* 113 (August 14, 1965): 147–148.

"Old men of 30, crones of 35 now feel first hiring bars because of age." *Business Week*, July 20, 1957, p. 38.

"Older and wiser may not help in job hunt." *Management Review* 83 (June, 1994): 6.

"Older men at work." *The Economist* 117 (December 31, 1955): 1196–1197.

"Older men barred from 59% of jobs." *New York Times*, November 19, 1932, p. 17.

"The older worker. *Time* 62 (October 19, 1953): 100.

"Older workers face hiring problems." *Office Management* 19 (June, 1958): 8, 12.

"Ont. bans age discrimination." *Canadian Labour* 11 (May, 1966): 116.

"The Osler dead line." *New York Times*, October 4, 1908, pt. 5, p. 11.

"Osler only half right says Dr. Felix Adler." *New York Times*, January 8, 1906, p. 6.

"Over forty." *Literary Digest* 122 (December 12, 1936): 13–14.

"Over forty." *The Economist* 176 (August 20, 1955): 608.

"Over-40 hiring bias tied to relief load." *New York Times*, May 28, 1951, p. 23.

"Over 40 project to advertise." *New York Times*, November 27, 1937, p. 22.

Palmer, Dwight L. and John A. Brownell. "Influence of age on employment opportunities." *Monthly Labor Review* 48 (April, 1939): 765–780.

"Pensions vs. jobs for older workers." *U.S. News & World Report* 28 (May 5, 1950): 18–19.

"Perkins asks work for those over 45." *New York Times*, September 7, 1937, p. 2.

Perkins, Frances. "Too old at 40." *New York Times Magazine*, March 13, 1938, pp. 3, 19, 22.

Perry, James S. "College students' attitudes toward workers' competence and age." *Psychological Reports* 42 (June, 1978): 1319–1322, pt. 2.

"Persons in fifties sell more goods, study finds." *New York Times*, September 2, 1937, p. 30.

Peters, Jim. "Alternative labor pool." *Restaurant Business* 86 (September 1, 1987): 183–187.

Petersen, Anne. "Challenge issued to remedy plight." *New York Times*, February 20, 1938, sec. 6, p. 5.

Pirie, Mary K. "No one over thirty-five need apply." *Independent Woman* 29 (February, 1950): 42–44.

"Pittsburgh club finds jobs for many over 40." *New York Times*, July 27, 1939, p. 36.

"Plan job survey for middle-aged." *New York Times*, September 4, 1930, p. 11.

"Plans to aid middle-aged." *New York Times*, March 13, 1930, p. 46.

"Pledges premier support of labor." *New York Times*, October 8, 1929, p. 3.

"Plight of the over-45." *America* 93 (September 24, 1955): 606.

Pollak, Otto. "Discrimination against older workers in industry." *American Journal of Sociology* 50 (September, 1944): 99–106.
Pollock, Channing. "Death begins at forty." *The Forum* 98 (November, 1937): 211–216.
"President urges hiring older idle." *New York Times*, April 4, 1941, p. 37.
"President's appeal for hiring of older workers." *Monthly Labor Review* 52 (May, 1941): 1151–1152.
"The problem of the employment of older workers." *International Labour Review* 69 (June, 1954): 594–618.
"Problem of the middle-aged is still far from solution." *New York Times*, October 20, 1929, sec. 3, p. 5.
"The problem of the older worker." *Canadian Unionist* 27 (April, 1953): 117–119.
"Problem of the older worker in the United States and Europe." *Monthly Labor Review* 48 (February, 1939): 257–270.
"Progress in dealing with problem of older worker." *Labour Gazette* 48 (January/February, 1948): 6–7.
"Protection of older workers against discrimination in Louisiana." *Monthly Labor Review* 39 (December, 1934): 1386.
Raffel, Dawn. "The search for jobs." *50 Plus* 24 (November, 1984): 72, 74.
"Raises spectre of unemployment." *New York Times*, October 2, 1929, p. 33.
Ransom, Roger L. and Richard Sutch. "The labor of older Americans." *Journal of Economic History* 46 (March, 1986): 1–30.
"Rate for older workers soar." *New York Times*, October 8, 1982, p. B7.
Reid, Dorothy C. "Pull yourself together." *Independent Woman* 21 (November, 1942): 333–4+.
Reiter, Mark. "Age discrimination in the workplace." *50 Plus* 25 (May, 1985): 14–15+.
"Revolt of the jobless middle-aged." *Literary Digest* 94 (September 10, 1927): 9.
Riddell, Mary. "Mary Riddell." *New Statesman* 127 (February 6, 1998): 13.
"Roosevelt asks jobs for citizens over 40." *New York Times*, April 20, 1940, p. 9.
Root, Norman. "Injuries at work are fewer among older employees." *Monthly Labor Review* 104 (March, 1981): 30–34.
Rosen, Benson and Thomas H. Jerdee. "The influence of age stereotypes on managerial decisions." *Journal of Applied Psychology* 61 (August, 1976): 428–432.
Rosen, Benson and Thomas H. Jerdee. "The nature of job-related age stereotypes." *Journal of Applied Psychology* 61 (April, 1976): 180–183.
Rosen, Benson and Thomas H. Jerdee. "Too old or not too old." *Harvard Business Review* 55 (November, 1977): 97–106.
Ross, Richard. "One way to get good workers." *Nation's Business* 65 (September, 1977): 39–40.
Rubin, Jeffery C. "McSeniors." *Time* 146 (December 4, 1995): 25.
Rusk, Howard A. "Retiring of workers at 65 producing vital problems." *New York Times*, April 23, 1950, p. 51.
Saks, John I. "Status in the labor market." *Monthly Labor Review* 80 (January, 1957): 15–21.
Sandford, Gillian. "Lawmakers seeking to fortify older workers' protection." *Congressional Quarterly Weekly Report* 47 (April 22, 1989): 891.
"Says employers bar many older than 35." *New York Times*, February 8, 1937, p. 6.
"Says workers dye hair in fear of losing jobs." *New York Times*, November 15, 1929, p. 32.
"S.C.A.D. finds gains in fight on age bar." *New York Times*, November 8, 1959, p. 13.
Scanlan, Burt K. "Effects of pension plans on labor mobility and hiring older workers." *Personnel Journal* 44 (January, 1965): 29–34.
Schiff, Lenore. "Is health care a job killer?" *Fortune* 125 (April 6, 1992): 30.
Schiller, Ronald. "Help wanted for the 40-plus." *Reader's Digest* 71 (July, 1957): 154–158.
Schuessler, Raymond. "Success begins at Forty Plus." *American Mercury* 82 (April, 1956): 54–57.
"Secretary Hull." *The Nation* 137 (November 15, 1933): 552.

"Sees a rush for city jobs." *New York Times*, April 8, 1938, p.19.

Seligman, Daniel. "Slipping." *Fortune* 122 (December 17, 1990): 183–184.

Seligman, Daniel. "The case against old age." *Fortune* 114 (November 10, 1986): 163, 166.

Sellett, Lucien R. "Age and absenteeism." *Personnel Journal* 43 (June, 1964): 309–313.

"Senate panel on aging, after a 2-year study, says retirement problem has reached crisis stage." *New York Times*, January 18, 1971, p. 11.

"Shall we starve men over 40?" *Literary Digest* 100 (March 9, 1929): 10.

Shanahan, Eileen. "Oil concern to pay age-bias settlement." *New York Times*, May 17, 1974, pp. 1, 8.

"65,500,000 jobs set U.S. record." *New York Times*, September 5, 1955, pp. 1, 6.

"St. Barnabas house aided 1,584 in year." *New York Times*, July 1, 1928, sec. 3, p. 7.

Stahler, Abraham. "Job problems and their solution." *Monthly Labor Review* 80 (January, 1957): 22–28.

Standing, Guy. "Labour flexibility and older worker marginalisation." *International Labour Review* 125 (May-June, 1986): 329–348.

"State ban on barring jobs to aged put off." *New York Times*, December 9, 1951, sec. 5, p. 8.

Stessin, Lawrence. "The ax and older workers." *New York Times*, June 23, 1974, sec. 3, p. 3.

Stetson, Damon. "Prejudice noted in jobs for aging." *New York Times*, December 11, 1959, p. 30.

Stetson, Helen Sloan. "You, too, can find a career." *Independent Woman* 20 (September, 1941): 270–271.

Stone, Julia E. "Age Discrimination in employment Act: a review of recent changes." *Monthly Labor Review* 103 (March, 1980): 32–35.

"Support rallied for handicapped." *New York Times*, November 2, 1948, p. 43.

Tavernier, Gerard. "The age of discrimination." *International Management* 34 (September, 1979): 18–21.

"Thomas advocates city job bureau." *New York Times*, October 11, 1929, p. 4.

Thompson, Clara Belle and Margaret Lukes Wise. "P. S. she didn't get the job." *Independent Woman* 18 (January, 1939): 9–10+.

"Thinking young." *Newsweek* 83 (April 29, 1974): 80.

"Thirty years later: attitudes toward the employment of older workers." *Journal of Applied Psychology* 71 (August, 1986): 515–517.

"Tobin attacks age ban." *New York Times*, January 24, 1952, p. 29.

"Too old for a job at 35." *New York Times*, December 12, 1936, p. 18.

"Topics of the Times." *New York Times*, November 9, 1937, p. 22.

"The truth about men over 40." *New York Times*, September 29, 1931, p. 20.

Tuckman, Jacob. "Experts' biases about the older worker." *Science* 115 (June 20, 1952): 685–687.

Tuckman, Jacob and Irving Lorge. "Attitudes toward older workers." *Journal of Applied Psychology* 36 (June, 1952): 149–153.

"250 elderly seek jobs daily." *New York Times*, May 18, 1930, sec. 2, p. 18.

"Unemployed and over forty—the new minority." *Labour Gazette* 77 (February, 1977): 54–58.

"Unemployment among older workers, 1945–1949." *Labour Gazette* 49 (November, 1949): 1392–1396.

"Unemployment of older workers in New York." *Monthly Labor Review* 49 (August, 1939): 364–366.

"Unemployment studied." *New York Times*, August 23, 1929, p. 11.

"Unions act to save older men's jobs." *New York Times*, November 27, 1949, p. 83.

"The unwanted middle-aged men." *New York Times*, July 17, 1927, sec. 7, p. 9.

"Urge jobs for men over 40." *Business Week*, July 16, 1938, pp. 24–25.

"Urges job analysis for older workers." *New York Times*, November 10, 1929, sec. 2, p. 6.

"Urges provision for older worker." *New York Times*, February 20, 1933, p. 4.

"Uruguayan bill would force employment of men over 45." *New York Times*, November 12, 1929, p. 10.

"U.S. to seek jobs for older women." *New York Times*, October 3, 1956, p. 35.

Varela, Raymond. "Over 40 ... are you really too old? *Financial Post* 51 (November 30, 1957): 44.

Vassallo, William. "The phony age barrier." *American Mercury* 88 (May, 1959): 76–78.

"We cast off men in prime of life." *New York Times*, March 15, 1931, sec. 3, p. 2.

Weaver, Warren Jr. "Age discrimination charges found in sharp rise in U.S." *New York Times*, February 22, 1982, p. A12.

Weaver, Warren Jr. "Harriman policy on aging scored." *New York Times*, October 3, 1957, p. 31.

Weaver, Warren Jr. "Harriman signs a ban on age bias." *New York Times*, April 16, 1958, p. 35.

Weaver, Warren Jr. "State puts curb on authorities." *New York Times*, April 20, 1961, p. 21.

Weaver, Warren Jr. "State urged to bar age bias in hiring." *New York Times*, January 27, 1957, pp. 1, 60.

Webb, Marilyn. "How old is too old?" *New York* 26 (March 29, 1993): 66–73.

Welshimer, Helen. "When employers say 'too old.'" *Independent Woman* 16 (October, 1937): 308+

Wiencek, Thomas J. "Washington targets benefits in fight against age discrimination." *Management Review* 80 (August, 1991): 31–33.

Willard, J. W. "Employment problems of older workers." *Public Affairs* 11 (July, 1948): 135–140.

Williams, C. Richard. "Is there a life after forty?" *Advertising Age* 43 (March 6, 1972): 39–40, 42.

Williams, D. N. "You can trust anybody over 50." *Iron Age* 204 (July 10, 1969): 64–65.

"Woes of the middle aged." *New York Times*, July 17, 1907, p. 8.

"Women in industry." *Monthly Labor Review* 39 (August, 1934): 336–343.

"Work for the middle-aged." *New York Times*, September 27, 1927, p. 26.

"Workers discarded too young, he says." *New York Times*, April 11, 1928, p. 8.

"Workers, jobless at 40, organize for fight." *New York Times*, August 20, 1927, p. 17.

"Workers over 45 backed as able." *New York Times*, May 26, 1957, p. 76.

"Workers past 40." *New York Times*, February 26, 1938, p. 14.

"Workers past 45 face lack of jobs." *New York Times*, March 10, 1957, p. 111.

"Would protect the idle." *New York Times*, October 2, 1921, p. 2.

"Wounded executives fight back on age bias." *Business Week*, July 21, 1980, pp. 109–110.

"Years prove handicap to women in business." *New York Times*, September 25, 1927, sec. 8, p. 15.

"Young and old at the employment office." *Monthly Labor Review* 46 (January, 1938): 3–15.

Zipser, Alfred R. Jr. "Industry revamps personnel policy." *New York Times*, January 28, 1951, sec. 3, p. 7.

Zipser, Alfred R. "Insurance no bar to older workers." *New York Times*, April 3, 1949, sec. 3, p. 9.

Zipser, Alfred R. Jr. "State law to aid older workers is off until 1951 session in Albany." *New York Times*, March 5, 1950, sec. 3, p. 1.

Index